Banker's Guide to New Small Business Finance

Banker's Guide to New Small Business Finance

Venture Deals, Crowdfunding, Private Equity, and Technology

CHARLES H. GREEN

WILEY

Published by John Wiley & Sons, Inc., Hoboken, New Jersey.
Published simultaneously in Canada.

For general information on our other products and services or for technical support, please contact our Customer Care Department within the United States at (800) 762-2974, outside the United States at (317) 572-3993 or fax (317) 572-4002.

Wiley publishes in a variety of print and electronic formats and by print-on-demand. Some material included with standard print versions of this book may not be included in e-books or in print-on-demand. If this book refers to media such as a CD or DVD that is not included in the version you purchased, you may download this material at http://booksupport.wiley.com. For more information about Wiley products, visit www.wiley.com.

Library of Congress Cataloging-in-Publication Data:

ISBN 978-1-118-83787-0 (Hardcover)
ISBN 978-1-118-94086-0 (ePDF)
ISBN 978-1-118-94085-3 (ePub)

Printed in the United States of America
10 9 8 7 6 5 4 3 2 1

This book is dedicated to the tireless women and men who perform the detailed tasks required to deliver financing to small businesses. To all those lenders and brokers who engage in countless conversations, answer thousands of questions, and drive hundreds of miles, and whose work takes them to diverse places like dry cleaners, convenience stores, doughnut shops, mills, loading docks, funeral homes, dentist offices, manufacturing plants, highway motels, and every other door on Main Street.

An innovation that is disruptive allows a whole new population of consumers at the bottom of a market access to a product or service that was historically only accessible to consumers with a lot of money or a lot of skill.

—Dr. Clayton Christensen

Contents

Figures and Tables

Preface

My introduction to the real world of banking, beyond lofty finance courses taken in college, was found on my first bank office desk in a stack of pages filled with columns of blank grids, matched with an adjacent column of accounting terms on the left side of the pages. These papers were spreadsheets, designed to be populated with numbers found in the hundreds of business financial statements collected by the bank from clients as obligated through their loan agreement covenants.

Behind these sheets were musty stacks of file folders of varying age, size, and degree of disorganization, which contained evidence used by the bank previously to decide whether to make each loan. Many of them actually had multiple financial statements inside while many were missing any such information.

My new purpose in life became to open and read every one of these financial statements and transcribe them by hand and pencil, writing every number from every financial account listed into the corresponding grid in every client file's respective spreadsheet. My hand began to ache just thinking about the task ahead. Should I have majored in economics?

These spreadsheets were organized to detail up to four years' balance sheets on the front side and four years' income statements on the back side, with succeeding years listed from left to right. At the bottom of the back side was space for calculating some financial ratios to measure working capital, liquidity, and leverage. Still more impressive was the fifth column on both sides of the page, which was reserved to include the latest year's industry average for each financial account, copiously transcribed from the fine print found in the Robert Morris Associates (now known as the Risk Management Association) Financial Statement Studies (cost = $29.95 in 1979—low whistle).

My boss thought his small-town bank was finally hitting the big leagues, just like the money center banks—*financial analysis*. How sophisticated! But others grumbled that a college kid with no lending or business experience had been hired to second guess or opine about credit decisions already made. They were right, of course, as I discovered in my first loan review discussion with one of the bank's most senior lenders, its chairman, who patiently illuminated how much I had to learn.

And so began my exposure to "the numbers," which today remains the central element of client information required to determine the risk and desirability of a funding transaction. But other than using a digital workbook like Microsoft Excel or other spreadsheet software, little has changed from those early years of my career when even small banks started aggregating more information and exercising more thorough analysis to underwrite credit to businesses.

For many years, technology enabled the commercial banking industry to originate, aggregate, manage, move, and account for cash and non-cash item deposits with dizzying efficiency that dramatically lowered costs, increased productivity, improved security, and saved millions of trees. While in college during the 1970s, a part-time job in the school bursar's office exposed me to check cancellation machines that could imprint "for deposit only" on thousands of student payment checks in a matter of minutes and capture the front and back images of these checks to be reproduced later on microfiche for future reference.

But strangely, applying any technology to its core business—*lending*—has been painstakingly slow for bankers. Other than being able to order credit reports online and access a few financial analysis platforms that still require substantial manual entry, business lending has been the last frontier for banking technology improvement.

Even now, a small business owner approaching a typical bank for a loan will most likely be asked to provide a handwritten application form, personal financial statement, and printed copies of a long list of information. And all these pages are then handled by two or more people who read, analyze, transcribe, copy, file, and retrieve them. As a result, banks frequently waste valuable time and information due to misfiling and losing paper.

Losing information is a byproduct of the overwhelming growth of requirements for more information used to screen potential loans. And since this information is on paper, it aggravates the already problematic system.

Missing at most banks are some of the simplest shortcuts that could manage this arduous process more efficiently, like online portals to gather and interpret much of the required information, digital financial statement forms that could be edited annually, and a centralized digital filing system to store all loan application data in the same way banks have stored checks for decades.

While recovering from the financial crisis that shook the industry in 2008, most banks have hunkered down to repair wounded capital, dealt with large problem loan portfolios, and tried to return to business as usual—that is, business as it was in 2006. The problem is that it's 2014. Part of that focus on recovery also meant deferred consideration of investment in technology assets and system upgrades.

As technology raced forward (recall that Apple's iPad was introduced after the financial crisis) and investors were scouring the Earth for new financial opportunities in the post-CDO period, a funny thing happened: Private equity discovered small business lending. Long the exclusive forte of commercial banks, a new crack appeared in the wall that defined turf of who would finance what.

That crack was widened by banks' reluctance or inability to take on seemingly moderate risks in small business lending since the crisis. Concurrently, the development of funding sources for small companies that could be obtained through fancy technology platforms have made bank applications look like what they are—a thing of the past.

Ironically, the limited number of small companies that have remained very healthy and attractive for bank funding since 2008 have actually fed a feeding frenzy among banks starving for earning assets. Many bankers shared stories with me of intensive negotiations for loans priced at painfully low rates that sometimes even had to include negative loan fees (think of it as a closing cost rebate) just to win the business. The recipient companies must have enjoyed being in funding heaven for a brief while.

Meanwhile, thousands of businesses that had been perfectly fundable for years had to turn to other non-bank lenders and were glad to pay interest rates and fees amounting to annual percentage rates (APR) in the 30 to 70 percent range just to get the growth capital needed. And most interesting is the fact that loan losses for most of these funders have not been much higher than those of the commercial banks, but the revenue sure was.

Literally hundreds of funding companies emerged over the past 10 years that are providing business capital in some very innovative ways. Collectively they have reexamined virtually every convention of traditional bank business lending, such as to whom to lend, how to underwrite risk, how to price risk, how to document credit/funding agreements, how to collect payments, and even where to fund the deal.

And, as with many other new technologies that have emerged in recent years, this sector has its own accompanying support industry of businesses that have popped up to originate and support the prospective borrowers who want to get funding, wherever the source.

Who are these lenders and from where did they come? Some have simply evolved from more seasoned ideas, like merchant cash advance companies, which started in the 1990s and have been much more willing to adapt better technology as it became available.

Some of these lenders are truly cutting edge technologies that have developed proprietary platforms, new underwriting theories, and interesting strategies to manage credit risks. They are funded by a combination of private equity, loan sales, and in a more limited way, through some bank funding as they begin to scale their early success.

Some of the companies in this space are adapting to evolving ideas, like crowdsourcing, and tapping into smaller investors. The investors under this umbrella have varying motivations (from empathy to fascination) and varying risk appetites (from measured to what-me-worry). The channel growing around the notion of crowdfunding is providing capital to new and old businesses, startups, and some good causes with a profit motive. As the name implies, funding is sourced virtually anonymously through the "crowd."

What do we call lenders that are described in this category? Many insiders, observers, and pundits have been using the tired label of "alternative lenders" to describe this growing list of funders and lenders that are differentiated from each other mainly by the distinctive lending models, client targets, or funding sourcing.

I reject that title because it's been used for two or three decades to describe two much narrower financing categories outside commercial banking known as *asset-based lending* (ABL) and its financial cousin, *factoring*. To me this new sector is definitely distinct from that world, which has shown little appetite for technology, product improvement, or expansion of a rather defined market. That worn category name, alternative, also excludes the support companies that are emerging, which can be an important source of growth for this new category and conventional lending companies as well.

Maybe it's presumptuous of me, but I propose to christen this business funding category as the *innovative funding* sector.

And what has been the banking industry's response to this surging new financial frontier, now labeled "innovative funding"? I would like to describe the reaction as disbelief, disapproval, or dismissal, but curiously, it is overwhelmingly undiscovered. Nobody seems to even know that it's there.

Having been involved in training hundreds of business lenders over the past three years, I asked many participants what they know about technology-driven lenders. I threw out a few company names, like the oldest innovative participant (since 2004!), most publicized company, or largest volume lender. I find there are few who have even heard of these companies or the emerging sector that has racked up about $100 billion of business funding.

Granted, most of that $100 billion would not have been funded by commercial banks anyway and in toto, the sum is not exactly a threat to the $3 trillion of outstanding commercial real estate (CRE) and commercial and industrial (C&I) loans presently held on bank balance sheets around the United States. But it's growing at a rapid pace no one seems to be tracking.

This book is an exercise in my interest and curiosity in this emerging sector and an attempt to chronicle its brief history as a means to understand its likely trajectory. Drawing from my career as a business banker, Chapter 1 of the book lays down a baseline on how the traditional banking industry has funded small business owners for decades (at least since I entered the business).

Then the challenges to prudently invest in small business loans is examined in Chapter 2, to illuminate how the obstacles banks face give rise to opportunities that are currently being exploited by this rising innovative funding group. Maybe the biggest obstacle is simply the restrictions imposed on all those cheap funding deposits they have to invest that are insured by the FDIC.

Chapter 3 offers my perspective of changes that occurred in the post-2008 capital markets and how we arrived to that point today. Despite concerted efforts of policy makers and the markets, small Main Street businesses are forced to seek funding alternatives due to the lack of viable options in the once-reliable banking sector. And the timing couldn't have been better for the many innovative funders that are described later in the book.

For background, Chapter 4 offers a layman's interpretation of what's happened in the digital marketplace that may shrink the playing field for many banking lenders who seem unaware of a marketing revolution that is threatening their market share. Chapter 5 describes how this perfect storm occurred as private investors began getting squeezed by low interest rates, a terrorized equities market, and the increasing competition in the angel investor marketplace.

In Chapter 6, the environmental changes described earlier are discussed in light of the concurrent emergence of unprecedented data collection, packaging, and distribution. This convergence spawned a flurry of new ideas that began flowing into the marketplace, introducing different ways to distribute capital to individuals and small business owners.

Chapter 7 discusses the new sector of funders and lenders that have begun to provide capital to different niches in the scramble to scale. Donors, innovators, lending peers, and investors are covered in Chapter 8 with the continuing development of crowdfunding, an old idea that has exploded across the globe.

Chapter 9 explores other innovative lenders whose technology may be conventional, but have introduced new ways to deliver funding to specific enterprises and whose growth will impact the increasing migration of capital assets away from commercial banks.

The rising group of service providers that connects funding to borrowers is examined in Chapter 10 with an analysis of what they do (and don't do).

Chapter 11 tries to make sense of all these changes and developments in the banking industry through the lens of a seasoned banker who has toured the other side. The challenges are real and threatening for some, but will offer many banks opportunities to grow market share, profitability, and other benefits outside lending.

Throughout the book the terms *funder* and *funding* are often used to describe the party that provides small business capital to business owners and the transaction through which it is delivered. Those generic terms are easier to default to rather than constantly having to clarify the differences between gifts, loans, non-loan funding, and equity investment.

Some may ask what the difference is between a non-loan funding and an equity investment. Non-loan funding is an acknowledgment that many companies, particularly the merchant cash advance sector, provide business funding that legally is structured or defined as an advance or purchase of an account receivable, income stream, or other asset. These companies are generally not registered with any state banking or finance regulatory agency or recognized anywhere as a lender and accordingly by law are not able to legally advance loans.

So now read it. This moment is an opportunity for banks large and small to understand this emerging market, take initiative to engage both technology and clients to protect and expand market share, and exploit natural advantages in this brave new world of innovative funding.

Acknowledgments

A lot of collaboration is needed to develop any book project, but even after six earlier titles, this one was most challenging in that it combined the principal business of my career (banking) with the technology cloud we've all been forced to acknowledge.

I wish to thank many different people who contributed minutes or hours to provide crucial links that helped me put this book together, including: Rodney Schansman and Lara Stegman (FTrans.com), Joseph Barisonzi (CommunityLeader.com), Brock Blake and Ty Kiisel (Lendio.com), Bob Coleman (Coleman Report), Robert Gloer (IOUCentral.com), Sara Watkins and Natalie Waggett (nCINO), Scott Sanford (LendingClub.com), and Rebekah Nicodemus (Atomic PR).

Special thanks go to Alicia Butler-Pierre (Equilibria, Inc.), who created the illustrations to help communicate this information more vividly.

And importantly, recognition to my partner at home, Angela Edmond, whose counsel and encouragement were instrumental, from early discussions about the concept all the way to getting this undertaking completed.

Lastly, I want to offer a special tribute to my dad, Joseph Henry Green (1919–2005), who taught me how to count money and the value of entrepreneurship.

About the Author

Charles H. Green is a seasoned finance professional with over 30 years experience as a commercial banker, mostly funding the small business sector. He founded and served as president/CEO of Sunrise Bank of Atlanta. Charles presently advises a broad list of financial service companies.

He has written extensively about business financing through articles and books including *Get Financing Now* (McGraw-Hill, 2012) and the bestselling *The SBA Loan Book*, 3rd Edition (Adams Media, 2011). He earned a BS in finance from the University of Alabama (1979) and a diploma at the Stonier National Graduate School of Banking (2009).

Charles teaches business lending through a number of channels including the Stonier National Graduate School of Banking, ABA's Graduate School of Commercial Lending, the Graduate School of Banking at University of Wisconsin, and Coleman SBA Webinars.

■ ■ ■

Illustrator

Alicia Butler Pierre is CEO of Equilibria, Inc., an operations management firm specializing in creating processes and systems that help companies reduce waste and minimize operational defects. She earned a BS in Chemical Engineering with minors in technical sales and chemistry from Louisiana State University (1999), and an MBA with concentrations in marketing and management from Tulane University (2004).

Survey of Funding
Small Business

How Small Businesses Are Funded

"**S**mall" business is the category still used to classify more than 99 percent of the 27 million business entities in the United States (although 75 percent of them have zero employees). Representing approximately 40 percent of all commercial sales, 50 percent of the U.S. gross domestic product, and over 55 percent of the nongovernment work force, small business is really *big* business.

This sector is credited for having created two out of every three new jobs in the United States for the past two decades, yet obtaining capital financing continues to be a challenge for most small business owners and entrepreneurs. And opposing logic, capital funding gets more challenging as the loan size decreases, rather than increases, at least as far as commercial banks are concerned.

DEFINING SMALL BUSINESS

Part of the ongoing confusion around small business financing is that there is no clear, absolute definition of the question, what is a small business? The federal government delegated the task of defining small business to the U.S. Small Business Administration (SBA) and they have stratified the response to make it necessary for anyone seeking an answer to that question to flip through a 46-page list of industrial codes to determine the agreed upon answer.

SBA defines small only according to the agency's determination of business size relativity. And even that size relativity gets subdivided into different determinants used according to their classification. Each distinct business category defined by the North American Industry Classification System (NAICS) is assigned a limitation by SBA, usually expressed as either the maximum annual revenues or the maximum number of employees, to determine whether they are officially deemed a small business.

As defined by the SBA's Table of Small Business Size Standards, *small* to some companies can be defined as maximum annual revenues of $750,000 (dry pea and bean farming) while for other companies that limit can be as much as $35.5 million (marine cargo handling). But other companies are adjudged small by a maximum of 100 employees (tire & tube merchant wholesalers) while some others can employ as many as 1,500 (aircraft manufacturing) and still be considered small.

All distinctions in this table are not as gaping, as is illustrated by Table 1.1, which highlights the range of income difference in one single category (Subsector 541—Professional, Scientific and Technical Services). In this group of industrial sectors, maximum allowable income to be defined as small ranges from $7 million to $35.5 million. And for some reason, in the middle of this list is one business defined small as having no more than 150 employees.

And still other sectors are determined to be small by metrics such as annual megawatt hours (power generation) or assets (credit intermediation).

There are about a thousand categories broken down among 19 sectors and 90 sub-sectors in the table, which inevitably offer capital providers one more barrier to navigate on the road to deploying resources. But since there is much non-lending public policy riding on the outcome of this definition, the SBA has an impressive Size Standards Methodology[1] that is used to guide these determinations; this is published and available on their website, and makes any category subject to review at almost any time for a variety of reasons.

Not lost on many persons trying to distribute capital is the additional confusion created by simply getting a business adequately categorized. The starting point, at least for existing companies, might be to check the federal tax return of the subject company to see what they have defined themselves to be in the eyes of the IRS, which requests business filers to add the "business activity code" in forms 1120 and 1120S, and a listing of these same NAICS codes is found in the respective instructions for both forms.[2]

But that category, which is usually declared by either the business owner or the tax preparer, is sometimes wrong. Many business owners simply don't want to be bogged down reading a long list of business categories and will choose the first reasonable sounding category they find. Many high-volume discount tax preparers simply speculate, based on a one-time engagement or limited history with the client and take a guess at what the business as named really does.

The confusion that surrounds the definition of what a small business is comes amid the massive communication streams in our digital society and the role public policy and advertising play in encouraging economic growth, regulating the financial sector, and trying to find a source of capital.

TABLE 1.1   Small Business Size Standards

NAICS Codes	NAICS Industry Description	Size Standards in Millions of Dollars	Size Standards in Number of Employees
Subsector 541—Professional, Scientific, and Technical Services			
541110	Offices of Lawyers	$10.0	
541191	Title Abstract and Settlement Offices	$10.0	
541199	All Other Legal Services	$10.0	
541211	Offices of Certified Public Accountants	$19.0	
541213	Tax Preparation Services	$19.0	
541214	Payroll Services	$19.0	
541219	Other Accounting Services	$19.0	
541310	Architectural Services	$7.0	
541320	Landscape Architectural Services	$7.0	
541330	Engineering Services	$14.0	
Except,	Military and Aerospace Equipment and Military Weapons	$35.5	
Except,	Contracts and Subcontracts for Engineering Services Awarded under the National Energy Policy Act 1992	$35.5	
Except,	Marine Engineering and Naval Architecture	$35.5	
541340	Drafting Services	$7.0	
541350	Building Inspection Services	$7.0	
541360	Geophysical Surveying and Mapping Services	$14.0	
541370	Surveying and Mapping (except Geophysical) Services	$14.0	
541380	Testing Laboratories	$14.0	
541410	Interior Design Services	$7.0	
541420	Industrial Design Services	$7.0	
541430	Graphic Design Services	$7.0	
541490	Other Specialized Design Services	$7.0	

(*Continued*)

TABLE 1.1   *(Continued)*

NAICS Codes	NAICS Industry Description	Size Standards in Millions of Dollars	Size Standards in Number of Employees
541511	Custom Computer Programming Services	$25.5	
541512	Computer Systems Design Services	$25.5	
541513	Computer Facilities Management Services	$25.5	
541519	Other Computer Related Services	$25.5	
Except,	Information Technology Value Added Resellers		150
541611	Administrative Management and General Management Consulting Services	$14.0	
541612	Human Resources Consulting Services	$14.0	
541613	Marketing Consulting Services	$14.0	

Source: "Table of Small Business Size Standards," U.S. Small Business Administration, 21. www.sba.gov/sites/default/files/files/Size_Standards_Table.pdf.

Megabanks are notorious for massive marketing campaigns targeting small business clients, who they seek for a myriad of banking services like checking accounts, merchant processing, and payroll services, as well as credit products. But no one ever clears these campaigns with the credit underwriters ahead of time and they often lead to a surge in loan applications that wind up declined.

Likewise, when politicians offer grandiose legislation intended to encourage stronger business growth or more capital funding, there is confusion around exactly who they are targeting. For example, national debates in recent years around income tax reductions have cited the need to relieve the onerous tax burdens on "small business owners."

That phrase may conjure up visions of the neighborhood café or convenience store owner and hence gain valuable popular support for the proposal. But that politician may actually be working at the behest of a hedge fund operator earning $50 million annually. Since that manager is organized as an S-corporation or LLC (limited liability company), he or she has every right to claim title as a small business owner, but obviously it's a mask used to hide the fact that a very wealthy person is pressing for a tax reduction.

Many larger banking companies, under pressure from politicians, regulators, and business advocates to increase lending, can easily mask how well they are stretching the limits to offer more funding to the small business sector simply by exploiting differences in what the Federal Deposit Insurance Corporation (FDIC) quarterly call report considers a small business loan (loans under $1 million) and how it's defined by the SBA. Technical default seems to be fair game in today's public relations communications.

In any case, those most often impacted by all the labels and confusion are the small businesses themselves. Often the average small business owner is woefully unprepared for the financial management of his or her company, much less acquainted with how or where to source third party funding.

For a staggering percentage of business owners who cannot read a financial statement or tax return beyond numbers disclosing their cash balances and taxes owed, targeting the appropriate funding source based on the business use is often beyond their recognition skills. Hence, when they see or hear "business financing," they flock to anyone.

And therein lies the most fundamental dilemma for borrowers and lenders: the lack of cognitive financial literacy on the part of business owners wanting to access third party financing. A very large percentage of the small business sector drives what might be surprisingly large companies on only their reading of a bank account statement. Many mistakenly think that "if there's money in the bank at the end of the year, they must be profitable."

These business people can't read basic financial statements. Typically limited to looking at the cash balance and net profit, they're content to let their tax preparers drive most financial strategies with the singular goal of reducing the impact of federal income taxes. At the expense of potential future business growth, they avoid business profits, retained earnings, and development of stronger financial metrics—what bankers want most—just to avoid paying taxes and accountants.

Plenty of lenders don't mind such an unsophisticated participant, so long as the fundamental conditions exist for a prudent lending transaction. But there is a natural limit to how much capital these less-informed entrepreneurs can access (see Figure 1.1), which is reduced by the quality of financial information they produce.

It's unlikely that business owners would ever pay for audited financial statements that they can't read. And they will never grow large enough to

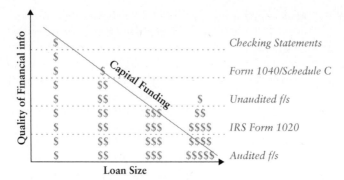

FIGURE 1.1   Quality of Financial Information versus Loan Size

need them anyway, so long as they rely only on internally prepared financial statements and annual tax returns to measure their financial progress.

ABCs OF SMALL BUSINESS FUNDING

Depending on the nature of a company and its balance sheet, and to some extent the planned use of funding proceeds, lenders seem to have an insatiable appetite for information. Banks in particular are sometimes intense in the volume and breadth of information they require even to decline a loan application.

Part of the banking sector burden is rooted in other regulatory concerns—some overzealous regulators at times seem to be applying many consumer loan protections to small business owners, so banks tend to look under every stone to ensure they have complied with many possible interpretations of the regulations.

In banker-speak, they concern themselves with gathering a healthy list of documentation and information with which they can assess loan applicants against the five Cs of credit: capacity, capital, credit, collateral, and character.[3]

The standard repertoire for general business lending requires at least three previous years of financial statements and tax returns, a personal financial statement from all business owners, credit reports, business plans, financial forecasts, detailed asset schedules, collateral appraisals, and a litany of business information provided on an application form or one question at a time.

As illustrated in Figure 1.2, the sometimes exhausting degree of application examination deters many qualified borrowers who would ultimately get funding. They can sometimes be simply too busy with the endless duties required to operate a business or overwhelmed by the administrative burdens required to gather and present what many banks required to consider a loan request.

Unfortunately, banks have not provided many solutions for mutual benefit. Too many banks are stuck in methodologies of the 1960s when it comes to gathering and analyzing application information. Very few companies have embraced integrated technology that could simplify the transfer and examination of borrower information for both borrower and lender.

And, it's fair to say that the analysis burden suggested by the regulators can also be out of proportion to the degree of safety it may actually add to lending, compared to the cost burden on lending in a hyper-competitive economic period with fewer deals deemed qualified to fund.

Outside banking, many companies have reformed their credit criteria and changed their outlook on risk, based on the nature of their lending or theories on funding risks. For example, non-bank working capital lenders long ago stopped obsessing over credit reports and other information for a simple reason—their lending relationships gave them control of borrower cash accounts. Late car payments and medical bills of the business owner were inconsequential as to whether they would be repaid.

Likewise, in the growing innovative funding sector, participants are looking at seemingly unthinkable borrower attributes and a range of other metrics (or semi-metrics) to define borrowing risks, measure repayment capacity, and price funding.

For many business owners, the essential information and strategies needed for small companies to be fundable are changing. The climate in which business owners now search for funding has been altered by an expanding number of capital sources that are more sharply delineated by the kinds of situations they fund. Most new capital providers are funding a narrower and more distinct business profile as a means of containing risk and targeting their marketing.

In light of the movement away from small business lending by the banking sector, many small business owners needing funding now elect to accept funding that in other times would have been considered to have outrageous borrowing terms, just to get the money and get their business going. But they often enter a financing arrangement without really understanding the true costs of funds. Sometimes such a leap works out well, even if it's unnecessarily expensive or restrictive. Sometimes things don't go so well.

These conditions will change and improve over time as the broader market discovers rich opportunities in meeting these credit needs, particularly

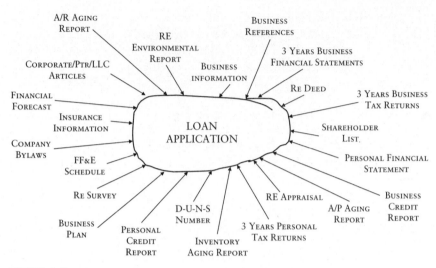

FIGURE 1.2   Common Loan Application Requirements

as technology assists in the delivery of capital. New funding strategies and underwriting methodologies will also change as a path to scaling more, smaller loans that have targeted uses and shorter repayment terms.

Traditional capital providers have not risen to the challenges presented by the information age fast enough, to provide sufficient funding for opportunities created by utilizing new technologies or meeting consumer service demands. This circumstance is likely to change.

USUAL SUSPECTS PROVIDING BUSINESS CAPITAL

Banks are sources that the general population, businesses, and non-businesses, assume will provide the majority of their business capital funding. Often, without considering the nature of their funding request or what should be well-known limitations as to what a bank can or will provide financing for, newly minted entrepreneurs and business owners flock to bank branches in every nook and cranny to get money.

According to the SBA Office of Advocacy, in 2010 approximately 90 percent of the $1 trillion of annual small business borrowing is sourced from banks ($652 billion), finance companies ($460 billion), and the SBA[4] (see Figure 1.3). They note that the sum of outstanding small business loans was higher in 2010 than in 2006. All other sources of financing (mezzanine, angel capital, and venture capital) account for less than 10 percent of small business funding.

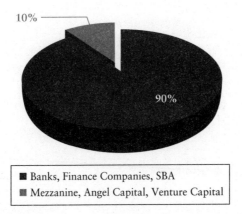

FIGURE 1.3   Sources of Small Business Financing

Pepperdine University's Graziadio School of Business and Management produces a quarterly economic survey titled "The Pepperdine Private Capital Access Index" (PCA). This index measures the demand for, activity, and health of the private capital markets. The purpose of the PCA Index is to gauge the demand of small and medium-sized businesses for financing needs, the level of accessibility to private capital, and the transparency and efficiency of private financing markets.

According to their PCA Index dated June 30, 2013, among those companies with annual revenues of less than $5 million that attempted to obtain financing during the previous quarter, most often banks were targeted, reported 59 percent of the respondents. The next highest responses were business credit cards (57.2 percent) and personal credit cards (49.9 percent), which are both also primarily funded by banks. Less than one-half of the respondents sought out personal loans (48.4 percent) or assistance from friends and family (44.2 percent)[5] (see Figure 1.4).

But the financing success among these businesses was found to be in the opposite order. Most often, funding was provided by friends and family (71 percent), followed by personal credit cards (58 percent), trade credit (57 percent), and business credit cards (54 percent). Bank loans trailed far behind at a miserable 27 percent.[6]

Yet despite this reality, 63 percent of survey respondents still think their likely source of business financing will be a bank, which is almost 1.5 times the number of companies expecting to rely on business credit cards (44 percent).[7] Telling, though, may be another statistic reflecting that 67.7 percent of respondents expect it will be difficult to raise debt financing in the next six months.[8]

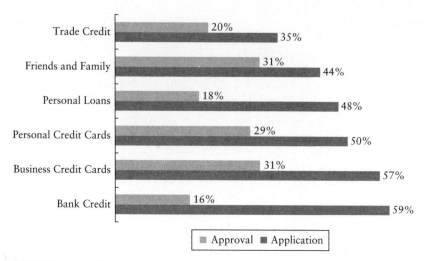

FIGURE 1.4   Small Business Financing Applications versus Approvals

These conditions parallel a similar study conducted by the Cleveland Federal Reserve Bank, which concluded, "The 15-year-long consolidation of the banking industry has reduced the number of small banks, which are more likely to lend to small businesses. Moreover, increased competition in the banking sector has led bankers to move toward bigger, more profitable, loans. That has meant a decline in small business loans, which are less profitable (because they are banker-time intensive, are more difficult to automate, have higher costs to underwrite and service, and are more difficult to securitize)."[9]

THE RISE OF ALTERNATIVE FINANCING

Part of the constantly changing landscape for business financing is rooted in the business prerogatives of the capital providers themselves. Over the years, the kind of businesses served and exact funding uses that banks would lend for changed frequently as several variables changed within the industry. Many factors led to such changes, such as economic trends, perceived risks, administrative costs, and profitability.

In decades past, many banks provided working capital loans to businesses of all sizes in the form of monitored lines of credit. These credit lines, called asset-based loans (ABL), required the bank to monitor daily or weekly company shipments and capture company payments directly from their customers. An agreed formula between bank and borrower defined how much the bank would advance against outstanding invoices that were monitored regularly with a borrowing base report.

ABL lending is provided to companies that are asset-intensive and require plenty of cash flow to meet the demands of a constant turnover of inventory and receivables. Known by some in the corporate sector as the lender of last resort, by its nature, ABL is expensive due to the many hands employed to supervise and manage lending and collections. Finance charges for ABL lending are usually presented to the borrower as a function of prime plus, but the real cost is obfuscated with a variety of fees and charges for every manual function provided to administer the loan and often includes contractual costs associated with the actual volume of use and annual commitments.

To be sure, there is plenty of non-bank competition for this kind of financing. ABL is used extensively in the manufacturing sector to allow companies to keep workers converting raw material into goods while payment is floated for 30, 60, or 90 days from buying retailers and wholesalers. Companies like CIT and former legacy lenders Textron and Heller have been strong competitors to banks over the years, though their costs of funds were generally higher and accordingly they took higher risks than banks.

Many bank and non-bank finance companies in this area also engaged in a different type of funding to provide working capital—that is they *factored* or bought a company's receivables rather than advancing loan funds against them. In a true factoring arrangement, the selling company (seller) sells the cash obligation of their customer to pay for goods they have shipped, and the factor (buyer) purchases it for a discount from its face value with no recourse to the seller. In other words, the seller can only collect the debt from the obligor and not the selling company.

With the constant communications required between borrower and lender on a daily basis during years devoid of personal computers, application software, or even fax machines, the company monitoring process required highly trained bank employees. These costs could not be scaled easily and eventually became significant enough for banks to question the profitability of this lending if they did not capture sufficient market share.

By and large, only larger banks offered asset-based lending as a product line because of the significant expertise required. And with the relative high cost involved, most banks were not interested in serving smaller companies that might be requesting less than $1 million. Besides generally being weaker credits, the banks needed to focus on more profitable accounts to cover the overhead of running a well-managed ABL operation.

These conditions gave rise to smaller, non-bank finance companies that formed with an eye to serving smaller borrowers who needed lines of credit ranging from $250,000 to $1 million. These companies were started with private equity that was usually augmented with a local bank line of credit. A broader range of smaller, regional banks generally are willing to fund these companies to provide lending capital for covering loan portfolios or to *re-lend*.

Today, the list of loans funded indirectly by banks has grown to include many other high-risk, high-priced lending categories, like payday lenders that advance money to consumers against the proceeds of their next pay-check. Whether it's due to our fear of bad publicity to fund these kinds of loans or to circumventing regulations to get higher yielding assets, lender financing adds to the complexity and costs of capital for consumers and small business owners alike.

The non-bank finance company sector has long been dubbed the alternative financing sector and was principally comprised of ABL and factoring companies. Over the years, though, this label seemed to be applied to any funding source that was not a bank. Today, it is even applied to funders ranging from micro lenders to municipal and state lending programs and to a broad group of technology-powered funding companies.

The alternative financing category is overdue for a makeover and, as indicated in the introduction, this book suggests defining technology-powered, data-centric small business funders and lenders as the *innovative funding* sector. It is an alternative of a different stripe, and hopefully the distinctive name will help business owners and other capital providers distinguish it from the usual suspects and factoring crowd as well.

Notes

1. U.S. Small Business Administration, "Size Standards Methodology," www.sba .gov/content/size-standards-methodology (accessed September 1, 2013).
2. Internal Revenue Service, "Instructions for Form 1120S," www.irs.gov/pub/irs-pdf/i1120s.pdf (accessed September 1, 2013).
3. Charles H. Green, *Get Financing Now* (New York: McGraw-Hill, 2012): 31.
4. U.S. Small Business Administration, "Frequently Asked Questions about Small Business Finance," www.sba.gov/sites/default/files/2014_Finance_FAQ.pdf (accessed June 29, 2014).
5. The Pepperdine Private Capital Access Index, June 30, 2013, Graziadio School of Business and Management, Pepperdine University, 24.
6. Ibid., 23.
7. Ibid., 41.
8. Ibid., 40.
9. Anne Marie Wiersch and Scott Shane, "Why Small Business Lending Isn't What It Used to Be," Federal Reserve Bank of Cleveland, www.clevelandfed.org/research/commentary/2013/2013-10.cfm.

CHAPTER 2

Elusive Nature of Bank Funding

Perhaps the biggest misperception among the greater business community is how the banking sector views commercial lending and the associated risk of funding a small enterprise. And to be fair to small business owners, where did they learn to expect certain lending patterns? Perhaps it was from watching a movie like *It's a Wonderful Life* or *Wall Street*?

Surely today's commercial banker would fall somewhere in between the sappy hometown banker George Bailey (played by Jimmy Stewart) and the conniving hedge fund operator Gordon Gekko (played by Michael Douglas).

Realistically, the many varied impressions of what typical lending terms should be have more often been fed by reality. Many business owners can cite plenty of instances of aggressive lending provided intermittently by start-up banks, government guaranteed lending run amuck, or an occasional money-center bank buying market share in a particular lending niche.

And like the inner child in all of us, when the business market sees one behavior or response to market conditions, such as 90 percent or 100 percent loan-to-value (LTV) advances on commercial property loans, it expects those terms should be forever available to them, too. They can never know the myriad factors that may go into a credit decision, but are convinced that because they know someone who scored a highly leveraged, unsecured, and low-priced loan, they can find one, too.

Of course, they never consider that their friend may be less than honest with them or has the benefit of some third-party intervention to qualify for favored terms.

The biggest problem with these scenarios is that these companies may be perfectly fundable on more reasonable terms (at least reasonable as deemed by the fund owners), but they exhaust themselves and exasperate many lenders with a long, fruitless search for financing terms that do not exist. They freeze themselves out of contention for many potential lenders until they finally give in to the truth at their last stop (the fifth, tenth, or fifteenth lender), disappointing several people along they way who may have found the core business proposition viable, but wasted time with a hopeless, misguided neophyte trapped in a false sense of reality.

RISK APPETITE IS AN OXYMORON

Collectively speaking, the banking sector doesn't really have an appetite for risk. Through multiple screening efforts, analysts, underwriters, credit reports, industry data, and seasoned horse sense, bankers obsess considerably to find all the potential risk in a proposal and sort out whether it can be answered by various compensating measures to avoid slow repayment, loan default, or worse, credit losses.

Real property deeds, collateral of all shapes and sizes, personal guarantees from business owners, government guarantees, third party guarantees, insurance, "dragnet" asset liens, borrowing base monitoring, lockboxes, negative pledges, loan covenants, and hundreds of pages of loan documents, security agreements, and collateral assignments are a few of the ways lenders attempt to make the price of default higher than the cost of loan repayment.

Yet banks—all banks—charge off a lot of loans each year. Even money-center banks that diversified in the post-Glass Steagall years into investment banking have found that there is no sure thing. In mid-2012, JPMorgan Chase suffered a massive $6 billion loss from aggressive trading in their European operations and their notorious heavy trader, the London Whale. Few, if any, underwriters ascend to a $6 billion lending authority.

To a seasoned credit professional, *risk appetite* is an oxymoron, because it's intended that risk be something discovered, measured, and supposedly eliminated. While acknowledged as a construct, bankers seek to erase risk through a series of screening, underwriting, and declination if necessary. Those transactions deemed to exhibit only inherent risk are then subjected to deal structures, agreements, security, and declarations that are intended to establish payment terms, operating conditions, and a litany of repayment sources that cannot fail to restore the bank's money at a mutually agreed time.

To suggest that there is an appetite for risk would suggest that bankers are willing to take an exposed gamble on longer odds of repayment, an idea that would be frowned on by most written loan policies, government supervisors, and the adult in charge. Bankers even speaking in such terms are subject to sowing suspicion among peers and superiors that can forever cast one's career into a tangential stalemate.

SOURCE OF BANK FUNDING LIMITS ITS USE

Banks have to be more measured with their lending activities and avoid most real and imagined lending risks due to the source of their funding—depositing customers. Gathering funds from the general public is an interesting business model, but is also a highly regulated business. Think about it—the general, anonymous public provides the primary source of inventory for banks to invest in various profit-making activities such as business lending. Figure 2.1 illustrates a typical bank funding/loan approval cycle.

And it's the only business in America where the federal government indemnifies the company's customers from loss, at least to a certain extent. The FDIC insures depositor funds up to generous limits to maintain confidence among the population storing the nation's cash supply in its banks, regardless of how many bank failures, loan losses, embezzlements, or robberies occur.

The price of this endless supply of deposit inventory is merely competition from the other 7,400+ banks trying to get their hands on a stake in it and the alphabet of bank regulators watching what is done with it. The United States has 50 state banking regulators and two federal regulators—the Federal Reserve (Fed) and the Office of the Comptroller of the Currency (OCC). In addition, the Federal Deposit Insurance Corporation (FDIC) partners with one of the other 52 regulators to double-team every bank in the country that relies on insured deposits.

These regulators provide general guidelines and myriad regulations intended to confine bankers in their methodology and practice of extending credit. The rules are much looser for business lending, compared to the protections afforded consumers, but there are plenty of ambiguous regulations that give rise to the supervisors letting banks know when they don't like something.

And certainly not lost on these bankers is that fact that most of their credits are subject to being reviewed, examined, questioned, and challenged by a person representing the respective agency who has never sat in front of a promising client or demanding bank president. That irony goes with the territory.

These kinds of forces are never really appreciated by the borrowing business public. Lenders are often restricted from some of the business opportunities they want to do by the reality of how their supervisors will react to it. Some bankers take these rules more seriously than others (considering the number of bank failures since 2007). Likewise, regulators tend to regulate in cycles that typically get very intense just after the latest economic downturn or financial crisis.

Bottom line—banks would not have many of the vast resources available to them to fund businesses if not for the public policy that provides the

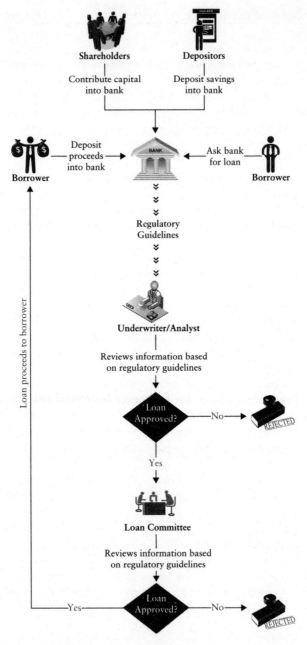

FIGURE 2.1   Bank Funding/Loan Approval Cycle

institutional structure that encourages the public to place cash on deposit and transfer most payments through a regulated channel that has public safeguards. But in the name of safety and soundness, that institutional structure limits—and at times chokes—the willingness of commercial banks to meet many needs of business owners.

SMALL BUSINESS CREDIT IS DIFFICULT TO SCALE

Most people outside the business credit sector might be stumped by the supposition that it's easier to provide a line of credit to The Coca-Cola Company than it is to make a small equipment loan to Joe & Sons Deli. Joe may only need $10,000, while Coke undoubtedly maintains billions of dollars of credit lines with dozens of lenders, available to them just in case.

Easy to recognize that Coke's financial history has been audited for over a century, and their management can account for every nickel of revenue and expense to any inquiring regulator, investor, analyst, or lender. In fact, there's a legion of people who are paid good salaries just to monitor, track, and report on everything Coke does, says, sells, or doesn't sell 365 days a year.

So, understanding the risk of lending or investing in Coke is fairly simple, given the transparency, reliable financial information, and analysis that is readily available.

But Joe & Sons Deli is a different story. Their modest enterprise, founded before there was an "& Sons," never had a reason to pay an accountant for financial statements. Since Joe had never borrowed any money through the company and couldn't read a financial statement anyway, why bother throwing away good money if it wasn't necessary? Besides, Joe faithfully filed a tax return and paid everything he owed.

So, when Joe's son wanted to borrow money from the local bank to buy a new oven, the bank had to begin a months-long consultancy of coaxing and coaching information out of the business owners to try to find sufficient metrics to understand whether the business would qualify for funding. And after all that, Joe expected to be considered a prime customer and get the best interest rate available.

Loans such as the one described to buy a single oven are more often made today with either a credit card issued to one of the business owners—who has no real sense or concern about whether the business is doing well or not—or by a non-bank captive finance company that may be a subsidiary of the equipment manufacturer.

This loan illustrates the fact that business banking is difficult to scale. While there are many more Joe & Sons than there are Coca-Colas, providing funding to them is frequently too onerous to do profitably, given the need for sound information against a backdrop of complying with a reasonable loan policy and banking regulations.

In 1979, a small bank's minimum loan might have been as low as $500, but even adjusting for inflation, it's hard to understand how that could have been profitable. Today, even with the credit enhancements offered with an SBA guarantee, a majority of participating lenders shy away from loans under $250,000.

With the actual cost of client recruitment and the many hands required to analyze, underwrite, approve, close, administer, and service a loan account, it's natural to expect that this minimum figure will rise higher in the years ahead with more complicated regulations expected after the Dodd-Frank Act is fully implemented.

Other than the obvious costs involved and regulations borne from deposit funding, many banks also suffer from lack of imagination. The lack of notable technological improvement in transaction acquisition and processing, a continuing one-size-fits-all general approach to underwriting prospective transactions, and failure to narrow the field of what constitutes the best lending opportunities have all contributed to the rising minimum size for loans as a means to respond to this scale problem.

With few exceptions, too many banks fail to consider building a higher degree of expertise within a few particular industries, business lines, or market areas in order to be better, more profitable distributors of capital. Too many banks sit back and wait to see who walks in the door. And their overhead, antiquated application processing, and unimaginative marketing aren't readily acknowledged as contributors to this dilemma.

So, small business owners pay the price for these industry structural problems by not being able to access lower cost bank funding unless they can qualify for and use a higher amount of funding than may be practical.

LOAN AND BANK SIZE ARE INVERSELY RELATED

Smaller banks have difficulty scaling most costs and are often more sensitive to the need to earn a positive return on every expense—hence, to ensure that the highest possible yield is garnered from the resources dedicated to generating business loans, small banks will more aggressively push for higher minimum loan levels and prioritize larger relationships.

However, given that the small company loans are more challenging to figure out and typically have a higher degree of credit risk, smaller banks have to dedicate a fair amount of resources to go *one-by-one* through these business owners to figure out whether funding is feasible. The bank's policies screen out most undesirable loans but the underwriters and analysts have to slog through the arduous process one-by-one to review and approve desired loans in the $250,000 to $2 million loan market. Strangely, many larger banks don't find these loans as appealing.

With more operational scale, larger banks don't have earnings pressure to such a degree that they focus on underwriting expenses as a narrow cost center, but do tend to face a different regulatory expectation to serve markets of all sizes. Smaller loans typically are managed at the branch level and considered retail lending, often serviced by branch managers and business specialists using credit scoring models and automated underwriting driven more by personal financial metrics than the borrower's business analytics.

Through the largest branch networks, the most recognizable brands, and the fact that larger banks are the primary issuers of credit cards, they can accommodate smaller business borrowers. Maybe the loans will not be as aggressive, but they are available in lower increments.

So, ironically, larger small business loans are easier to fund at smaller banks while larger banks are more likely to deliver a greater volume of funding for smaller business loans in small increments.

CHAPTER 3

Capital Market Disruptions, Post-2008

The new millennium seemed to get off to a roaring start despite the fact that the twentieth century fizzled out with the dot-com bust and the tumultuous weeks following 9/11. Overall, the years leading up to 2007 seemed to be the most robust of any age for capital creation. It was merely a matter of inventing new ways to create money.

During these years a combination of game-changing financial deregulation, new product innovation, unprecedented global portability of money, and a surge of optimism inevitably created the capital market's swelling to titanic proportions. Too much of a good thing cannot be good for any of us and, alas, it was not.

Former Federal Reserve Chairman Alan Greenspan made a half-hearted effort to calm folks down with a paltry reference to the market's *irrational exuberance*, but frankly there was just too much inventory and potential in the markets. Everyone was determined to get their share of it before it was gone.

The Federal Open Market Committee minutes from late 2006 reflect that they didn't seem concerned about housing market conditions that were evolving from a classic case of too much money crowding in to finance a shrinking demand for housing. The resulting price inflation eventually exploded among mortgage-backed security holders globally, whose insatiable demand for easy profits made them vulnerable marks for the oldest economic fraud on record: selling anything that glitters as gold.

DIDN'T ANYONE SEE BUBBLE COMING?

New home development was growing at mammoth proportions everywhere, but could barely keep up with the investment demand for mortgage-backed securities during this cycle. In their collective zeal to get ahead of the game and "grow the book," bankers tinkered with borrower qualifications to make funding available for people who normally shouldn't have been considered qualified. No income verification, no documents, no problem (the so-called *liar loans*). It is still amazing to recall all the wild angles some mortgage banks used to attract more loan volume.

Suddenly everybody was a real estate investor, notwithstanding the fact that many were concurrently barely able to pay for their own homes. A single mother with two children, struggling every week for cash to pay for day care owned two rental properties? Weeks after graduating law school, a newly minted $150,000/year attorney and first time homeowner buys a $400,000 Atlanta condo with 100 percent financing, payable at interest only?

How did these two scary deals exist? It's simple—because each found a willing banker working for a company brazen enough to lend the money in these circumstances or on these kinds of terms. Many people-turned-homeowners–and-investors got lured into the game by real estate brokers, mortgage originators. and even property owners looking to lock in their profit early. Plenty of accomplices facilitated the transition from fascinated sucker to owning an unneeded, overvalued house or condo with no tenant. But the borrowing terms and upside promised rewards that were just too good to be true.

The funding for all this exuberance was simple, or actually genius, depending on which side of the debit or credit one found oneself. Pool all these very weak loans with a smaller collection of high-quality mortgages in a bond with a dizzying array of multitiered risk tranches and an alphabet of investment holding priorities. Rebrand the bond as a *collateralized debt obligation* (CDO), sell them to rubes who had never heard the word *tranche*, and purport to balance the lower and higher grade loans for everyone's protection.

Better yet, buy a certified AAA rating for this amalgamation of confusion and slap some pretend insurance on the CDO called a credit default swap (CDS). The insurance served to convince the CDO buyer that if the security went down, someone else would get stuck with the tab (never mind who's writing the insurance and what their true financial picture may have been).

For sport, many sellers of these devious financial contraptions couldn't contain apparent unbridled greed, but went one step further from earning a diamond's commission on a piece of cheap coal—they couldn't resist betting against these very same assets. Investment bankers actually took a short position to profit from the predicted failure of the securities they were paid well to *underwrite* and sell.

How many ways can be invented to separate good people from their hard-earned cash?

The first wave of widespread mortgage defaults came to light in mid-2007 as some of the most egregious mortgage producers started failing because they could no longer sell their rotten loans. Like everything else in today's nanosecond capital markets, when the scent of rotting paper first began to waft through the air, everybody headed for the door.

By the second quarter of 2008, Wall Street was teetering on the front end of a liquidity crisis. The CDO market dried up quickly and the first wave of CDS claims started testing the holders of all that insurance. AIG became a household word among millions who had never heard the word *derivative*.

To be fair to the more level heads during this period, a combined communique from the Federal Reserve Bank, the FDIC, and the Treasury Department sounded a warning to the commercial banking sector as early as 2005 (that was repeated in 2006 and 2007). They were growing concerned about real estate value inflation and bank lending concentrations, but the warning was focused on *commercial real estate* (CRE) rather than housing.

Collectively they urged banks to begin diversifying assets and lowering exposure to high volumes of debt ostensibly secured with commercial properties and real estate developments. While that warning may have been too late, perhaps it would have garnered more attention if it had been followed with firmer regulatory actions, cracking down on some obvious loan concentrations and the capital exposure many banks had tied to speculative land development and new home construction.

THIS TIME WAS DIFFERENT

It has only been about six years beyond some of the darkest days of our modern financial banking system, days in which many bankers arrived to work each day pondering what else in the world could go wrong.

The year 2007 was full of events caused by the tumultuous effects of the steep descent of the housing market, including the bankruptcy of more than 100 mortgage lenders. But these failing companies remained in the background as most eyes were following the rapid fall of the industry's poster child for subprime lending: Countrywide Financial.

On January 11, 2008, after months of speculation, Bank of America finally announced an all-stock deal to acquire Countrywide for $5.50 per share, a pittance of the company's value only one year earlier when it still sold north of $40/share. While in any other year that announcement might have been the turning point in the mortgage debacle, this time was different. The rescue of Countrywide by the nation's largest bank did not slow down the unfolding crisis.

Soon afterward the venerable investment house Bear Stearns would narrowly miss bankruptcy in March through a fire sale to JP Morgan Chase.

TABLE 3.1 The Costs of 90 Days of Financial Chaos

Date	Sinking Ship	Lifesaver	Capital Impact
Sept. 7	Fannie Mae and Freddie Mac	FHFA	$6,000,000,000,000
Sept. 14	Merrill Lynch	Bank of America	$50,000,000,000
Sept. 15	Lehman Bros.		$639,000,000,000
Sept. 16	AIG	Federal Reserve	$209,000,000,000
Sept. 25	Washington Mutual	Office of Thrift Supervision	$62,900,000,000
Sept. 29	Wachovia	Wells Fargo	$15,100,000,000
Oct. 3	Banks with troubled assets	TARP	$700,000,000,000
Oct. 13	Nine Largest Banks	TARP	$125,000,000,000
Nov. 23	Citicorp	Treasury/Federal Reserve/FDIC	$326,000,000,000
Nov. 25	Student Loans Auto Loans Credit Cards SBA Loans	TALF	$1,000,000,000,000
		TOTAL 90-DAY CAPITAL IMPACT:	$9,127,000,000,000.00

Regulators shut down IndyMac in July when the bank could not sell loans in the market and customers began pulling out deposits after public comments concerning the bank's shaky condition were aired by Senator Charles Schumer (D-NY).

But more ominous events still lay ahead that culminated in the fall. The negative financial impact will never be entirely accounted for but Table 3.1 illustrates some of the immediate costs at street level. It seems surreal to recount all that happened over the course of the 90 days between September and November 2008:

- September 7: The Federal Housing Finance Agency (FHFA) placed Fannie Mae and Freddie Mac into conservatorship, with a combined $6 trillion of affected mortgages, over concerns over their inability to raise capital and debt, which could disrupt the U.S. housing finance market further.
- September 14: Bank of America announced it had agreed to acquire the venerable Merrill Lynch for about $50 billion in a transaction that would later spark controversy by the absence of disclosures of Merrill's

pending fourth-quarter losses and the bank's contention that it was pressured by regulators to complete the deal.

- September 15: Lehman Bros. filed the largest bankruptcy in history for $639 billion after a tumultuous year-long struggle with portfolio losses arising from leveraged positions as high as 31:1 in subprime mortgage tranches, which quickly eroded their capital as the mortgage market headed downward.
- September 16: The Federal Reserve rescued private insurance company AIG with an $85 billion investment paid for an 80 percent stake in the company to resolve a liquidity crisis created by about $58 billion in structured debt securities backed by subprime loans. The Fed would eventually add another $124 billion of investment exposure to this company.
- September 25: The Office of Thrift Supervision seized Washington Mutual, the largest bank failure in world history, following a nine-day runoff of nearly $17 billion of WaMu customer deposits.
- September 29: Wachovia Bank, reeling from mortgage-related losses that stemmed from its controversial purchase of Golden West Financial, ended a silent run on deposits and avoided pending failure only by being pressed by regulators to enter an open bank transfer of ownership to Citicorp, which was soon to be succeeded by a negotiated sale to Wells Fargo for a paltry $15 billion.
- September 29: After the highly charged House of Representatives voted down a bank rescue package proposed by Treasury Secretary Henry Paulson in the waning days of the U.S. presidential campaign, the Dow Jones Industrial Average (DJIA) fell 777.68 points, its largest single-day point drop ever.[1]
- September 30th: The final day of the government's fiscal year was a significant turning point for SBA-guaranteed loans, as the spreading financial crisis caused the secondary market for these loans to collapse. For 2008, the number of approved loans fell 30 percent from the previous year, totaling a 10 percent drop in dollar volume. By the end of 2009, small business loans would fall another 27 percent.
- October 3: Congress passed an amended 169-page Emergency Economic Stabilization Act that granted the Treasury authority to purchase or insure up to $700 billion of troubled assets from banks under the Troubled Asset Relief Program, to be known as TARP.
- October 13: Treasury Secretary Paulson met with CEOs of the nine largest U.S. banks and pressured them to accept a $125 billion preferred stock purchase from the TARP program to shore up balance sheets among the weakest of them, while not exposing the identity of the true target (Citibank) to the public.

- October 31: The DJIA finished October having lost a total of 1,526.65 points during the month, making it the worst month on record for the index, which included two trading days marked as among the worst 5 in NYSE history.[2]
- November 23: Even after shedding 92,000 jobs during the previous 18 months and having already received $25 billion in TARP funds in October, the Treasury Department, Federal Reserve Bank, and FDIC announced that the federal government would guarantee $306 billion of Citicorp loans and securities, as well as invest another $20 billion to keep the company solvent.
- November 25: The Federal Reserve announced the creation of the Term Asset-Backed Securities Loan Facility (TALF), which was intended to acquire securities used to fund student loans, auto loans, credit cards, and SBA loans. Advances were offered without recourse. While the announcement was made for a $300 billion fund, the Fed eventually purchased more than $1 trillion through TALF.

As if there weren't enough troubles, the creation of TARP set off a public backlash, redefining the banking system rescue as more of a private enterprise bailout that did more harm than good. To be fair, both sides of that argument have many facts with which to bolster their arguments. Ironically, TARP itself was dwarfed by other guarantees and lending limits; analysis by Bloomberg found the Federal Reserve had, by March 2009, committed $7.77 trillion to rescuing the financial system, more than half the value of everything produced in the United States that year.[3]

Any one of these events could have been the most remarkable story in any year during normal circumstances, but for all these apoplectic events to occur in such a short time span reflects how close the U.S. financial system was to a complete meltdown.

Six years later the economy remains in recovery, with a lethargic growth rate insufficient to overcome or turn around millions of job losses. Consumer confidence remains below what's needed for sustainable growth and for a while actually spurred gains in the national savings rate. While normally a positive development, during those first post-crisis years it reflected that consumers were hoarding cash at the expense of consumption thought to be needed to fuel growth.

Total home equity in the United States, valued at $13 trillion at its peak in 2006, had dropped to $8.8 trillion by mid-2008 and was still falling in late 2008. Total retirement assets, American's second-largest household asset, dropped by 22 percent, from $10.3 trillion in 2006 to $8 trillion in mid-2008. During the same period, savings and investment assets (apart from retirement savings) lost $1.2 trillion and pension assets lost $1.3 trillion.

Taken together, these losses total a staggering $8.3 trillion.[4] After peaking in the second quarter of 2007, household wealth was down $14 trillion.[5]

WHERE DID MAIN STREET FUNDING GO?

The commercial banking sector began choking on a similar variety of problems. Many community banks (those with under $1 billion in assets) bet heavily on more land speculation, residential development, and commercial construction than could possibly be absorbed in one good economic cycle. Sunbelt banks that had enjoyed bulging population growth during the previous two decades, in states such as California, Arizona, Nevada, Texas, Georgia, and Florida, were hit particularly hard.

During the 2008 crash months, as several major commercial and investment banking companies either failed or were forced into a quick sale, even large survivors like Goldman Sachs, Morgan Stanley, and American Express were feeling the heat. With the cooperation of the Federal Reserve, they quickly sought refuge in the more regulated commercial banking system and were approved for charters virtually overnight. This enabled them to access plentiful, cheap funding for liquidity and convert billions of client dollars to insured deposits to stave off sudden migrations of capital away from the markets. It also signaled the expectation that they would be protected from failure through federal intervention, if necessary.

It was ironic to realize early in the fourth quarter that Main Street investment broker Raymond James was suddenly the largest such company in the nation, since the Wall Street titans of capitalism ran for cover under Uncle Sam's banking umbrella.

Concurrently, as new home construction and home sales fell off sharply in late 2007, a global recession emerged that affected virtually every business sector. In the United States, 15 million jobs disappeared and the unprecedented millions of home foreclosures that followed ensured the real estate market crash would be felt for the foreseeable future.

After several healthy years following the 1990s S&L crisis, this crash caused hundreds of bank failures starting in late 2007. Even in 2014 and beyond it's expected that more failures lie ahead that are rooted in the changes of fortune dating back to the crash. Many of the surviving banks were severely weakened by capital depletion caused by either suddenly devalued loan portfolios or the lack of sufficient revenues in the face of severe interest rate reductions. As the business sector became too weak or too timid to borrow money, most banks' primary source of revenue was severely curtailed.

Small business capital financing evaporated almost overnight for most entrepreneurs. According to Federal Deposit Insurance Corporation chair

Sheila Bair,[6] more than $2.7 *trillion* of credit lines collapsed during this period, which made business growth and economic expansion virtually impossible.

The federal government's stimulus efforts through the Troubled Asset Relief Program (TARP), the Small Business Jobs Act, tax cuts. and expansion of U.S. Small Business Administration (SBA) programs have all contributed to soften the blow but there is still much work to be done. To get the United States and global economies back on track to a more encouraging growth rate will require more business. Capital financing for that growth is far from certain.

SBA—MAIN STREET'S FEDERAL BAILOUT?

TARP, originally hailed by many community bankers, turned out to be an accurately criticized tool with which the Treasury Department and Federal Reserve could pick winners and losers. First proposed by Secretary Paulson on a four-page memo as a bad bank fund that would be used to purchase bad real estate loans from commercial banks, it was partially sold to Congress as a way many smaller institutions could recover from a crisis that was not their making.

Evolving rules promulgated by the Financial Accounting Standards Board (FASB) since the 1990s dictated that bankers were required to recognize loan asset values based on their current risk conditions or as similarly referred to in the investment world, *mark to market*. When there were clear signs of deteriorating loan quality or performance disruptions, banks were expected to evaluate their exposure, which often meant obtaining an updated real property appraisal. Often that meant that the banks would be forced to increase loan loss reserves or write-down loans for potential losses on many performing loans that were not necessarily in default.

During the years immediately following the crash (2008–2010), these write-downs, accompanied by a 5.25 percent reduction in the prime interest rate crippled many community banks with painful loss reserves and led what had been healthy banks into problem bank status. Some legacy banks that survived the Great Depression ultimately failed in the face of the aggressive push for recognizing potential losses that was stressed over managing the accounts through these rocky times.

The brief ray of hope in late 2008 was that TARP would be available to purchase these loans that were underwritten and funded by good bankers doing a good job and who had been lending money secured by good real estate for decades with the same results: good profits. Although succored through many admirable, prudent bank lending cultures and seasoned with decades of experience, many bankers simply failed to recognize the severity or breadth of this crisis. The formerly reliable banker's lore that "you can't get hurt if you have the dirt" was suddenly hollow and devoid of refuge by a collapsing real estate market.

On December 31, 2008, Secretary Paulson[7] made it official through a report to Congress that he was betraying the promises that the most vulnerable banks would participate in a portion of the government's rescue by declaring that TARP funding would be limited. As redefined, TARP was available only to banks that qualified through stress testing and with conditions that kept it out of reach to many.

Basically it was a matter of winning approval of the Emergency Economic Stabilization Act with one set of promises and then implementing it with an entirely different strategy. Except for the strongest, many community banks—and therefore many of the primary banks serving Main Street— were on their own to navigate out of this mess.

Another wrinkle in the history of this situation was that on November 5, 2008, American voters elected Barack Obama as president, and on November 6 a transition to a new government started that would be grappling with these issues that were still unfolding in real time. Regardless of who won the race, the new president's administration would have to step up quickly to assume the financial reins in precarious times and unavoidable was the fact that whatever happened, they would shoulder some blame that may have been owed to their predecessors.

To its credit, the Obama administration included small business capital funding in the recovery portfolio from the very beginning. In February, 2009, scarcely 45 days in office, the Obama Administration championed the $787 billion stimulus package, known as the American Recovery and Reinvestment Act of 2009 (ARRA), which among other provisions, included $730 million for the SBA to expand lending and investment programs.

A portion of these funds was used to eliminate program fees for borrowers and lenders, and raise the guaranty percentage on eligible 7(a) program loans to 90 percent. This higher level of coverage and free price for borrowers was intended to encourage more bank lending and borrower acceptance of the SBA guaranty. It is still common for many business owners to avoid SBA financing due to misperceptions about how participation may result in closer government oversight or that the guaranty is an admission of financial weakness.

The ARRA funding was followed in September 2010 with the Small Business Jobs Act, which extended the higher loan guarantees and fee elimination for another year and answered SBA advocates' plea to increase the loan size to higher limits in recognition of a growing economy. The size limits of the flagship 7(a) loan program and 504/CDC debenture financing program were both increased to $5 million from $2 million. In addition, the agency expanded business size standards in many industrial sectors as defined through the National Association of Industrial Code Standards (NAICS), thereby making more than 122,000 additional businesses eligible for SBA financial assistance for the first time.

The combined effects of these two actions opened more flexible, long-term capital options to not only many business owners but to many new transactions as well. These owners suddenly had access to capital to buy more, build more, and grow more. And as a bonus, while the 2004 elimination of the 7(a) program subsidy had driven loan guarantee fees to an eye-popping 3.75 percent on larger loans, under the ARRA allocation, for a limited period these loans would have a 0 percent fee to borrowers.

While the SBA guaranty doesn't turn a bad deal into a good one, it does make good deals more affordable to a company's cash flow by giving lenders the flexibility to extend a longer loan term. The SBA guarantee is equivalent to the full faith and credit of the United States government, meaning that financially speaking, it is as safe as a Treasury bond. So the loan guaranty on a 25-year real estate loan that is priced at some spread over prime rate can be sold off to a secondary market of willing buyers who enjoy low risk at rates much more attractive than typical government bonds.

The effect of this legislation for banks and other SBA lenders was that suddenly they had the SBA available to partner to dizzying new heights with a 150 percent increase in the program limits for guaranteed loans. The loan sale premiums, additional loan interest, and elevated servicing fees made many community bankers swoon as they aggressively began marketing these ARRA loans while the funds were available.

But some lenders had another strategy. Regardless of their earlier focus (or lack of) on SBA lending, many saw these larger limits and cheap conversion costs as a way to refinance existing portfolio loans into longer-term SBA loans. That conversion was intended to benefit both the banks and borrowers, depending on their respective situations.

For banks, refinancing to SBA was a way to (1) provide relief from the unknown (or perhaps known) credit exposure they had and place the credit under SBA's shared risk umbrella, and (2) generate some badly needed non-interest fee income by selling the guaranteed loans off. The combined effect was to lower bank loss exposure and generate some quick profits that could address the squeezed capital pressure many banks felt.

For borrowers, refinancing to SBA was a way to (1) get some cash flow relief by rescheduling their loans over a longer term to lower payments, and (2) if they happened to be better off financially than their banks, maybe get some additional funding that might have been resisted earlier.

A bonus for some of these banks may have been providing relief to deserving customers under financial pressure and avoiding the consequences of having to categorize the loan as a troubled debt restructure (TDR), since the more liberal SBA loan terms were standard. But for some banks, marginal loans that were converted to SBA loans still defaulted—many within 18 months of being reworked with SBA. And for them, they may still yield problems with SBA ahead if the loan account problems resurface.

One other provision of the Small Business Jobs Act was to budget $10 million for the SBA's Office of Inspector General (OIG) to monitor the new crop of 90 percent guaranteed loans by the ARRA and its extension, to ensure that lenders did not abuse it.

In January 2013, PNC Bank[8] became the first high-profile bank to face prosecution under the False Claims Act for lending abuses relating to ARRA 90 percent loan guarantees, which resulted in the bank paying a $7.1 million fine plus the loss of the SBA reimbursement for loan losses. And OIG has made it clear in the months since that these ARRA loan audits will continue as the results of many of the loans reveal that their warnings were valid.

SUPPLY VERSUS DEMAND—DID ANYONE ASK FOR A LOAN (AND WHAT WAS THE ANSWER)?

SBA industry's most prominent observer, publisher Bob Coleman, has pointed out in many national interviews that "SBA didn't require a bail-out."[9] He is largely right because there was never a crisis at SBA requiring immediate federal intervention for their seasoned model. Essentially the SBA 7(a) program operates as a credit insurance fund with extensive actuarial history with which to plan future funding reserves. The 504 / CDC program is funded by investor purchases of long-term debentures, and before the crisis operated for many years without a subsidy to cover loan losses.

But to be fair, SBA was the recipient of some extra help. In 2004, the Bush administration gutted the 7(a) program's subsidy—then a paltry $72 million—and passed along the full cost of the program to borrowers through guaranty fees that nearly doubled (from 2 percent of the guarantee amount to a sliding scale up to 3.75 percent), and a first time ongoing assessment on lender servicing fees totaling 55 basis points of collections for the life of the loan. Some corners correctly recognized these changes as a tax increase with another name.

The Obama administration provided direct relief to borrowers by eliminating the guarantee fees paid by borrowers in fiscal years 2010 and 2011 with subsidy funding for the 7(a) program totaling $562 million. Beginning October 1, 2011, the normal program fees resumed but the agency braced for higher loan losses ahead. As a result, the loan program budget was again subsidized[10] with $363 million in FY 2012 and $351 million[11] in FY 2013 to cover these anticipated higher losses. The FY 2014 budget called for a return to the $0 subsidy for the 7(a) program.

Was that a bailout? Not really, but it was extraordinary funding that had to be appropriated from the federal budget to support a projected level of small business funding because losses in the guaranty fund were rising higher than historical trends. Given the modest dollars involved (at least in federal budget terms), it might be best expressed that the program got a *hand-up, not a hand-out.*

Compare the total SBA subsidies during these years (approximately $1.3 billion) to the massive federal capital infusions provided from a combination of TARP, FDIC, and the Federal Reserve[12] into the top three recipients: Citicorp *($476 billion)*, Bank of America *($336 billion)*, and distant third Morgan Stanley *($135 billion)*, the SBA 7(a) program subsidy costs were virtually equivalent to a rounding error.

But despite all the Obama administration's effort, the small business sector remains fairly tepid. After countless tax breaks and no fewer than three separate legislative acts aimed to pump business capital toward the 26,500,000[13] American companies with less than $7.5 million revenues, from 2010 through 2013 this market was largely a dry well, frustrating efforts of policy makers, bankers, and those concerned directly with job growth.

And all the while, there seemed to be a constant battle to write an accurate narrative explaining this situation. In the financial press, there was a constant barrage of stories highlighting business owners frustrated at the lack of capital financing available at their neighborhood banks, advocacy and trade groups haranguing the financial sector for holding their reins too tight, and a plethora of surveys and studies proving this angst with hard numbers.

Pepperdine's PCA Index[14] probably provides the most comprehensive set of data gathered during these years to measure the supply and demand for capital among business owners. Segmented into two distinct silos based on revenue size: <$5 million (which are the results cited here) and $5 to $100 million, this quarterly survey was conducted nationwide beginning in 2009 and offers a compelling story about demand during these years.

Clearly the pressure of the Great Recession was felt far beyond the financial sector and lasted much longer. This survey even revealed that about one-third of respondents reported slower trade account collections during the previous quarter.[15]

While 70.5 percent of respondents said it was still difficult to raise new external debt financing during this period,[16] only 26 percent of respondents had even attempted raising outside financing since the previous quarter.[17] Extrapolating the data reveals that actually only 18 percent of the total number of respondents found it difficult to raise capital. While it's still 70 percent of those who tried, the point is it's less than a fifth of the entire survey response.

Of the 26 percent attempting to secure outside financing, 43 percent of respondents sought funding for growth or expansion and 27 percent for working capital fluctuations. Some 6 percent cited worsening conditions, and 1 percent sought to replace equity with debt financing.[18] The latter borrowers were unlikely to obtain financing in a good economic period for the cited use of funds.

Of the 74 percent of the businesses on the sidelines not looking for external capital, the reason most (70 percent) cited as to why they were not attempting to find external financing was that "they had sufficient cash flow or financing already in place." The most frequent "other" response was because of a "weak economy."[19]

Finally, the survey revealed that only 29 percent (+11 percent) of respondents had the intention to raise capital in the succeeding six months,[20] and the main purpose for 89 percent of them was to fund growth or augment working capital. Tellingly, 66.4 percent of the respondents planning to ask for credit expected that raising debt financing would be difficult.[21]

The Pepperdine data provides some hard numbers from which some context can be extracted—information that was rarely reflected in the media during the past two or three years. It seems that the demand for capital was rather muted as a percentage of the whole survey population. Quite simply, the small business sector wasn't asking for capital mostly due to the fact that they didn't need it. Suffice it to say that the lack of interest may have been largely owed to the stagnant economy but still, these businesses were getting along.

Lenders and investors rarely bail out failing business owners as their companies are dying. The Great Recession had many victims, but it was ludicrous to think that banks had an inclination or obligation to deploy funding when the risk of default was certain, much less reasonably high.

But on the side of the supply argument, bankers too had plenty of statistics to support the notion that they were doing all they could to increase lending. While sitting on perhaps the largest cash reserves in the history of banking, a reported $2 trillion[22] on bank balance sheets, many bankers issued quarterly declarations that loans to small businesses were growing. Bank of America even announced they hired 1,000[23] new business lenders while Wells Fargo claimed to have added 1,500[24] business lenders between the years 2012 and 2013. Bravo!

For the record, in 2012 Wells Fargo did become the first single lender to underwrite $1 billion of SBA loans[25] in a single year, taking credit for 5 percent of the entire program, which counts about 3,000 qualified lenders with access to program funds.

Of course the real answer was that both sides were technically correct. Larger U.S. banks consistently increased lending to the small business sector in years 2011 through 2013, but some closer analysis of the numbers reveals that they were taking business from the community banking sector to do it.[26]

One Atlanta bank president described the dilemma: Their bank had for years focused on small medical practice loans to doctors and dentists who wanted to acquire buildings to house their practices. These loans were lower risk in that with a thriving practice, the income and profits were fairly predictable and stable. The bank could attract the business with a reasonably priced loan with a margin of 1 to 1.5 percent over the prime rate that was stuck at 3.25 percent for more than four years.

Then one of the nation's top-10 ranked banks took aim at this product niche, offering dentists a 20-year term loan at 2.75 percent fixed until maturity. That larger bank could make these attractive terms available because they had the multiple sources to acquire long-term capital funding to lend well beyond the immediate community's depositor base, which is where the smaller bank had to source most of their funding.

So did that larger bank's lending to the small business sector increase? Yes. Was it driven by greater demand from that sector? No. This bank simply used its financial pricing advantage to cannibalize good loans already being provided by a smaller bank, and offering a lower fixed-rate price to the borrower to win the business.

Other obvious supply problems for small business owners included the generally tighter loan standards imposed by many banks as the recession began in 2008, which have never really changed. The reliability or confidence that many business owners had developed over the years with a local banker simply evaporated and has not yet been restored.

Deflation and uncertainty in the real estate markets also lowered a ready supply of capital for many business owners who had grown accustomed to using their real estate equity as an ATM for business funding. The disappearance of the home equity lines of credit (HELOCs) particularly was felt among the very smallest companies.

Other barriers to capital included the sheer number of failing banks that canceled tens of thousands of existing financing relationships with business owners and diverted even the best borrowing customers into an extended period of uncertainty. Many companies felt the faltering financial effects of the recession, which meant that restarting a banking relationship would become very challenging, even if the applicant had never defaulted on previous payment obligations.

Add to these barriers the evaporation of personal investment portfolio gains, retirement plan losses, and lower business revenues and it's no wonder that business owner confidence hit the skids. Who would want to try to expand a business as Rome was burning?

Whether there was a supply problem or a demand problem for capital financing to small businesses during this period will likely remain a matter of perspective dependent on the lens used by the viewer. But it's probably most accurate to say there was a problem with both elements that contributed to extended post-crisis doldrums in the U.S. economy.

POST-CRISIS REFLECTIONS ON FINANCIAL REGULATION

Beginning in 1980, the United States entered a period accentuated with banking deregulation, including the Deposit Institution Deregulation and Monetary Act (1980), the Garn-St. Germain Depository Institution Act (1982), and the Secondary Mortgage Market Enhancement Act (1984).

No doubt, after U.S. monetary intervention of the 1970s to fight inflation, which raised interest rates to historic levels, many of these changes seemed to be good ideas. Savings & loan associations (S&Ls) were struggling under their historic model of long-term lending with short term deposits. But Congress (with the assistance of a legion of industry lobbyists) effectively deregulated S&Ls into banks without the same rules, business experience, or management capacity and alas, S&Ls are largely a quaint recollection of the past.

Following the first wave of these relatively rapid and radical banking system changes there were 2,935 bank failures from 1980 to 1994, following the S&L crisis. That rate slowed from 1994 to 2007 to a mere 58 bank failures, but in the aftermath of the Gramm Leach Bliley Act (GLB), passed in 1998, and the Commodity Futures Modernization Act (CFM), passed in 2000, 505 additional banks failed since the beginning of 2007.

Some pundits, like the conservative think tank American Enterprise Institute (AEI), blame the housing crash on the Housing and Urban Development (HUD) programs encouraging home ownership or the Community Reinvestment Act (CRA), which was intended to require banks to lend money in the neighborhoods where they gathered deposits. But that argument ignored a broader consensus that illiquid non-insured mortgage securities brought the market to its knees. AIE's call for market-based reforms failed to recognize the evidence of exactly what had just happened.

Ireland and Spain also had severe housing busts without HUD or CRA, but they did have the same actual impetus: easy money that was provided by the aggressive securitization of mortgages through these exotic financial instruments.

Recall that Ginny Mae began trading securities backed by Government Sponsored Enterprises (GSEs) in 1968, through residential mortgage-backed securities (RMBSs), a bond secured by thousands of residential mortgages bundled in tranches with the same structure and loan terms. But in 1984, the landscape changed with a market-based reform (permitted by the Secondary Mortgage Market Enhancement Act) when Salomon Bros. introduced a housing finance securitization vehicle without GSE supporting guarantees.

According to former IMF chief economist Simon Johnson, the volume of private RMBSs (excluding GSE-backed mortgages) grew from $11 billion (1984) to $200 billion (1994) to $3 trillion (2007).[27] They exceeded GSE-sponsored mortgage volume in 2004 with lower lending standards (i.e., low-doc, no-doc, and no income verification loans), thereby securitizing low quality and high-risk mortgages.

No federal housing policy mandated a single bank to create, sell, or compete with these products to their disastrous end. Hence, arguably there was an element of these market-based reforms in housing finance that contributed to the crisis.

Blaming the government masks the true cause of the financial crisis: insufficient financial regulation. The real villain may have been GLB, which among other provisions, repealed the Glass-Steagall Act, removing the 65-year-old barrier between commercial banks, investment banks, and insurance. It gave us the "too-big-to-fail" banks that collectively aggregated more than 78 percent of U.S. bank deposits in the largest 20 banks.

A close second place would be CFM that exempted derivative products from being regulated as securities. It was the collapse of the CDO market that led to the financial crisis. Based on the numbers, blaming GSEs rather than Wall Street simply allows a predisposition to hold the federal government's action as the root-of-all-evil to override facts. Whether that's philosophical or ideological reasoning doesn't matter—intellectual honesty has more evidence to support this case.

Most economists, academics, and investigators, notably the Levin-Coburn Report[28] and the highly politicized Financial Crisis Investigation Commission,[29] concur that the meltdown was caused by a liquidity collapse attributable to CDOs issued through a shadow banking system.

The CFM exempted regulating CDOs as securities. Combined with credit default swaps and the rating agencies' complicity, banks began hustling these securities with unfathomable success between 2004 and 2007 to fund Alt-A and subprime mortgages. The rest is history and could not have occurred without GLB or CFM.

To be clear, GSEs were not without blame. Fannie Mae originated as a federal program in the 1930s to provide liquidity to small banks that wanted to meet the demand for housing loans but could hold the exposure to a 15- to 30-year mortgage. The enterprise went public in 1968 through the sale of stock (and ending the explicit federal guarantee of their holdings) and in 1970 was authorized to buy private, non-government guaranteed mortgages. In 1981, Fannie Mae issued its first mortgage-backed security, and while it was clear that their instruments were subject to market risks, the buying public always relied on a clear perception that an implicit federal government guaranty protected their investments.

Throughout the 1990s and well into the Bush II administration, Fannie Mae was subjected to competing Congressional intervention to make it more—or less—accessible by various housing policy standards. During this time the agency became enmeshed in politics, fielding the largest team of lobbyists and outspending all others to influence Congress.

It's been well documented that Fannie Mae gamed most of the policy goals set for them during these years and racked up their own accounting scandal. They were found to have overstated earnings by more than $6 billion, which resulted in more than 100 criminal indictments since 2011 against senior managers, whose handiwork was created in order to inflate their bonuses.

Maybe former FDIC Chair Sheila Bair best summed up the quandary in a 2010 speech: "In hindsight, the implicit government backing enjoyed by the mortgage GSEs, where profits were privatized and the risks were socialized, was an accident waiting to happen."[30] While most agree that sufficient long-term capital is not available to fund growth in the U.S. housing market without some government participation, all those possibilities are laden with the risk of abuse that comes with easy profits.

The expansion of Fannie Mae through a public offering and their leading the charge to create better financial products to fund the housing sector were done in good faith for laudable public policy goals. But the problem with sole reliance on market-based reforms may be that the short-term profit compulsion by many participants, often aided by illegal tactics, has repeatedly proven to create severe consequences for the financial and banking systems and their stakeholders: depositors, borrowers, investors, taxpayers, and the economy at large.

Policy makers do not purposely create malfeasant solutions but are often complicit in bad ones when they allow campaign contributions to dictate industry-driven exemptions and exceptions to balanced constraints. Such contortions usually result in skewed outcomes from well-intended regulation.

Deregulation produced many positive results and certainly excessive regulation can stifle bona fide economic opportunity. But likewise, mis-regulation happens when policymakers are totally disconnected from the realities of what happens on the ground among those subject to regulation.

The well-intentioned people who pine for a less-tethered market must provide an alternative, workable solution for an unregulated environment that protects all participants from the abusive products, tactics, and profiteering witnessed on the heels of most earlier regulatory reforms. Much of the rising economic expansion that resulted from earlier deregulatory efforts did not benefit any party beyond the previously regulated one.

Consumers have been pummeled by higher costs and worse service by the telephone, airline, bank, and energy industry deregulatory efforts. Did they get more product choices? Yes. Did the price of these services double and triple costs? Yes again. Is anyone completely satisfied with their phone service, baggage fees, bank services, or electric bill? It's very unlikely.

Those advocating for reasonable regulation must work toward the prevention of abuses often seen as crony oversight, which invariably originates from the to-be-regulated seeking to insulate the effects or soften the impact of the very regulations intended to establish boundaries. Often they are able to stifle competition and evade accountability in the process of proliferating rules. These realities undermine well-intentioned and needed rules, while fueling public sentiment in favor of some political cronies who would simply drop all the rules.

Strangely, it's to the defense of the to-be-regulated class that many of the most vicious cries for a free market are heard, spoken by those who argue for policy reverence to the Austrian Economics theories. And while they purport to be more representative of actual market participants, those companies constantly occupy themselves with efforts intended to rig the system to avoid regulation or competition in exclusive ways to the detriment of competitors and customers. In other words, their actions are not so free-market.

Profits in the financial sector are a very good thing when transparent and exchanged between a willing buyer who has the benefit of information that is the same as information available to all other buyers, and a seller who fairly represents exactly what is being sold with adequate disclosure to present the true risks. But deregulation confirmed that our economy needs protection from some who can't be trusted to act even in their own best interests.

Alan Greenspan conceded before a House committee that he placed too much faith in the self-correcting power of the free market. "Those of us who have looked to the self-interest of lending institutions to protect shareholders' equity, myself included, are in a state of shocked disbelief," he said.[31]

All the major components of this entire narrative enraged some. There were advocates railing against deregulation for the predictable impact they would have on ordinary bank clients, small investors, and the cost of financial products. Likewise, there has been howling from big banking interests and their advocates about being blamed for the crisis and the new regulations intending to rein them in.

The extraordinary financial deregulation of the 1990s, made during the term of former Goldman Sachs Co-Chairman Robert Rubin as Treasury secretary, lowered government supervision and regulation of the financial markets to their lowest level in more than a half-century. Interestingly, the ensuing crisis was only survived through the greatest U.S. government financial market intervention in history by another Goldman Sachs alumnus, former CEO and then-current Treasury Secretary Henry Paulson.

In the ensuing years since the crisis, the Dodd-Frank Act was adopted to close many of the obvious gaps that existed in financial regulations, through which most of the various abuses occurred despite earlier attempts to reasonably deregulate the financial markets. Fiercely opposed by the very industry that was arguably saved by the federal government's printing press, four years later there remain hundreds of regulations still not written as directed by the bill.

The actual, comprehensive effects of this legislation will not be fully known for decades; meanwhile, many observers predict that its final tally of bureaucracy will amount to more than 30,000 pages of rules. It's to this degree that lobbyists, lawyers, and industry proponents insist on carving out nooks and crannies to permit them to avoid much of the original intention of the law. In other words, it will be business as usual to a large degree.

Notes

1. Julie Hirschfeld Davis, "Bailout Bill Slapped Aside; Record Stock Plunge," Yahoo! News, Associated Press (September 29, 2008).
2. "Dow Jones Industrial Average Historical Data," Dave Manuel.com (accessed September 30, 2013).
3. Bob Ivry, Bradlay Keoun, and Phil Kuntz, "Secret Fed Loans Gave Banks $13 Billion Undisclosed to Congress," *Bloomberg Markets*, November 28, 2011.
4. Roger C. Altman, "The Great Crash, 2008—Roger C. Altman," *Foreign Affairs*, January/February 2009.
5. "Americans' Wealth Drops $1.3 Trillion," CNNMoney.com, June 11, 2009.
6. FDIC, www.fdic.gov/news/conferences/sbl.html (accessed September 30, 2013).
7. http://web.archive.org/web/20090429194236/,http://www.financialstability.gov/docs/AGP/sec102ReportToCongress.pdf (accessed September 30, 2013).
8. Department of Justice, www.justice.gov/opa/pr/2013/January/13-civ-109.html (accessed September 30, 2013).
9. ColemanReport,www.colemanreport.com/wp-content/uploads/2012/10/coleman report082211.pdf (accessed September 30, 2013).
10. SBA,www.sba.gov/about-sba/sba_newsroom/fiscal_year_2012_budget_summary (accessed September 30, 2013).

SURVEY OF FUNDING SMALL BUSINESS

11. SBA,www.sba.gov/sites/default/files/files/1-508%20Compliant%20FY%202013%20CBJ%20FY%202011%20APR(1).pdf.
12. Final Report of the Congressional Oversight Panel, March 16, 2011, 33.
13. U.S. Census Bureau, www.census.gov/econ/smallbus.html (accessed September 30, 2013).
14. Pepperdine University, "PCA Index Survey Responses, Second Quarter 2013."
15. Ibid., 19.
16. Ibid., 22.
17. Ibid., 20.
18. Ibid., 25.
19. Ibid., 26.
20. Ibid., 35.
21. Ibid., 40.
22. Forbes,www.forbes.com/sites/robertlenzner/2013/07/16/householdscorporations-and-banks-are-hoarding-14-trillion-cash/ (accessed September 30, 2013).
23. Bank of America, http://newsroom.bankofamerica.com/press-release/promotions-and-appointments/ (accessed September 30, 2013).
24. CPA Practice Advisor, www.cpapracticeadvisor.com/news/10941069/wells-fargo-enhances-small-business-lending-and-services (accessed September 30, 2013).
25. Wells Fargo,https://www.wellsfargo.com/press/2013/20130620_WFUSSBALarge LenderoftheYear (accessed September 30, 2013).
26. *Inc.*,www.inc.com/jeremy-quittner/lending-big-banks-federal-reserve-small-business-administration.html (accessed September 30, 2013).
27. Simon Johnson and James Kwak, *13 Bankers: The Wall Street Takeover and the Next Financial Meltdown* (New York: Pantheon Books, 2010), 76.
28. www.hsgac.senate.gov//imo/media/doc/Financial_Crisis/FinancialCrisisReport.pdf?attempt=2 (accessed September 30, 2013).
29. www.gpo.gov/fdsys/pkg/GPO-FCIC/content-detail.html (accessed September 30, 2013).
30. www.fdic.gov/news/news/speeches/archives/2010/spoct1310.html (accessed September 30, 2013).
31. "Greenspan Concedes Error in Judgment," *New York Times*, B1, October 24, 2008.

PART TWO

A Perfect Storm Rising

CHAPTER 4

A Paradigm Shift Created by Amazon, Google, and Facebook

Our presumptions of markets must be rethought.
—Chris Anderson, Editor-in-Chief, *Wired* magazine

While the timbers were falling in the U.S. housing market and the financial sector was on the ropes, another transformation was occurring in the U.S. economy at the same time: We actually arrived in the digital age. More than memory typewriters, wireless telephones, and voice recognition software, the world was moving, sorting, and fully trusting information in the "cloud"[1] like never before.

It's become quaint (and finally rare) to occasionally learn about a 60-year-old acquaintance who "doesn't do e-mail." But we should be paying more attention to the fact that members of Generation Z (not to be confused with the Millennial generation) aren't doing e-mail, either. In fact, they barely "do" telephones. They text. E-mail just became "too bothersome and too formal."

Many folks are puzzled at this evolution and continue to defiantly cling to laptop keyboards in the face of all those flying thumbs-to-mobile-device, and that's okay. But ignoring the reality of the accelerating technological changes and pondering where they will lead will be business suicide in most business sectors, particularly banking.

In the early 1970s, automated teller machines (ATMs) introduced bank depositors to the convenience of withdrawing cash from a dispensing machine 24 hours per day. No more standing in line to cash a check. Simply insert the plastic card, punch in the personal identification number (PIN) and voilà, cash spits out to fatten one's wallet again. For this young banking student, it was also a source of interest-free overnight loans. Whenever Mom mailed a check to school, the offline ATM of those days was good for a $25 or $50 unsigned, unsecured, and interest-free advance to celebrate instantly with friends at a local bar.

Customer acceptance was slow, however, since the first iteration of an ATM rolled out in about 1960, with several versions and schemes failing before a model that was affordable for the bank and simple for the customer to use was finally settled on. There were about 25 years between conceptual introduction to the time that virtually all banks offered ATMs and a majority of customers used them in the mid-1980s.

AMAZON CREATES DIGITAL TRUST

Consumer choice is a challenge that many companies in all industries have struggled with since traders were importing Asian spices and silk to Europe during the Middle Ages. Business owners know that multiple choices cost more to produce and therefore put pressure on prices to compete and earn profits. Many business models are built to produce single choice products, making them as attractive as possible to consumers with other attributes like pricing, features, and frills.

Consider McDonald's—this company targets children with playgrounds, cookies, ice cream, and the Happy Meal, but children are not great decision makers. Alas, McDonalds makes meal decisions for them, like having their hamburger dressed with ketchup, mustard, and pickles. A Big Mac includes two all-beef patties, special sauce, lettuce, cheese, pickles, onions, and a sesame seed bun. Special orders at McDonald's are a money-losing proposition.

But Burger King built a different business model. Remember "Hold the pickles, hold the lettuce. Special orders don't upset us. All we ask is that you let us serve it your way!" Their franchise turned the rigidity of other restaurants into their advantage by attracting consumers who insisted on choice. Likewise, Wendy's took that model even further with their Single, Double, and Triple patty sandwich designations.

McDonald's is doing just fine, but choice remains important to many consumers and needless to say Burger King and Wendy's are vibrant competitors. The food industry adapted much earlier than most industries to the demand for choice, but maybe the most transformative change occurred with booksellers.

In 1995, Jeff Bezos started Amazon.com on the front end of the digital revolution to sell books. But for this revolution to succeed, consumers had to graduate from a recently acquired trust of a machine retrieving cash from their bank accounts to giving an unseen, unknown company their credit card number over the Internet. While that seemed like a higher hurdle compared to the acceptance of ATMs, it happened much faster.

Today, consumers use Amazon to buy tens of thousands of products and many retailers connect with buyers around the world whom they would otherwise never have reached. How did this happen? Bezos was an early visionary of what has become known as the *long tail* of commerce. He wasn't alone, but his company has been the most successful at not only providing customers with almost limitless choices, but they actually introduce consumers to new targeted choices that relate to each consumer's preferences, indicated by his or her buying patterns.

What is the long tail? It was the notion held by a few that with the rise of unlimited shelf space in the digital marketplace, old restrictions on commerce would be removed and forever change product distribution by allowing all consumers to buy exactly what they wanted, rather than goods that were chosen for them to select among.

The best explanation of this economic theory is found in the 2006 book *The Long Tail*, written by *Wired* magazine editor Chris Anderson, which is recommended to anyone interested in understanding the digital marketplace.

Anderson explains how his consciousness about digital product distribution was stood on end in a 2004 conversation with Ecast CEO Robbie Vann-Adibé. Ecast was an online jukebox service that provided restaurants and bars with an almost unlimited playlist of music for their customers to select.

Vann-Adibé asked Anderson to guess how many tracks of Ecast's 10,000 album playlist were played at least once each quarter?[2] Drawing on the commonly held economic rule that 80 percent of all sales comes from 20 percent of all products (the 80/20 rule), Anderson guessed 20 percent. He was wrong—it was 98 percent. Obviously, digital was different.

Conventional wisdom may challenge the fact that Vann-Adibé's reference to a single album track play per quarter hardly seems to be a sufficient response to build a company around. But when put in context of the cost of situating that track as a consumer choice, storing it in their platform and playing it on demand, suddenly it's not such a crazy idea. When the total results of small sum selections are added up against thousands of choices, the total revenues match and often exceed the results of offering a much smaller selection that would get more individual sales.

In his book explaining the long tail, Anderson offers the example of how music recordings used to be distributed. Remembering the local record store as recently as the 1980s, the music selection for consumers was limited by the cost of real estate. We grew up in a greatest hits world where in fact 80 percent of all record store sales represented 20 percent of the titles available. Why? One principal contributor to that statistic was that the store owner loaded up on inventory of the 20 percent, since they were expected to sell better.

Imagine a 3,000 square foot store full of waist-high bins filled with record albums. Total inventory was limited to the linear feet of space available to stack records, so the front half of the store was full of the 20 percent selection and the remainder was filled with the 80 percent. Most specialty categories like classical, jazz, folk, and international music were usually crammed into a single section since they did not turn over frequently enough to deserve more space.

Essentially, the 3,000-square-foot store intentionally created scarcity due to the owner's business plan, the real estate market, or financial limitation. It was an economic bottleneck that limited record distribution and missed sales opportunities due to distortions on the supply side rather than the demand side.

At the time he wrote the book, Anderson described how the "average Walmart carries around 4,500 unique music CD titles."[3] Their selection was broken down in the various categories like Rock/Pop (1,800), Latina (1,500), Christian/Gospel (360), Country (225), and Classical/Easy Listening (225) based on their relative popularity measured by sales. Considering that there were 30,000 new albums released annually in those years, Walmart only added about 750 (or 2.5 percent) of them to its shelves. Their total 4,500 titles offered to consumers represented less than .5 percent of the music available.

"Scarcity, bottleneck, distortion of distribution and tyranny of shelf space all wrapped in one big store. But walk into a Walmart and you might be overwhelmed by abundance and choice," continued Anderson. Meanwhile, Amazon listed about 800,000 music titles.

The essence of the long tail is that the list of available goods beyond the 20 percent greatest hits (called the *head*) can be almost infinite, and that the demand for them is equal to or can exceed the demand for the head if the marketplace is free of artificial limits, barriers, and mitigated interference of buyer choice.

Whereas a typical big box bookstore used to carry about 200,000 titles, Amazon has unlimited shelf space in the digital cloud and can offer an unlimited number of titles. Finding a book at one of those megastores might require hunting a category section (Business) and then a subsection set of shelves (Management). At that point, consumers had to scan dozens or hundreds of titles to either search among choices or to pinpoint one book.

At Amazon, finding a particular subject or title is as easy as typing in the name of a title, author, or subject area. Plus, algorithms then analyze the individual consumer's demographics, preferences, and buying patterns over time in order to locate and suggest related topics and titles that may be of interest. Wandering around a bookstore suddenly changed into a whole new experience.

While it took almost six years to become profitable, Amazon.com has not only turned the bookselling world upside down, it has transformed retailing. UPS and the USPS have benefited greatly from the migration of consumers going online to buy regular goods (from music recordings, to computers, to health and beauty aids) rather than getting in the car and driving to a local shopping center. For many online retailers, fixed rent is out and shipping costs are in.

While it was easy to recognize Bezos's success with books, overlooked was his personal mission to *transform retailing*. His model would be easy enough to emulate with a super retailing site for virtually any and every product we demand. But the problem of trust would become a barrier to everyone—who to trust with the home address, telephone number, and credit card ID (CCID) number from the back of a credit card.

Bezos recognized that the real sell was *trust*—he designed Amazon to be the world's most recognizable retail checkout counter. No need to enter confidential buyer, shipping, and payment information with every single retailer online—just one. Using Amazon as a retailing search engine, simply find what you need, select from a variety of vendors with competing prices, and trust that Amazon will facilitate payment for you.

Amazon offers a familiar face to purchasers and allows each customer to maintain several payment options in their site, ready to allocate as directed on each sale. Shipping information is stored as well, which makes multiple transactions quick and safe. Thousands of small online retailers and service providers now use Amazon as their pay station, to give their customers comfort in the trust of a known brand and convenience of not having to duplicate their delivery instructions.

eBay.com started around the same time as Amazon.com and morphed into an online garage sale. Most of what was traded there was not available in stores, and likewise, eBay didn't become a success emulating the inventory found in established retailers. But within 10 years, eBay.com was managing the sale of a volume of goods online equal to Walmart's sales through its thousands of stores. More impressive, eBay averaged about $5 million revenue per employee, nearly 30 times that of Walmart.[4]

Since most eBay sellers were individuals who could not negotiate sales with a credit card, another payment solution was required. PayPal introduced a payment intermediary platform that provides its customers with a limited online deposit account and payment dashboard where individuals can make and receive cash transfers. This platform was important enough to eBay that they bought PayPal in 2002.

WHO ANSWERED ALL THOSE QUESTIONS BEFORE?

In 2012, there were approximately 1.8 trillion[5] Google searches, or an average of 5.1 billion per day. Given that the global population is estimated to be just over 7.1 billion[6] and only 2.4 billion[7] of us have access to the Internet, when did everyone get so curious to ask Google an average of 2.1 questions per day? Who answered all those questions before Google?

Google as we know it is the most efficient and successful search engine to find and decipher information for users in the Internet cloud for no apparent cost. Since its founding in 1998, they've added an e-mail service, office suite, picture editing, web browser, and dozens of other information/media related services and products that feed into their insatiable appetite for information about the global population. But focus on that word *apparent*.

No one pays for Google's search engine, e-mail, picture management, or a host of other free products with a single dime, but they do pay a price: privacy. Signing on to any one of these services requires acknowledgment and consent to Google's agreement, but few if any patrons ever choose to read or object to the dozens of pages of endless legalese. Buried there, though, are the terms by which users allow Google to extract unlimited gigabytes of data that paint an accurate picture over time of the user that might shock many people.

So without visible revenue from these billions of searches and all the free e-mail and storage space, how did Google generate $50 billion of 2012 revenue? Over 95 percent of it comes from advertising. Who knew that at a time when television, radio, and print media advertising revenues were fractionalized by the explosion of cable channels, Internet streaming, and the 24-hour news cycle, that there was $50 billion to be found?

Google reinvented advertising. They overcame the rapidly rising high cost of selling advertising—which essentially is limited space or time in various media sources—sold in inches and minutes person-to-person. Imagine the number of people required to distribute tens of millions of advertising dollars for major companies like General Motors or Nabisco. With so many markets and advertising outlets, it meant that many people had to be involved, requiring that much cost would be incurred by both the buyer and seller of advertising.

But Google developed a customer driven system that is loaded, targeted, and timed when the buyer wants it and ranked by the offered price. Advertisers bid for search rankings and can target their ads based on keyword searches that are relevant to what they are selling and who they are trying to sell to. Google's system prioritizes who should see what advertising and can even rank tangential messages according to the degree of accuracy key words might suggest.

By tracking the websites a computer user visits and the questions or information the user seeks through the world's most popular search engine, Google created the stronger advertising targeting infrastructure that would lower the cost for both parties of an advertising transaction. Likewise, advertising messages were developed around a keyword template designed to allow the advertiser to send messages to those with certain interests that may not be apparent in their service or product category.

YOUR OPINION IS (IN)VALUABLE

Among the recollections of the freedom discovered when renting my first post-college apartment, there was the regular activity of starting to domesticate my life in various ways, at least so far as a $12,000 annual salary would allow. A new Sears charge card filled my small abode with all sorts of new lamps and small appliances to add a touch of home to an otherwise barebones masonry-block cell. Back then, new appliances like can openers, blenders, and toasters were accompanied by a printed, unstamped postcard that invited buyers to register the purchase with the manufacturer to validate coverage through the product's warranty.

More often than not, these postcards would be doubled up with a fold in the middle and suggested a staple or taping before mailing. In the folded side would be a multiple-question consumer survey. Most were composed of very similar questions, like "indicate your general interests (check all that apply)," and would include 20 to 30 topics such as magazines, hunting, sports, and music.

Other questions might ask whether you own or rent, own a car or not, have children or not, and other seemingly innocuous questions about habits, needs, and preferences. Over time the questions became more intrusive, such as education level, cost of home or rent, marital status, and income range.

And like a robot, this household would complete and mail all these warranty postcards to be sure that the appliances were covered by any warranty benefits, and like trying to understand a freak car accident, for some reason I couldn't stop myself from answering the silly surveys. (Full disclosure: Yes, I also faithfully responded annually to the Publisher's Clearinghouse Sweepstakes).

It took me several years to realize that my self-important stature in the business world wasn't the reason that so much unsolicited mail arrived at my home. A decade of completing surveys had drawn a fairly detailed profile of me from all those postcards paid for with my postage stamps. Who knows how many data collectors were involved, but no one was refused. Welcome to the foothills of metadata.

How many friends can anyone really have? According to Facebook, the nation's most popular online social media site, the number can be as many as the 5,000 direct friend connections allowed on their site, but so far as fans are concerned, there is really no limit as to how many folks can "like" you in your cause or company page.

Facebook started on the Harvard University campus as a somewhat sexist public evaluation of campus women for the benefit of the men on campus choosing a date. As late as 2005, it was still restricted to .edu web domains, meaning college and high school students. Many adults (like me) took their step into the Facebook community as a clandestine effort to keep an eye on their children's social life and friends.

Today, Facebook is a public company with one of the most notorious IPOs in history, albeit successful, raising $38 billion on opening day, an incredible feat. The company boasts of over 1 billion users around the globe, although most of them can't explain the company's revenue model. Hence, most Facebook users don't understand that they are Facebook's product, not client.

Adults, companies, and other promoters have chased many younger people away from Facebook, a sizable number of whom recognize that its cool status has passed if you are younger than 23. After all, what better way to curse your friends with buzzkill than for a funny joke or posting among teen friends to be interrupted with someone's Aunt Sally chirping in with comments exposing that she has no idea what's being talked about. Alas, it's painful to admit that my profile (business promotion) has twice as many friends as my children's accounts combined.

Most traffic there (posts) seems to be messages either blatantly promoting business or screaming about politics. There are margin advertisements and algorithms that rank your friends to decide what order their posts are presented in for your viewing. Dozens of games and applications provide lowbrow entertainment for many ("Farmville," "Buy Me a Drink," and "Godfather Wars" among the favorites that my "friends" asked me to join), but basically it seems to be a cross between lots of people who need to talk to someone and others who are going to blanket them with birthday wishes, event invitations, shared ideology, and idle chatter.

Facebook is about information. As benign as the incessant details of the life of an average high school teen, college student, or mid-20s working person may seem, "there's gold in them thar hills." And that hill (really it's a mountain) is data. By offering a free web-based hangout destination for users to communicate, cruise, disclose, advertise, promote, and express, Facebook is paid in reams of data about their users and their ever-widening circle of "friends."

While originally targeting younger users, there are 70- and 80+-year-old people online in Facebook, which has replaced the old-fashioned party-line telephone, where several families actually shared the same phone number. For Facebook, an older, mature audience probably means it gets more valuable data that can be distributed at a higher value in the near term.

Users freely reveal everything from nicknames, birthdays, birthplaces, current cities, phone numbers, pictures, friends, political leanings, fashion preferences, social causes, relationships, dispositions, aspirations, and even tragedies—and more. The more people talk, share views, post pictures, and exchange messages, the more Facebook can complete a profile of who people are, what their preferences are, and what kind of trajectory they are on as consumers.

Perhaps more ominous, Facebook has also been a leading developer of face recognition software, meaning that names and faces are being put together in metadata for future reference. Today, it means that they may volunteer the names of those people whose photos you post on Facebook, but obviously this technology has many more implications.

Imagine that your customer service representatives could have the name, credit report, and financial profile of a prospective customer pop up on their screens when the person enters the bank. That scenario is already happening, at least with names, by using cell phones as the identifier. Surely it will not be far behind that face recognition will be transmitted from all those security cameras placed in your office.

Of course, Facebook is not alone but they have certainly changed the way and depth in which data can be gathered. Competing data aggregators are snatching up any and everything about people, institutions, systems, budgets, capital markets, weather, economics, census, and most other information, to be parsed, sorted, analyzed, and interpreted in a variety of ways.

According to ProPublica, "Some companies collect lists of people experiencing 'life-event triggers' like getting married, buying a home, sending a kid to college—or even getting divorced. Credit reporting giant Experian has a separate marketing services division, which sells lists of 'names of expectant parents and families with newborns' that are updated weekly."[8]

Some companies are collecting data to identify your hobbies, the purchases you make, and what books you read. Some monitor lists of people who donate to international aid charities and a subsidiary of Equifax, the credit reporting company, can collect detailed salary and paystub information on roughly 38 percent of employed Americans.

Data can be monetized in many ways to many different buyers who are hungry to find their markets in the hundreds of crosstabs, sorts, and lists that can be created. The analysis can be used to identify consumer needs before the consumer may know or decide to buy something. Sorting can create targeted lists for sales, marketing, or advertising for many different kinds of products or campaigns. In 2012, micro-targeting of data was credited with helping President Barack Obama find households and individuals most likely in favor of his campaign to pledge support, make donations, encourage friends to join them, and turn out to vote. It really works.

HOW DO THESE CHANGES AFFECT
SMALL BUSINESS LENDING?

The nature of business lending has not changed much in the last 30 years. Other than the quick computations of Excel, the Internet access of credit reports, and word processing to assimilate all those loan write-ups, the commercial banking industry has embraced few improvements to enhance its productivity to acquire, underwrite, and deliver funding to business owners.

Other industrial sectors—and even some other bank departments—have been quicker to adapt to technological advances and strategies to grow their client volume and markets, lower the human intervention required to process information, and create simpler paths to realizing income. Business lending in many corners still hands out paper applications and requests millions of paper documents every year.

One exception focused on upgrading lending technology is nCINO. The technology offers a loan application/management platform to load various client data into, provides many processing features, and shares information with the multiple parties that need access to it at various stages of the business lending process. Business developers, underwriters, decision makers, closers, and others can view application information, appraisals, title reports, closing documents, and any portion of the client file in a digital format on demand from their desks.

nCINO was born out of the desire for a more dynamic service platform that would add efficiency and support, lending growth beyond what could be squeezed from the tired processes used over the past 20 years. The principals at LiveOak Bank, which was founded only in 2008, were no strangers to banking innovation and determined to grow their bank with a smarter adaptation to technology, even if they had to build it themselves. So they did.[9]

This lending platform operates in SalesForce.com, a respected technology that provides a safe, secure environment needed for banking operations without having to reinvent anything. What the nCINO platform is designed to do is simply:

- To dissect lending processes down into the many specific tasks, to ensure that the responsibility of each function is clearly assigned to a specific participant
- To manage information with a conforming template that offers short-cuts and efficiencies to accelerate processes
- To reduce the time required to process a transaction by sequentially managing the many responsibilities that must be performed

- To provide one digital file folder to store transaction documents, which can be accessed only by authorized participants, when appropriate
- To provide clear communications to all parties concerned at every step of the transaction, from application to closing

Participants are encouraged to create notes along the way to keep everyone up to date in real time about deal progress, to lower the time and effort of e-mails and phone calls. When questions need answered, they can be posted in the platform, which notifies the appropriate party and gives the information to all concerned in real time.

A document manager and a checklist keep everyone up to date with what's missing and who's trying to get it. Alarms can be used to notify appropriate parties when benchmarks are reached and transparent accountability is the hallmark—everyone knows the deal status at all times and who is responsible for progress, or lack of it.

Document labels are automated by the platform, which can read the contents and decipher an appraisal from a title opinion. This prevents PDF files from being automatically named by Adobe and stored with a name that might appear as 193EF0593858383829294.pdf.

Finally, this platform tracks outcomes. If a particular loan officer or loan broker always seems to submit transactions that are declined, or default quickly after approval, these details become apparent much faster. Loan volume, credit quality, and portfolio performance are tracked in several ways, which adds important tools for management.

While this platform was developed for SBA-guaranteed lending, it's being made adaptable for conventional commercial and industrial (C&I) lending, too. In fact, the company plans to roll out versions for mortgage and consumer lending as well.

To date, the company has shared this technology with more than 40 bank installations, with interest growing. That's a good beginning to move business lending out of the dark ages.

And for whoever's wondering, yes, company officials concede that some regulators (and bankers) have security concerns about putting this kind of information in the cloud. But frankly, addressing those concerns and ensuring that information is protected will probably be cheaper than relying on the 1970s-era methods of underwriting a mountain of paper.

Lending Diversity?

While a commercial bank cannot offer an unlimited number of choices of different loan products—there is a finite limit to how many ways a debt instrument can be structured—there is a lesson to be found in Amazon's long tail. Business lenders—whether banks, commercial finance, or leasing companies—tend to fight it out year after year over the same greatest hits, be it commercial real estate loans, equipment loans, or particular industry sectors needing A/R funding. That is, they are all scrambling to get a share of the same loans without any thoughtful strategy diversion to focus on particular market sectors or offering a different way to approach the same tired loan structure.

A business loan is typically structured with four major elements that must be negotiated with the client: (1) dollar amount, (2) interest rate and fees, (3) repayment term, and (4) collateral and guarantees. Most lenders make these loans exactly the same. Since "all money is green," the only differentiation the client usually sees in competing offers or lenders is the personalities involved. Or, in some radical departures from the norm, one party feigns aggression to offer a ¼ percent lower interest rate to win the business. Wow.

Why not break the mold and compete with something other than price, like the loan term, collateral leverage, or loosening restrictive covenants? Or, why not focus on a smaller part of the industry and intentionally structure a better deal offer that earns a larger share of the market that may offer lower servicing or management costs?

Surely the entire 100 percent of an existing client base may not embrace any particular new approach and neither will all the prospective clients. But chipping away at some competitors' business with Alternative Idea #1, and a few more with Alternative Idea #2, and so on, may shift the competitive edge without relenting on pricing. For too long bankers have cannibalized each other's customers (and their own profits) by only competing with lower rates.

Offering a longer list of choices, which may be as simple to administer as a checklist of alternate documents, can give clients and prospective clients choices. One shoe size does not fit all, and likewise fattening up the various loan structures, pricing schemes, and general terms can win business when the competitor is stuck in 1970. The cost to the lender will generally be moot, given that pricing can be easier to protect (and even grow) and modest changes in other terms get lost in the greater portfolio, which absorbs any particular exposure that may marginally increase for a few credits.

Amazon proved that there is as much business in the long tail as there is in the head and that pays equal to or even in excess of the greatest-hits business. For business lenders, exercising some inventiveness to think beyond "how we've always done it" does not automatically mean greater credit risk or structural risk to any loan or portfolio. It does require dissecting typical deal structures and deciding how many terms and conditions could be modified slightly as a business development tool to protect loan pricing. It will surprise many what choices clients will make if they are offered.

Google unlocked a faster route to extracting information from the droves of open-book, digital information sources that have continued to multiply each year, so much so that the entire knowledge base of mankind is doubling almost annually. Google has turned that search function into a user targeting tool, meaning that lenders, like everyone else, can begin searching for prospective clients on the web based on target client profiles.

Prospecting strategies, whether using Google Ads or targeted banner ads, are sold much like print advertising except you can actually pinpoint the demographics of who will see a particular ad. With Google, it means that ads will be seen when buyers in a particular geographic area search for a particular term, like *business loan* or *equipment lease*. Spare yourself the wasted effort of using those particular terms, however. The former phrase search identifies 242 million results, so it is safe to say that too many parties have chased that idea, including nine of the first 12 that are lenders.

But thinking more strategically, why not search for clients investigating what you are interested in financing? If you lease Mack Trucks, popping up among people searching for them might be a better bet. The search identifies only 5,300,000 results, but none on the first page are finance companies or banks.

Likewise, using the names of equipment brands, real estate developments, or other assets needed by the parties identified as prospective clients can accelerate finding them. And sometimes that discovery will be ahead of their decision to buy, which is fine. Getting their attention and interest ahead of a full-scale search can be an advantage to winning a client.

Compiling information and data is nothing new in the process of analyzing and underwriting a business loan. But strangely, little progress has been made by the financial sector to broaden that search for more or better information in this digital age, when there is more information than ever before about people and companies. In addition, there are many more information sources available to bypassing the client to get additional, meaningful data that's reliable and easy to obtain.

The real teaching moment in regard to data may be further in this book, where innovative funders who are underwriting loans based on bank checking account data are discussed. Read that sentence again.

Think about it. For existing customers, banks have a trove of financial data that is routinely ignored except in limited circumstances to measure the client relationship: How large are average client deposits (aka the client's loan to the bank)? And within that same report is the raw sum of cash collections for a business that could be parsed by the day, week, month, or quarter, alongside the average disbursements that could be evaluated as to their regularity by the day or week. Average monthly bank deposits and average account balances provide immediate vital signs about a company's operations in real time, but are not recognized by a majority of banks that rely solely on months-old, self-prepared financial statements when pondering the client's financial condition.

With the volume of government-issued statistical data published monthly on an ever-growing range of subjects, and pertinent statistics concerning public oversight of a variety of matters that could weigh into a credit decision, few banks have embraced the regular sourcing, mapping, and use of plenty of information that could shape better results, both in transactions and strategies.

The days of waiting for customers to walk in the door to be offered the same product year after year is antiquated and will be self-defeating. A new generation of business owners is discovering alternative funding sources that may cost more but also deliver more. And "more" may be getting a credit decision in two hours rather than two months, the latter of which is not uncommon at some banks.

Just the decision to develop more thoughtful, creative products and terms to meet client needs and preferences is a competitive advantage, because few in the business lending sector recognize a need to do so. Targeting clients who are interested in certain business topics or who are exploring strategic assets is a conversation starter that beats buying a stale mailing list and spending thousands of dollars on postage.

Business lending that has always been done a certain way, with a tired, stale requisite list of information that must be gathered, probably will not change much this decade. But augmenting that list with available, free information that can be effortlessly sourced in seconds and provide qualifying encouragement or reveal evidence of concern is a no-brainer.

Notes

1. The "cloud" is an expression used to describe a variety of computing resources that involve a large number of computers connected through the Internet and accessible to retrieve data on demand in real time.
2. Chris Anderson, *The Long Tail* (New York: Hyperion, 2006), 7.
3. Ibid., 154–156.
4. Ibid., 202.
5. StatisticBrain.com, www.statisticbrain.com/google-searches/ (accessed September 5, 2013).
6. U.S. Census Bureau, www.census.gov/popclock/ (accessed September 5, 2013).
7. InternetWorldStats.com, www.internetworldstats.com/stats.htm (accessed September 5, 2013).
8. ProPublica, "Everything We Know About What Data Brokers Know About You," March 7, 2013, www.propublica.org/article/everything-we-know-about-what-data-brokers-know-about-you.
9. "Our Story," ncino.com, www.ncino.com/about/ (accessed December 30, 2013).

CHAPTER 5

Private Equity In Search of ROI

Investors invest. While large salaries, high commissions, and capital gains are all appealing paths to generating wealth, they can be fleeting events that are more difficult to replicate and repeat. Over time, the compounding results of redeploying accumulated funds have the ability to magnify the earlier acquisition results with true wealth.

While billionaire status is the new (inflated) version of what was once bantered around as the more common aspiration of becoming a millionaire, relatively few people attain the actual accomplishment of accumulating $1 million net worth of real equity. And for clarity, that term should appropriately only be used to refer to actual value, not the kind of wealth heard about on a 24-hour looping infomercial trying to sell books about how to become rich on expected real estate inflation and a steady stream of unsteady rents.

Living in one of the world's top economies, brimming with opportunities to earn profits and leverage success, literally millions of people have accumulated a legitimate claim to being a genuine millionaire, whether by hard work, vigilant saving, lucky breaks, or inheritance. There is no lack of reverence about anyone's accomplishments intended, but millionaires *aren't what they used to be.*

Many of today's well-to-do have been accelerated to that status through the lowest income taxes in three generations, aggressive capital markets that created many short-term equity bubbles, and persistent real estate inflation. These conditions built a nice nest egg for many, but realistically often relied equally on public policy or capital market manipulation rather than sheer hard work or talent alone to create a path to wealth. In many instances, somebody lost money in order for the market to reward someone else.

THE FED'S LOW INTEREST POLICY AND THE EFFECTS ON THE PRIVATE INVESTOR

Regardless, one constant condition of wealth is the need or demand to generate a continuing stream of income from it. Idle money loses value at the rate of inflation plus the cost of lost opportunity. Through the middle of the previous decade there were ample places to park capital and earn a decent return, with even insured bank deposit rates exceeding the rate of inflation most years.

But the Federal Reserve Bank's monetary policy response to the financial crisis changed that era. Lowering the Fed funds interest rates 5.25 percent over the 14-month period between October 2007 and December 2008 was a desperate Hail Mary stimulus to encourage private sector lending and borrowing.

By drastically lowering rates, the Feds were injecting some profits into well-managed banks that could take advantage of funding costs that dropped faster than lending rates. In addition, they were lowering the cost of outstanding debt to businesses, credit card holders, and others to provide a softer landing from plummeting sales and their loss of profits as the globe bounded into the Great Recession.

It was investors who got stuck with much of the tab. The sudden rate changes left many investors better off in the very near term (particularly fixed-rate depositors and bondholders), but many were abandoned at maturity with precious few options that paid anything close to the inflation rate. Many retirees who used a conservative earnings estimate of three to four percent suddenly found themselves drawing down on principal. Thousands of them were forced to return to the working ranks in order to replenish or augment devalued holdings.

Later, the Fed's quantitative easing policies, intended to extend low interest rates into other sectors by buying up a large share of freshly issued government debt, forced investors to seek other opportunities to increase returns. The shared goal was to stimulate capital distribution into riskier ventures in order to encourage growth in a moribund economy.

The full results of these policies will be studied for decades ahead, but the best we can say today seems to be that maybe we avoided having things get worse. And that "maybe" will certainly retain detractors who will forever challenge the net effects. The equity market rebounded nicely from its darkest hours during the crisis, but that recovery may be owed to many other conditions that changed during these years and the reality that it had nowhere left to go but up.

WALL STREET ISN'T MAIN STREET

Casual observers might agree that there appear to have been some fundamental shifts in the traditional equity markets that began decades ago, but spiked suddenly during the crisis years, and it will be interesting to watch the evolution. The stock market, long hailed for its democratization that increased the number of U.S. shareholders[1] from 1 percent to 52 percent of the population in just 98 years, never prepared Mom and Pop for the roulette world of trading.

Something happened between the years when Charles E. Merrill and Edmund C. Lynch partnered up to establish an investment banking firm on Wall Street. When Merrill Lynch recommended opportunities to their clients, they were fully invested individually and corporately with their own capital at risk in these transactions. There was a common interest and intention for mutual shared benefit. When the company did well, its customers did well.

Those days are long gone. Today, client capital represents a fading percentage of a typical investment bank's business and revenue. They are principally focused on trading on their own accounts, and throw off scraps to their "muppets"[2] (an alleged disparaging reference to clients by Goldman Sachs traders). During the financial crisis, many firms were found to have first sold their clients exotic, translucent securities loaded with toxic mortgages and then later taking short positions on the same securities, effectively betting on the eventual failure of what had been laid off on unsuspecting customers.

While the many investment bankers still pitch *investing*, really they are *trading*. The storied, patriotic refrain that describes "aggregating capital to invest in productivity, build companies and drive the world's greatest economy. . ." today is a fantasy in the broader stock markets. Bankers there are gaming for trades and are paid the same to buy and sell. They are the bookies who win regardless of whether investors come out ahead or behind and concentrate their efforts on keeping the trade volume growing.

Today's typical investor is looking for a quick score. Buying and selling is a means to an end. According to the tax code, a short-term capital gain is the profit on any investment that's held less than a year. But for many investors, *short term* might refer to minutes or even seconds of programmed ownership. Trading is a strategy of buying an asset at one price and selling at another (preferably higher) price. Investing and actual investors who buy into a long-term horizon have left the room.

Early technology advances gave rise to day traders, who could step into the role of being a stock trader with direct access to trading data, analyst reporting, and the floor broker. Continuing advancements led to some institutional investors being able to program trading decisions into an algorithm that automates buying and selling much faster than a roulette wheel.

These technological advancements in and of themselves led to the infamous "flash-crash" on May 6, 2010, when the market plunged more than 1,000 points (9 percent) in midafternoon, only to recover minutes later. It was the largest one-day decline on an intraday basis in the history of the Dow Jones Industrial Average.

Technology also enabled a 24-hour trading day that never sleeps. Beyond telephones and telefaxes, traders and investors move capital and investments around the globe with amazing speed in an integrated marketplace that is closed only a few hours for the crevice of a weekend break just past the International Date Line.

Now the exchanges are hunkered down with a series of mergers, consolidating various trading markets across continents and oceans, reflecting their asset runoff and new competition of alternative trading channels to date. Technological bloopers and programming errors have resulted in trading blackouts, overheated robot trading ignited massive selloffs causing mini-crashes, and most famously, the heralded Facebook IPO fiasco shut out thousands of traders for much of the stock's inauguration.

These market changes, investment banker disregard for clients, and the volatility witnessed in the 2008 crisis crash shocked many of those 52 percent of Americans who began to question the wisdom of investing in a trading market. Tens of thousands of participants have been migrating out of the market since 2009 and the lowered inflow of new money continues. The workers investing their nest eggs are not alone—many seasoned investors also have begun to rely more heavily on direct investment into real companies rather than playing the slot machine formerly known as Wall Street.

The trading market has scarcely noticed. They've recovered most of the ground lost during the crisis and are busy inflating the next bubble. As an example, in September 2013, LinkedIn.com launched a second offering to sell $1.2 billion of shares that some analysts likened to a feeding frenzy. Their original IPO launched in 2011 for $45 a share.

Shares closed on the 2013 sale day at $252.17. "At that price, LinkedIn, which had just $688 million in revenue for the first six months of its 2013 fiscal year, had a market value of nearly $33 billion, according to Google Finance. As for earnings, something Silicon Valley typically scoffs at, LinkedIn was making money, but its previous quarter net income was $26 million, which begs the question how a company producing profits at that level can possibly be valued at such an outsized market capitalization," according to DealBook's Steven Davidoff.[3]

LinkedIn at this level was trading at a price-to-earnings (PE) ratio of 722x. For comparison, on the same day, Facebook stock was at a PE ratio of 165x and Google was 27x, both of which had much stronger revenues and profits. Nuts.

FIRST BUY IN, THEN INVEST UP

Many disgruntled investors joined the emerging trend of investing directly into small companies and startups as *angel investors*. The angel investor trend started informally a couple of decades ago among retired entrepreneurs and business executives who were interested in investing in small, early-stage businesses for reasons that went beyond purely a financial return. It was a way to keep abreast of current developments in a particular business sector, mentor another generation of entrepreneurs, and use their experience and network on a part-time basis.

It used to be that venture capital met the demand for early-stage startups and truly entrepreneurial companies that needed high risk capital to chase big ideas and growth strategies. Back in the late 1970s and 1980s, venture capitalists aggregated together in partnerships that gave birth to companies like Intel, Apple, Hayes Microcomputer Products, and Microsoft, and led the first leg of innovations that resulted in the information age.

But somewhere in the 1990s and beyond, venture investing attracted too many investors and too much money. It lost its edge and lowered its tolerance for risk. Everybody throwing $250,000 or $500,000 in the pot was suddenly expecting a 20 percent guaranteed return. That changed the focus of this sector into a fund mentality with professional managers, where the arbiters of capital were really handling other people's money rather than placing large gambles with their personal funds.

Instead of starting and building great companies, venture capital became the third or fourth stage investor—with the higher-risk (and higher return) initial rounds left to the angels. Today they only seem to invest in proven concepts, technologies, and products that need growth capital for penetration and territorial expansion.

It's not a bad situation for innovators, though, being left to the angels. In addition to funding, angel investors can provide valuable management advice and important contacts to assist the company seeking investment. Because there are no public exchanges listing these securities, private companies search for angel investors in several ways, including referrals from the investors' trusted advisors and other business contacts, investor conferences, and at a variety of organized pitch events aimed to foster face-to-face meetings.

Angel investments bear extremely high risk and are usually subject to dilution from future investment rounds. As such, they are structured to provide very high returns for the investor. And because a large percentage of these investments are lost entirely when early-stage companies fail, seasoned angel investors aim for a potential return of at least 10 or more times their original capital contribution within a five-year horizon, which equates to about a 60 percent return on investment.

These returns are planned through the investment company's defined exit strategy, such as an initial public offering or through acquisition by a targeted acquirer. After taking into account the cost of failed enterprises and the multiyear holding period for the successful investments, however, the effective rate of return for a typical angel investor's portfolio is typically in the 20 to 30 percent range.

While the investor's demand for a high rate of return on these investments can make angel financing seem to be an expensive source of funds, cheaper sources of capital, such as bank financing, are usually not available for most early-stage ventures in good economic times. After the fallout from the 2008 crisis and prolonged low interest monetary policy enacted for recovery, angel investments began to attract a much broader interest among people who formerly had much lower tolerance for risk.

For comparison, there are estimated to be more than 250,000 angel investors and just fewer than 900 venture capital funds in the United States. In 2010 there were approximately 61,900 angel investment deals totaling over $20 billion and 2,750 venture capital transactions contributing another $22 billion of equity.[4] These statistics illuminate the importance of angel investors to the early-stage business sector.

The challenge for these companies may be that only about 5 percent of the U.S. population are accredited investors, only 5 percent of that number are angel investors, and only 5 percent of those investors join angel investor groups. There are about 170 angel groups nationwide but there are no universal terms, strategies, or investment criteria although a majority of angel investors make investments along with other angels, not necessarily as an organized group.

Angel investors generally contribute $25,000 to $50,000 per deal that aggregates to a total deal size ranging from $300,000 to $2 million. According to Angel Resource Institute, in the first quarter of 2013, the median angel round size was $680,000.[5] Presently, angels fund an average of 16 percent of the transactions they personally review, although most might only contribute to two or three deals per year.

Some of the angel investments that emerged during the post-crisis years were aimed at innovation of capital itself. Rather than investing in the invention of a new gizmo, several entrepreneurs explored how capital itself was distributed and looked for ways to use existing technology to organize the millions of requests for funding into an automated sorting process. In doing so, they were looking to exclude the most expensive and often most vulnerable link of the entire small business lending process: the *loan officer*.

Online banking and growing retail sales online with credit cards proved that consumers were finally getting comfortable with providing confidential information over the Internet when a secure, credible company was asking. Credit card companies had been gathering client applications online for years, in addition to using credit bureaus' data searches to find prequalified prospects based on nameless financial profiles, delineated with attributes like credit scores, ZIP codes, and home ownership to define potentially desirable cardholders. Why not try this approach with a small business owner?

Virtual nonbank funders began coming online to facilitate business capital funding and have been growing steadily since 2008. Using tested, familiar technologies, portals opened that could gather needed information to process requests for business capital in a clean, standardized application format.

Driven entirely by the customer (or approved loan intermediary), this new application channel provides funders with a more efficient gathering operation and a much lower operating cost. The platform is left with the task of coaxing complete details and correct data entries required from the applicant, otherwise the application doesn't move. That avoids the frustrating task usually reserved for humans in traditional lending.

Ironic that an economic crisis that cast thousands of financial institutions into a capital panic has hastened the development, refining, and expansion of a rival funding delivery system that has reached only a tiny fraction of its potential use and impact.

And the potential is huge. While there is no official accounting available from these nonpublic, nonreporting companies, the aggregate capital purveyed through these channels is estimated to have already exceeded $100 billion since 2005. While that figure is a scant ripple in the entire pool of supply or demand for business capital, what may speak volumes about the future upside are several trends and demographics in their favor:

- **Continued growth in acceptance and use of technology.** The global march of technology and the Internet continues as major online companies seek to expand through establishing free Internet networks in many developing countries. In the United States, census reports[6] revealed that in 2011, 243 million households were connected to the Internet, reflecting a 107 percent growth since 2001 and including an average gain of 56 percent across major ethnic groups. And, several U.S.-based innovative funders are targeting less-regulated markets outside the United States.
- **Continued growth in entrepreneurship.** While dipping slightly in 2011, entrepreneurship and business startups are at the highest level since the mid-1990s. "The Great Recession has pushed many individuals into business ownership due to high unemployment rates," said Robert Litan, vice president of research and policy at the Kaufman Foundation.[7] And the share of 55- to 64-year-old entrepreneurs has risen to 20.9 percent, reflecting the aging U.S. population.
- **Smaller is the new normal.** In a quarterly survey, the "Main Street Pulse Report,"[8] intended to reflect business owner outlook and the response by capital markets, OnDeck Capital reported that the median borrowing need

of small business owners was $44,000 in mid-2013. While large banks will remain the primary credit supplier to larger companies for the foreseeable future, there is ample opportunity for new channels to supply funding to small businesses, long avoided by many banks anyway. It's safe to say that there will be a higher growth potential among these companies than in larger enterprises.

- **Dodd-Frank Act.** Many pundits expect that new banking regulations will add more burdens on community banking that will pressure their participation in small business lending. According to *U.S. News & World Report*, the "new requirements will be disproportionately costly for small banks and small credit rating agencies."[9]

- **Capital markets.** While it remains to be seen how the shakeout of major equity exchanges and the community bank sector will turn out, investor motivations and demands will not significantly change. That said, it is getting increasing difficult to envision how well smaller banks, particularly those measured with less than $1 billion in assets, will be able to generate sustainable profits and therefore attract sufficient new capital for growth and future opportunities. Without growth as an option, many have few options but to roll up with similar sized companies to exit.

Another opportunity for investors in the rise of the innovative funding sector is likely to be the need for equity to build more platforms and develop additional infrastructure as the viability and market share of these companies improves. Portfolio growth will also require a steadily increasing supply of funds, and like banks that must grow deposits, these innovative funders can tap into an ever-growing list of suppliers.

Today most of these funders are dependent on private equity investors and hedge funds to fuel the portfolios they originated with a cost of capital that has kept their retail funding rates high and poised as a barrier to profitability for many of these funders. When they finally break into profitability, they should be able to source funds from the banks that offer lender finance, a valued business line that for decades has been funding various alternative lenders, consumer finance, and leasing companies. These funds will be considerably cheaper than private investors.

In addition, with more experience and exposure, confidence will grow among more conservative investors, like money managers, pension funds, and individuals who will step up to buy into portfolios to boost their own rate of returns with short-term loan strips, participations, and portfolios.

Opportunities in this space are not restricted to large investors. Peer-to-peer lending platforms provide ample opportunity for smaller investors to buy into smaller consumer loans. With returns averaging in the 6 to 8 percent range, this platform affords a chance for many to escape the doldrums of bank deposit accounts and avoid the gyrations of the stock market when playing with smaller sums.

The consumer debt market is approximately $2.8 trillion[10] and it's in play as debtors have found a lower cost option to refinance higher-priced loans. The dominant peer-to-peer lending platform, out of about 50 world-wide, is LendingClub.com.

A CAUTIONARY NOTE ABOUT A 72 PERCENT APR

Much of the growth and virtually all the strenuous competition of this sector today has come from the higher risk, much higher priced merchant cash advance (MCA) sector and, to a lesser extent, some of the lending companies. MCAs purchase future credit card income streams from their client that's recovered with a daily deduction of an agreed percentage of revenues directly from the client's credit card processor.

In observed transactions, some MCAs present a straight offer of advancing X dollars in exchange for a total repayment of Y dollars. While most pundits might assume that the storied entrepreneur would busily calculate the cost of funds and decide whether to accept it based on an analysis of ROI and alternative sources, they would be seriously wrong.

Surprisingly, a vast majority of small company owners consider their checking account statement as equivalent to a financial statement: If there's money in it at the end of the year, they assume they're profitable. Many fail to get bank or other financing assistance simply because they're flying blind without a basic understanding of their own profitability or cash cycles.

So when an MCA suggests a $100,000 advance and requires repayment of $136,000, most business owners quickly deduct they are paying 36 percent.

The Projected MCA ROI Calculation is:

$136,000 (repayment) − $100,000 (advance) = $36,000 (net financing cost)
$36,000/$100,000   = 36 percent

But what these business owners overlook is the time value of money. In underwriting their advance, the MCA recognizes what the client is generating in monthly credit card revenues and accordingly requires that a flat percentage of these revenues be diverted daily from the credit card processor to repay the advance. For example, if the business averaged $200,000 of credit cards each month and the MCA required a 12 percent of revenue repayment rate, each month, approximately $24,000 would be captured by the merchant processor and forwarded directly to the MCA to repay the $136,000 sum required to repay the advance.

Most bankers can calculate this scenario in their heads: The entire advance will be repaid in less than 6 months, meaning that the annualized yield to the MCA is really closer to 72 percent. Obviously, if the business owner did the quick presumed calculation to derive a 36 percent cost of capital, they knew they were expected to pay well beyond prime rates. But the appropriate question to ask is whether they would have accepted the same funding at 72 percent.

This question will become a focus point of participants and policy makers as this sector grows. Business is business and the axiom we all enter this economic system with is "buyer beware." MCAs will quickly point out that by using a flat percentage of daily revenues as the determinant of how fast funds are repaid, calculating the final cost in terms of APR is impossible. Additionally, they are legally advancing funds for a fixed fee return, so use of an interest calculation equivalent is not legally applicable to them.

While both of these conditions are true, they avoid the question of how much transparency MCAs and other lenders using a similar model should provide clients concerning potential funding costs.

Some innovative funders operate with a questionable practice that will likely draw either client or public policy backlash: "name your commission." One lender in particular uses this approach to determining the price of third party origination if the deal cash flow will sustain loan repayment at that price.

Many of these innovative funders have built an extensive network of third party originators, loan brokers, and independent sales originators (ISOs) to identify prospective clients, gather application information, and forward everything to the lender for evaluation.

As part of the transaction profile, these third parties are invited to name their commission or tell the lender what level of compensation they expect to be paid if the transaction is approved and funded. Brokers are given their choice of commission rate between 1 and 15 percent of the final loan size.

While this lender is operating easily within its legal constraints, the obvious conflicts, potential indiscretions, and long-term reputational risks go well beyond their company alone. Obviously these higher potential costs are borne solely by the borrowing companies, which distorts the availability of funding and compromises growth prospects with a higher cost burden solely because a broker was selected that placed its own exaggerated interests ahead of the client's.

Widespread knowledge of such shortsighted pricing schemes will run off customers and raise suspicions in the marketplace about all technology-based funders. Should there be any high-profile objections, editorials, or business failures, an invitation for more regulation can be initiated by any one of hundreds of politicians who may take interest.

The innovative sector and their investors might take note of these potential risks and cool their zeal for the 72 percent short term return in exchange for being left alone in a market that will gladly embrace funding costs well above prime rate. Remember, *pigs get fat, hogs get slaughtered.*

Notes

1. PBS, "The First Measured Century," www.pbs.org/fmc/book/14business6.htm (accessed October 1, 2013).
2. Greg Smith, "Why I Am Leaving Goldman Sachs," *New York Times*, March 14, 2012, www.nytimes.com/2012/03/14/opinion/why-i-am-leaving-goldman-sachs.html?pagewanted=all&_r=0.
3. Steven Davidoff, "A Trading Frenzy Over Oh-Oh-So-Hot LinkedIn Shares," *New York Times*, September 10, 2013, http://dealbook.nytimes.com/2013/09/10/a-trading-frenzy-over-oh-so-hot-linkedin-shares/?_r=0.
4. "Angel Investing—An Overview," a program of the Ewing Marion Kaufmann Foundation, 2006–2011.
5. Angel Resource Network, www.angelresource.org/research/halo-report.aspx (accessed October 1, 2013).
6. U.S. Census Bureau, www.census.gov/prod/2013pubs/p20-569.pdf (accessed October 1, 2013).
7. Kaufman Foundation, www.kauffman.org/newsroom/annual-new-business-startups-study.aspx (accessed October 1, 2013).
8. MarketWatch.com, www.marketwatch.com/story/ondeck-main-street-pulse-report-reveals-73-percent-of-small-businesses-are-optimistic-about-the-economy-2013-08-07 (accessed October 1, 2013).
9. *U.S. News & World Report*, www.usnews.com/opinion/blogs/economic-intelligence/2013/01/07/10-ways-dodd-frank-will-hurt-the-economy-in-2013 (accessed October 1, 2013).
10. Randall Smith, "Not Banks, but Still Lending Money and Drawing Investors," DealB%k, August 7, 2013, http://dealbook.nytimes.com/2013/08/07/not-banks-but-still-lending-and-drawing-investors/.

CHAPTER 6

First Change the Marketplace, Then Change the Market

There isn't much sympathy for business developers in the banking industry these days but anyone who's done that job can relate to the challenges of wrestling business away from competitors while satisfying ever-changing internal requirements as to what constitutes a good deal. It's reminiscent of Abbott and Costello's legendary comedy routine "Who's On First?"[1] (also viewable on YouTube):[2]

Costello:	So, you the manager?
Abbott:	I'm the manager!
Costello:	Well, you know, I'd like to know some of the guys names on the team so when I meet 'em on the street or in the ballpark I'll be able to say hello to those people.
Abbott:	Why sure I'll introduce you to the boys. They give 'em funny names though, nicknames.
Costello:	Oh I know they give those ball players awful funny names.
Abbott:	Well, let's see, on the team we have uh, "Who's" on first, "What's" on second, "I Don't Know" is on third.
Costello:	Are you the manager?
Abbott:	Yes.
Costello:	You know the guys' names?
Abbott:	I sure do.
Costello:	Then tell me the guys' names.
Abbott:	I say, "Who's" on first, "What's" on second, "I Don't Know's" on third and then you . . .
Costello:	You the manager?
Abbott:	Yes.
Costello:	You know the guy's names?
Abbott:	I'm telling you their names!

Costello: Well who's on first?
Abbott: Yeah.
Costello: Go ahead and tell me. . . .

Sometimes business lenders can feel trapped in a similar maddening circular path that can be a part of the process to getting loans approved in a commercial bank. This dilemma comes from the endless round and round characterizations of the bank's credit culture when articulated by competing voices.

For example, many managers and bank leaders will argue that their primary driver of credit is cash flow, so lenders screen good cash flow as the primary litmus test of probable credit approval. Then the frustration starts after the deal is submitted to underwriting, where the chief loan approver declines the loan due to inadequate collateral.

Business developers are stuck in the middle as to which of the bank's lending criteria are really most important, *cash flow* or *collateral*?

And so it's easy to illustrate that markets are never perfect. From the highest to the lowest volume marketplace for anything, there are plenty of participants in all of them who can tell you about their ubiquitous challenges. From big box retail stores to the small town five-and-dime, most markets have unique characteristics that are efficient in many ways and satisfy customers on some level. Capital markets are no different.

Borrowers complain about the arbitrary nature of bank credit and endless lists of documentation that stifle business owners and prevent them from getting funding. Companies wanting to sell equity shares to the public get the rude awakening as to the costs and complexity of launching an offering of any size. Yet these two markets do things the way they do for many valid reasons that have been tested over time and are entrenched for most participants.

Banks are by far the most dominant first source that comes to mind by most business owners when thinking about the search for capital financing. But according to some surveys, banks disappoint almost 75 percent of loan applicants by declining their requests.

OLD THINKING/TECHNOLOGY CAN STIFLE CREDIT

Credit risk aversion, scaling loan sizes, and all the red tape customers must endure due to the government's conscription of banks into the war on money laundering and loan discrimination make bank credit a perilous minefield of frustration for borrowers. And since there are usually dozens of loan applications in process simultaneously, it might take the bank 60 to 90 days to navigate through their normal process only to turn away the borrower with a declination or learn that the borrower has moved on to another lender.

All the documentation required for a bank to develop the borrower's life story, financial history, and interpretive character assessment is often distorted by a comedy of errors. There can also be communication mistakes, incorrect or incomplete details, and even a lack of motivation by thousands of intermediaries stretching from the front door to the credit decider.

The holy grail of bank underwriting—*character*—the fifth of the five Cs of credit through which banks filter loan applications, can be unintentionally distorted by any number of mistaken impressions or misinterpretations by inexperienced or callous bank representatives. Borrowers with different accents, more reserved communication skills, or who were acclimated into business with differing customs might be judged to be distrustful or dishonest.

Banks are often overly reliant on FICO credit scores as a significant screening barrier, often establishing minimum approval scores that cannot be breached. Many participating bankers don't know what information the FICO score is derived from and accordingly misunderstand what a score may indicate concerning a credit applicant.

The score was originally developed to evaluate borrowers requesting long-term residential mortgage loans. FICO scores measure such diverse elements of a person's credit experience metrics as repayment history, credit type mix, credit utilization, and the length of time elapsed since the individual began borrowing. They were never intended to predict behavior in a horizon of less than two years.

Most users—ranging from bankers, landlords, and prospective employers to law enforcement officials—assume the FICO score is a simple measurement of someone's debt repayment history and that a lower score indicates that someone hasn't faithfully repaid his or her debts. Not only is that reasoning false, the consumer's credit history only comprises about a third of the FICO score's composition.[3]

Mortgage lending credit is heavily tilted toward viewing someone as a consumer. Such orientation is different in many respects than business lending, but often FICO scores are cited as the reason to decline business loan applications. These borrowers are often punished by credit denial or higher interest rates due to what some might objectively define as a lender's misplaced reliance on the FICO score beyond what analytics may merit.

As an example, FICO measures *credit utilization*, which compares the percentage of credit used to the amount of credit available (for example, a $6,000 outstanding balance on a credit card account with a $10,000 credit limit would reflect a total utilization rate of 60 percent).

This measurement is an imperfect assessment of consumers' behavior that might indicate they are accumulating more debt than they can handle, using more credit than before, or are getting close to the top of their credit limits. Or none of these conditions may exist at all.

FICO also doesn't take into account the consumer's income or net worth in their score, so often their grade is a poor reflection of reality. Think about a very wealthy individual who had committed the unimaginable sin of not borrowing money for 20 years—his or her FICO score might be zero.

Another issue that can lower the credibility of a FICO score was the decision by the major credit bureaus a few years back to allow collection agencies to post names of their working files into credit reports. FICO then began incorporating these items into their scores,[4] predictably bringing most of them down.

Why is that an issue? For many files it was appropriate and a fair reflection of other creditors that don't necessarily report regularly to the credit bureau. But for other debtors, it's abusive due to the sloppy reality of how many debtors wind up with collectors in the first place.

Experience teaches that thousands of unpaid invoices are sent to collection agencies annually without the holder ever billing or contacting the responsible party—or should I say patient? Medical practices are widely known for wholesaling their unpaid invoices to collectors as soon as the medical insurance company responds to the bill without giving their patient any notice.

The results? Doctors discount these typically small invoices, which may be cheaper than trying to collect. Collection agencies, who buy them for pennies on the dollar, don't try to collect many of them, but rather just post these invoices as a collection item with the credit bureaus and wait for the phone to ring.

Blindly leaving an alleged unpaid obligation that's reported as delinquent on a debtor's credit report does wonders for scorching his or her credit score. This unjust process senselessly affects that debtor's future mortgage rates, credit availability, and reputational risk for the many parties that may be given access to the credit report.

No one ever accused the collection industry of virtuous business practices. To make matters worse, in circumstances where the collector uses the credit bureau as the shotgun approach to collecting a debt, it's often hard to contact the listing collection agency from information provided by the credit report. And even once the debtor satisfies the invoice, there's no assurance that the records will be updated with the credit bureau in a timely manner, if ever.

FICO is also unsympathetic to consumers who get caught up in the schemes of unscrupulous credit card issuers who use bait and switch tactics to snare borrowers into unwittingly paying severe interest penalties. When the borrower refuses, the credit report gets downgraded, while the misleading lender is overlooked.

What tactic does this refer to? Retailers began using branded credit cards more than 20 years ago to create a funded spending allowance for consumers to walk in, buy merchandise, and walk out with the goods and a monthly bill. Not content with merely providing more buying incentives and convenience, many retailers, like Best Buy and the Apple Store, began to use credit card terms to sell their stuff.

No Interest Until 2015! Ads screamed that consumers could buy that new sound system or flat-screen TV with no money down and 12 months to pay at no interest cost—0 percent. That part of the deal offer was the bait. It worked very well then and still does, judging by ads in the Sunday newspaper.

The gambit begins, though, by the card issuer sending a credit card statement to the purchaser for a minimum payment with $0 interest charged. Of course there's no suggestion to actually pay an equal monthly sum that would satisfy the purchase amount in the 12-month interest-free period.

Rather, the borrower is billed for the customary 36-year amortization amount that is practiced by most credit card issuers. Okay, so buyer beware, right? But even for those cardholders who are a little more savvy, there's a trap in this scheme intended to switch that interest-free offer to a high-interest penalty.

For example, what happens to a consumer who has made a $1,000 purchase and pays at least $83.33 each month to repay the entire principal amount within the 12-month interest-free period? Suppose the purchase was made on June 1, 2012 and the first statement arrives with a payment date due on July 10th. Statements generally arrive 10 to 15 days ahead of the payment due date.

Even though the borrower dutifully pays the outstanding sum down well ahead of the billing rate, sending in the twelfth and last payment by the due date on their statement—June 10th, 2013—results in an interest charge for the entire sum from the date of purchase.

Some readers will call that legitimate business while others will recognize it as the root of why banking has the distinction of being the least trusted business on the globe.[5]

When the principled consumers refuse to be conned, the card issuer begins dinging them with late fees, ugly letters, and maybe even sells the "debts" to a collection agency later on. The FICO score gets hit with the cascading 1-over-30, 1-over-60, and so on. Who's really got the character issue in this scenario?

And hapless FICO and the credit bureaus ignore the $1,000 principal repayment and punish the consumer for the <$100 unpaid interest charges that were accrued from a chartered, regulated bank. That's wrong.

But even with a positive repayment record, there's no assurance that FICO will provide a positive credit score. If the consumer purposely chose to only use one credit card account and maintained an outstanding balance near the account limit, regardless of the ability to pay it off entirely or the ability to obtain additional accounts, his or her credit score would be lowered due to this automated judgment.

Another weakness might be the FICO's inclination to favor revolving credit as a measurement of positive credit activity over term debt. In other words, consumers score better with more activity generated from credit cards than from auto, education, or other installment debt. And a proven means to lift someone's score in a short period is to acquire another credit card. That doesn't make sense.

FICO is a good tool but is overused and overly relied on by many bankers as an automated substitute for what formerly was known as underwriting. It should always be augmented with additional information. Borrowers, particularly business borrowers, get shortchanged when this robotic tool disqualifies them from access to credit due to errors, illogical design, or lax lenders unwilling to peer behind the score.

To be fair to FICO, they have developed more helpful tools to assess consumer behavioral patterns and other characteristics that they claim can predict likely payment outcomes of potential borrowers based on a larger data pool. This additional information draws on such information as rent payments, utilities, and other non-creditor information beyond credit card payment records.

The lending community loves dumbing down this kind of information because it's cheaper and no one requires training to perform it (except knowing how to count numbers sequentially), but there is still plenty of room for error and abuse.

Many outlier consumers who should qualify for credit will still get crushed in credit scoring because the modeling assumes the creditor/reporting source is always right and it's often next to impossible to correct the information.

Managed Solutions

There has been a growing alternative source of information to support small business lending in the form of a cooperative organization to collect and redistribute credit information about the business itself, rather than just the owner's consumer credit history. Although the collection of a critical mass of this information took considerable time to complete (10 years), the value of this source is really beginning to become better known and used in just the past three years.

In 2001, a group of leading small business lenders organized the Small Business Financial Exchange® (SBFE), a nonprofit company formed for the express purpose of aggregating loan performance information on smaller companies and sharing it with its membership. Rather than creating a new reporting agency, SBFE chose Equifax as the facilitating reporting bureau.

This enterprise bills its mission as providing a blind exchange of small business financial data, with give-to-get requirements, data use safeguards, self-governance, and compliance oversight. It's the only independent industry-governed consortium of its type. SBFE members continue to own the data they share in the exchange. To date, credit histories on roughly 24 million companies have been aggregated in this database to provide members with critical hard-to-get information about small companies.

SBFE membership is open to any financial organization that originates small business financial obligations, owns the paper related to small business financial obligations, or services the receivables for small business financial obligations. Members are required to report all their small business lending portfolios to the SBFE Data Warehouse™ on a monthly basis and pay annual member dues.

For their purposes, a small business is defined as a business entity with revenues of less than $10 million and loan exposure with the financial institution of less than $2.5 million, but they allow members to report loan portfolios based on each member's definition of a small business transaction.

The SBFE provides a picture of a small business's financial exposure across multiple financial institutions and portfolios. Key data elements include small business name and address, account type and status, date account opened, credit limit, high credit, balance, and payment history. Members use SBFE data to:

- Underwrite decisions, with a more complete picture of the business' financial obligations
- Manage and review portfolio risks of existing customers' credit performance
- Prevent fraud by contributing small business address, telephone number, tax ID number, and principal's name
- Enhance collection efforts by supplying the most current contact information for small businesses and their owners

Members may access the SBFE data for credit scoring model-building, although the data is restricted to those members who chose to opt-in for the inclusion of its data in the development of generic industry models.

Their site states that members are strictly prohibited from using data to build or augment marketing lists and that member usage is monitored for compliance.

While this enterprise did not represent an innovative shift in technology, or even in business thinking, it was an important development to the rise in innovative lending as we've witnessed. There was no financial incentive to aggregate data on 24 million companies for technological advances that were not imagined at the time. SBFE arose strictly to meet the needs of its organizing members.

Credit bureaus started in local communities where various credit providers—banks, credit unions, and businesses selling on open account—would share information to a disinterested third party for redistribution. They mainly evolved as consumer agencies because the subject's identification would more easily be tracked over decades with the same date of birth and Social Security number.

Business credit information had been more difficult to obtain since companies can open and close easily without understanding where common ownership exists. Lenders had to do considerable due diligence to ferret out whether multiple businesses were owned by the same party. And even then, before SBFE, they were largely unable to track the credit performance records, since the information was fragmented with no common point to gather it.

That problem is largely solved with SBFE, and with almost 15 years of record collection, a viable database is available to use in a variety of ways to strengthen business lending and lower credit risk. This data has been an important source of research for many innovative lenders over the past 10 years and will be tapped by more parties in the years ahead to improve their underwriting and risk management.

One of the largest beneficiaries of this information is FICO. Their business credit score—the Small Business Scoring Service (SBSS Score) is a model more appropriate for assessing the likelihood of business repayment, although it does include the consumer score to an unknown degree to derive its conclusion.

This scoring model is widely used and apparently, according to several commentators, is considered to be very reliable and accurate. It received a huge boost starting on January 1, 2014 when the U.S. Small Business Administration began requiring that every loan submitted to them for guaranty under $350,000 must be screened by SBSS.

MORALITY AND MONEY

Another issue that detours many business lenders on the path to credit approval is when a bankruptcy filing appears in the borrower's history. Bankruptcy is a component of the U.S. legal system that provides protection to borrowers whose liabilities have overwhelmed their ability to meet those obligations. As much as protecting the borrower, the framework of bankruptcy protects lenders from each other's competing claims and turns the question of claim priority over to the court to sort out who gets paid first.

Many people in the finance trade see bankruptcy as a self-inflicted financial failure caused either by the lack of competence or capability to succeed. Worse, some equate bankruptcy to a morality issue, rather than comparing it to similar resolutions such as a lawsuit. In this line of thinking, the presumption is that debtors have simply abandoned their responsibilities in favor of an easy escape that leaves lenders and other obligors holding worthless legal contracts that originally reflected an agreement to pay.

Missing from that latter presumption held by some bankers may be that life intervenes for many people in unpredictable ways, such as accidents, illnesses, and natural disasters, to name a few. But aside from that detachment aimed at consumers, many formerly illustrious companies have detoured through bankruptcy without lingering effects, and in some cases, survived only because of it.

Companies including Johns-Manville (1994), Delta Airlines (2005), and Chrysler Corporation (2009) filed Chapter 11 bankruptcy (reorganization) for a variety of reasons. These reasons generally amounted to a business strategy that they were unable to work out without the engagement of an independent arbitrator, which ultimately was the bankruptcy court.

Is it hard to reason that if bankruptcy can be used to break employment contracts, pension obligations, liability claims, and occupancy contracts in order for a business to survive, it is also possible to use the same code to rearrange debt and equity financing? It's not a morality issue.

The bottom line is that bankruptcy in and of itself shouldn't be an automatic disqualifier to accessing the debt market. But the due diligence required in order to decide the root cause and effects, and whether those factors inhibit the creditworthiness of a business is obviously difficult to scale or perform inexpensively.

For those who may disagree, consider the irony that the only American colony settled by prisoners freed from Great Britain's debtor prisons (Georgia), became the state that led the nation in bank failures during the financial crisis between 2008 and 2013.

THE UNINTENDED CONSEQUENCES OF OLD LAW

One frustration suffered by multiple segments of American society is when laws and regulations are adopted to discourage and prevent egregious, damaging actions by some people that lead to unfair disruption to others. And, much like the old saying "a locked door keeps honest people honest," most of these efforts tend to punish the majority who obey the law and have good intentions.

With bank lenders, that frustration is that many bank regulations intended to prevent discrimination or other lending disparities have unintended consequences. Some of the procedures required by the FDIC actually can prevent business owners from getting capital or at least getting a timely response to their request for capital.

While supporting the laudable effort to provide transparency in the process of interfacing with prospective borrowers to prevent overt discrimination, the FDIC sometimes goes overboard. This agency requires bankers to defer judgment or discouraging obvious unfundable loan requests until a physical loan application or package has been presented, a credit report has been obtained at the expense of the bank, and a formal declination can be mailed to the applicant. It's an exasperating waste of everyone's time.

Likewise, capital markets can get hamstrung on the very regulations intended to protect investors from getting swindled. Well-intentioned requirements to provide in-depth transparency and disclosure about companies (and the individuals who run them) becomes an extraordinarily expensive proposition over the course of *years* ahead of a hoped-for offering of securities to investors.

Virtually all of America's security laws governing the sale of equity and debt in public and private exchanges are rooted in the 1930s era reforms intended to put an end to brazen fraud that was perpetrated on its citizens. Of course, not only were the world and the capital markets much simpler and different then, we also didn't have as many securities lawyers.

All of today's high costs to offer securities that pay for attorneys, investment bankers, and auditors don't necessarily raise a dime of capital financing, but rather just increase the chance to "legally" get in front of investors someday to beg for capital.

Another challenging element of the securities law requires that when a company's ownership was shared by more than 500 people (recently revised to 2,000 by the JOBS Act), it must become a public reporting company. That means that the company is required to file quarterly financial statements to the Securities & Exchange Commission and make certain disclosures about company matters that may impact the value of its shares.

Improving the access of small businesses seeking to tap into more investors for smaller capital sums has been stifled by this cap due to both the high cost of public reporting and the lower sums that investors may be willing to invest in younger, early-stage businesses.

Another element of the old securities regulations essentially required securities dealers to pitch investment opportunities through personal connections. Meaning, they were supposed to have a client relationship with the potential investors in any transaction and were prohibited from soliciting the general public or even those unknown to them as a client or client prospect.

This law was adopted when only about 1 percent of the population owned stock, versus 50 percent today, and has been used to prevent the industry from *general advertising*, that is, securities cannot be promoted in newspapers or other forums that could attract buyers. It accounts for the aggressiveness of stock brokers, particularly newer ones, who network at various places and work to get their hands on your business card.

Existing securities regulations govern what is known as forward-looking statements, which essentially require that any disclosures provided to support the sale of securities must limit their language to the present, at the time it's made. This regulation means that any sale prospectus discussion about the company's potential to perform must be watered down so heavily with caveats, qualifications, and disclaimers that companies seem to be trying to convince people not to invest.

It seems as though there should be more common-sense middle ground to protect investors while allowing companies to tap into capital that's seeking opportunities.

CAPITAL MARKETS GO DIGITAL

Now, many of the former legal restrictions are beginning to evaporate as new digital paths to connecting private investors' capital to business owners are being created. Many traditional impediments, including screening tools, regulations, and attitudes are changing as new funding organizations are offering more innovative and efficient means to acquire, qualify, underwrite, and deliver capital financing.

On April 5, 2012, President Obama signed the Jumpstart Our Business Startups Act, or JOBS Act, into law. This law was constructed from a number of competing bills to incrementally change various security laws, to open up the equity markets more for smaller companies and in particular facilitate crowdfunding for equity.

The net effect is intended to provide greater access to capital funding to smaller companies through digital markets and from a greater pool of potential investors. If proponents prove to be correct, it will aggregate more equity capital for companies that otherwise would have been shut out of these funds, due to the cost of pursuing them or clearing the intermediaries standing between investors and companies.

And, thinking about the long tail in terms of the number of potential investors, it means companies will potentially be exposed to many more investors than their investment bankers could have ever pitched. Organizing markets through digital markets to allow investors to research and consider more companies should lead to more targeted investing and expansion of funding potential for the companies.

On the debt side of capital funding, innovation has led to the emergence of dozens of new lenders who have rethought and modified small business financing in ways never considered. Nonbank lenders have turned every component of the hunt for clients, including gathering applications, analyzing data, underwriting loans, and funding companies inside out, with new tactics to scale the delivery of funding to companies long shunned by banks.

In what promises to far exceed the production delivery of new digital equity markets, these new breed lenders are carving out fascinating products to purposely fund specific niche markets when funding has been scarce, and to date are as successful as traditional banking in terms of important metrics such as loan currency, loan default levels, and credit losses.

PATTERN RECOGNITION—DATA IS THE GAME CHANGER

Maybe the most significant change in the innovations of delivering capital through technology is the rising development and use of new metrics to fuel decisions drawn from lending data. Data? Yes, boring, flat, and unimaginative data is being mined for patterns among different data components and, alas, *metadata* is created.

What exactly is metadata? Basically it's the data that is developed from data.

Lenders collect plenty of data about loan customers that is stored in many places like spreadsheets, financial statements, and application forms. Some of this data (borrower name, address, date of birth, etc.) is sent to the credit bureau, which collects similar information from thousands of other sources and produces an aggregate report of the individual's accounts with all reporting creditors that is called a credit report.

That credit report is a collection of data. When that data is used to produce the FICO score, that score is an example of metadata.

Metadata offers information that is not apparent to the naked eye staring at thousands of lines of data. It may reveal that previous presumptions are wrong. It may offer new insight into an unknown risk or opportunity.

Most commonly, metadata can illuminate subtle risk differentials among business types, business owners, business locations, and virtually an unlimited other number of business attributes where the data is available.

Similar to the DNA code, portfolios can be analyzed in many different ways to discover patterns of repayment, default, and loan losses as a means to discover how to improve future decisions. And since more data continues to be generated, it's possible to use the analytical templates employed to monitor actual performance in a manner to constantly upgrade or modify credit policy, marketing efforts, and approval standards according to trends that can be detected.

Maybe more strategic is the ability to prove old theories wrong—positively or negatively—and change policy or underwriting models to adapt to new thinking ahead of the competition, like opening up credit to a certain demographic market—previously shunned by your organization and competitors—ahead of the competitors after discovering that the likely results will be much better than previously believed.

Meaning? Suppose the market minimum FICO credit score for business owners was established to be 660 among a majority of market bank lenders and anyone with a lower score would be immediately disqualified regardless of other application attributes. What if there was a method to reliably test a broad swath of data to determine whether 660 was the most appropriate number? Of course there are reams of data available to test such a question.

So, if the data showed that a marginal number of loan defaults did not begin to materially rise until borrowers with 630 scores were involved, it would lead to the decision of whether to lower the bank's minimum threshold score. Lowering the minimum threshold may improve the bank's appeal with more borrowers and thereby generate more business.

Likewise, if the data showed that credit scores at 700 greatly improved loan performance, it might raise the question as to whether the bank should continue to allow borrowers to have credit with only a 680 FICO score.

There is much more data to mine that can reveal much about loan risk and while it's never a good idea to block the eligibility of entire borrowing sectors, having good intelligence about how specific groups perform can lead to policy alterations to account for the exposed risk. Lenders can tighten lending standards on those sectors or charge higher interest rates to allow for the higher risks.

For better or worse, FICO has introduced a business loan product to the marketplace geared to provide credit decisions from a cloud-based platform called FICO Liquid Credit. Drawing information from consumer and business bureaus along with specific client application input, the platform gives lenders an automated credit decision complete with recommended pricing.

It's likely that FICOs built their model using the same reams of metadata that's rented out to other online lenders when developing their platforms. Credit scoring theoretically looks at every deal through the same lens and takes into account more micro bits of information that's been suggested through research to predict outcomes and the potential for loan default.

Lenders can customize their scoring approach by setting specific standards on several elements of the model, which customizes it according to the lender's credit policy.

The benefits of this system are obvious—it standardizes credit decisions using what information is available and applies a consistent pricing discriminant to deliver consistent decisions. It works faster with existing metadata available on the subject and responds to the client lenders faster than they could process in-house.

These attributes help moderate cost, particularly if the lender is a larger bank, with thousands of branches that each field dozens of micro business loan applications each week. And, regulators probably like it due to the consistent management of lending in this area and the depth of metrics collected that can be helpful to management to monitor compliance with lending regulations.

The downside is that this model relies heavily on FICO's own consumer credit score, with its inherent weaknesses, which will penalize many small business owners. Additionally, while this platform makes sense for borrowers seeking capital up to a certain size threshold, larger loans should be manually underwritten to account for more factors than can be captured by averaging data.

Where is that threshold? The answer will be unique to each different bank or lender, but is probably in the $350,000 range or higher.

DIFFERENT PROCESSES AND DIFFERENT VIEWS

New discoveries always lead to innovation but sometimes in totally unexpected ways. The idea that computer geeks would discover new ways to match (and occasionally surpass) the performance of hundreds of years of collective wisdom of the business finance industry is hard enough to swallow. But consider more assertive ideas that are completely turning over the conventions on which the industry has always stood: the basic credit model.

While *Merriam-Webster's Dictionary* doesn't define *finance* with these words, in its essence, finance is the allocation of scarce resources. For the finance world, that scarce resource is money. Since banks and other business funders depend on leveraging their capital with additional resources from depositors or other lenders, they have to exercise a certain degree of prudence when entering loan transactions.

Loan transactions inherently present a risk to the lender that the borrower will be unable to repay the loan, for one of possibly dozens of unforeseen reasons. The failure of the borrower to repay directly impacts the lender's capital and subsequent ability to make the same volume of loans in the future. Hence, the finance industry developed many practices over the years to lower the risk of borrower default.

The practices were designed to manage the lending risk either by setting standards and conditions the borrower must meet to be approved for the loan or by establishing a path to additional repayment sources should the borrower be unable to perform, such as personal guarantees, collateral, and the threat of legal action.

The digital finance marketplace began creating different ways to manage these risks, but at least one company hit on a new lending theory: *Credit risk is a line-item expense.*

While civilians may not think that such thinking is a big deal, to most commercial bankers that line of reasoning is heresy. Credit risk in the banking world is what they have spent decades developing practices to eradicate. But the digital marketplace, without the constraints of regulation, public deposits, and centuries of convention has evolved to just make credit losses a budget number.

What does that mean? For one thing, it accepts loan losses as the cost of doing business, and rather than obsessing over how to prevent losses and recover defaulted loans, innovative lenders strive to understand what the cost will be and chalk it up to the cost of doing business, to be covered with more stout charges assessed to all funding recipients.

Obviously, such an outlook is easier when the average deal size is less than $50,000 and there are no federally insured deposits involved. But the other advantage is how this strategy lowers other operating costs. Think about how banks often kill marginal deals and miss out on viable revenue in order to hold their credit operations to higher standards.

Likewise, how much management time is spent on negotiating tougher loan terms, managing defaulted loans, and collecting bad debt? If that time could be redirected toward making more loans, it would dramatically change their business as well.

In addition to new ideas, innovation enables new processes as well, and the freedom from regulation and convention facilitates many more efficiencies for innovative lenders than commercial banks can realize. Using technology from startups, innovators get the advantage of movable information that can be sorted, evaluated, analyzed, distributed, and filed easily—and even redirected at a later date.

The digitization doesn't have to be universal, though. Some innovative lenders continue to get paper applications from borrowers and brokers and they are happy to facilitate them—for a modest charge. One funder faxes paper application forms to a processing center in Costa Rica (since they have no Bank Secrecy Act (BSA) compliance to contend with) for the information to be permanently digitized.

Once entered, the due diligence of credit reports and other third party investigation or verification starts on the signal of one key. And as the information is received, the platform scores it instantly into a *Yes-No-Maybe* decision tree for further processing automatically.

In the digital world, applicant information is always taken at face value and verified later through a number of digital channels, with fraud detection that's fairly reliable. Once (and if) the underwriter decides on the transaction offer, the deal is communicated to the business developer and only then do real negotiations begin.

Applications are not one-size-fits-all. Smaller loans get an abbreviated list of information required and the list only grows as the loan size request does.

These funding platforms also monitor the transaction originator and grades them according to approval rates and deal performance. This information is used in the future to determine deal pricing, priority, and whether there is any push factor available for deals sitting on the threshold.

Finally, the innovator funders are more aggressive about acquiring deal flow. One rich source of business is their own book: When funding transactions are paid down to about 50 percent of the original amount, these funders begin "pinging" the client to determine whether more money would be useful.

CROWDFUNDING VERSUS THE CROWD THAT GOT FUNDING

In the 1970s, commercial banks were the primary source of capital for something like 90 percent of American companies. That number has been eroding ever since, thanks to many factors:

- There are simply more businesses today (28 million) and the average size of the business is smaller.
- Conversely, there are fewer banks today thanks to many factors including the consolidation that followed the end of "unit" banking in many states, liberalizing state banking laws to allow branches in other states, and the failure of thousands of banks following the S&L crisis in the late 1980s and hundreds that failed following the financial crisis of 2008.
- Banking and financial deregulation that started in the early 1980s has enabled a broader range of companies to begin making loans.
- Small and medium size banks began largely shunning certain loan products, such as auto loans, credit cards, and asset-based lending due to the inability to scale these efforts relative to the cost to deliver them, which conceded much business to non-bank competitors.

Among several channels that have emerged in the past 10 years to provide funding to small business owners, one is actually a recycled idea dating from the late nineteenth century: *crowdfunding*. It was not labeled as such back then but had the same characteristics as the process we have seen emerge boldly since 2005.

Many aficionados will define earlier acts of gathering resources from a community as crowdsourcing—think about barn raisings, where colonial era settlers would gather for several days of construction to help a neighbor in their community to build a barn. Likewise, today crowdfunding is a gathering of shared resources from a community to accomplish something that on some level is valued by all participants.

Crowdfunding is not really new, just the name is. The essence of crowdfunding is that social capital is converted to financial capital. It is very niche oriented—think clean energy, Native Americans, Beatles fans, or Chattanooga, Tennessee. Members in each community all have something in common, be it their beliefs, their location, their ethnicity, or whatever other attribute is at the heart of a shared interest or affinity.

History contains many forms of crowdfunding, albeit in varying forms. During the Middle Ages, with no access to banks, enterprising Jews turned to the elders in their synagogue. Chinese grandmothers customarily left their possessions to their granddaughters rather than their daughters, purposely skipping a generation to share resources into the future. And even Benjamin Franklin created a group called Junto, which pooled money through subscriptions to organize America's first library.[6]

In 1884, the city of New York was struggling to gather funding to construct a base for the newly gifted Statue of Liberty to the citizens of the United States from France. Newspaper publisher Joseph Pulitzer took a personal interest in this embarrassing dilemma and turned away from conventional fundraising of the time—government grants and corporate gifts—and instead went directly to the readers of his *World* newspaper to ask, beg, and cajole gifts from average citizens.[7]

It worked. Within six months, the campaign raised $102,000 from more than 120,000 small donors—at less than $1 each. Lady Liberty had a new perch inside Fort Wood, situated on Liberty Island.

That story is an excellent example of crowdfunding, where a funding need was put before a community that had an interest in the outcome and willingly participated with funding to see that need fulfilled. In the case of Pulitzer's campaign, it was a contribution for the greater good of the city, state, and nation. Gifts were, on average, very small, but with an influencer such as Joseph Pulitzer using the power of his newspaper's front page and editorials, the response was overwhelming for that era.

Fast forward to 1997 when the Internet was just beginning to take hold. A group of fiercely loyal American fans (the "Freaks") of progressive British rock band Marillion was hopeful that the band would tour the United States again to promote their ninth studio album, *This Strange Engine*.[8] But the band's American record company, Red Ant, had recently filed for bankruptcy and couldn't underwrite the trip.

The disappointing news was delivered through online list serv discussions from band members. Fans organized a grassroots fundraising campaign through e-mail and list-servers without a website or a sponsoring organization, and without the band's sanction. The campaign raised more than $47,000 to cover the expenses of the band's 21-city U.S. tour.

That stunning feat was witnessed by many other organizations in the arts and culture sector and in the years that followed, was replicated by many efforts to raise money for charitable and social causes.

In 2005, IndieGoGo launched a website-oriented platform to facilitate crowdfunding for anyone. Their portal offered the screening of potential campaigns to assure potential donors, a standard pitch page where campaigns could offer information and videos to entice their communities to participate, and a common payment window to collect donations that were offered and held until the campaign's conclusion.

By 2012, according to Massolution.com's 2013CF Crowdfunding Market Outlook Report,[9] more than $2.7 billion was raised in a single year through hundreds of crowdfunding sites across the globe, with participants making donations or buying new products with a future delivery promised. And, as of September 2013, this marketplace was opened to selling equity and debt securities thanks to the JOBS Act.

Suffice it to say that crowdfunding is rapidly changing the marketplace for gathering funds for benevolent causes, social enterprises, artists, some local for-profit enterprises, and other big ideas.

Conceptually, crowdfunding is no different than a bank—pooling resources of many to provide capital to curated ideas, projects, and purposes. The bank—like crowdfunders—becomes the gatekeeper to screen participants and protect the integrity of the greater community's resources.

But the rise of the digital community has allowed more participants to find and join with their communities and disrupt these older forms of crowdfunding in unique and interesting ways, which will continue to evolve.

THE RISE IN ALTERNATIVE PATHS TO SOURCE FUNDING

As many new funding choices emerged in this brave new digital landscape, so did the market intermediaries who began searching for both borrowers needing capital and funders seeking more borrowers. These digital brokers began arising to help both parties meet and directed them to a new range of choices that previously didn't exist in the search for funding.

These intermediaries have added value to business owners in a variety of ways, from helping to sort borrower funding needs more clearly in order to route them to the most appropriate funding source, to building online application profiles and applications, and to advising them on the construction of their application information, to provide funders with more complete information up front.

Ranging from simple "link farms" to companies that offer a full service one-on-one consultation with a trained lending advisor, the digital intermediaries have successfully scaled the loan brokering business in some interesting ways. With technology, they can serve as a trading post for companies seeking capital while simultaneously serving as a recruiting station for capital funders.

The evolution of intermediaries and other service providers will continue to grow, particularly as crowdfunding becomes more mainstream and equity can be sold over the Internet. Already there are coaches who can be engaged to organize a crowdfunding campaign, videographers who specialize in a quick three-minute pitch for funds, and an assortment of functionaries to facilitate the search for funds.

BILLIONS WENT MISSING AND NO ONE NOTICED?

Perhaps the oddest ending to this story of an altering landscape for capital distribution is how many participants in the old, established capital markets are completely unaware of this changing marketplace.

It is impossible to calculate an official tally on exactly how much capital has been channeled through these new lenders and crowdfunders, since most for-profit ventures are privately owned and will not disclose their volume. But one market participant CEO estimated that since 2003, more than $100 billion of funding has crossed through these digital markets largely unseen by the commercial banking market.

Obviously that is rapidly changing, and to be sure, many banks have noticed and began engaging in this sector to get a foothold in the new territory. Several money-center banks are reported to have already invested in several ventures and others have been an active lender-finance source for dozens of innovative funders, particular the merchant cash advance companies. It's only logical to expect that many will follow suit in the months and years ahead.

One notable exception is Nathaniel Karp, chief economist for BBVA Research, U.S. Unit. In their second quarter 2013 U.S. Economic Outlook,[10]

Karp provides some insight and analysis about crowdfunding, at least the two kinds used for peer-to-peer lending and equity sales. He concludes:

> *Crowdfunding is a disruptive innovation that commercial banks cannot ignore. Perhaps, for the first time in history, business and individuals have access to an unprecedented source of capital created from the small contributions of millions of individuals around the world.*
>
> *This is good news for individuals and entrepreneurs, who may never have to worry about not being able to access traditional lending sources or using more expensive funding solutions to finance their projects. It is also good news for small investors seeking a higher return than conventional investment products.*
>
> *For banks, crowdfunding poses a challenge. From here on, they will face a new competitor with lower operating costs, a different approach to risk management and a simpler product offering. To what extent crowdfunding platforms will displace commercial banks in the retail and small business segments remains to be seen. However, banks should be prepared for this trend and make it work to their advantage.*

It will be interesting to watch how many voices join Karp from the banking sector and how many follow his suggestion. It's obvious advice that banks should be paying attention and probably should engage in the development side of this new phenomenon. To the degree possible, it's a good idea to buy in as an investor of a sufficient stake in some of these innovators to get a clear view of the results. If it works, the banks can buy out the prize down the road.

Notes

1. MetroLyrics.com, www.metrolyrics.com/whos-on-first-lyrics-abbott-and-costello.html (accessed November 4, 2013).
2. YouTube.com, www.youtube.com/watch?v=airT-m9LcoY (accessed November 4, 2013).
3. "What's In Your Score," MyFico.com, www.myfico.com/crediteducation/whatsinyourscore.aspx (accessed November 4, 2013).
4. "Collections—How to Manage Them and What They Do to Your Credit," MyFico.com, www.myfico.com/crediteducation/questions/collections.aspx (accessed December 29, 2013).
5. "Trust in Financial Services," Edelman.com, www.edelman.com/insights/intellectual-property/trust-2013/trust-across-sectors/trust-in-financial-services/ (accessed December 15, 2013).

6. "Overview," LibraryCompany.org, www.librarycompany.org/about/index.htm (accessed January 2, 14).

7. "Pulitzer and the Pedestal—Or Why Crowdfunding Needs Influencer Marketing," Beth's Blog, www.bethkanter.org/crowd-funding/ (accessed November 4, 2013).

8. Dean Golemis, "British Band's U.S. Tour Is Computer-Generated," *Chicago Tribune*, September 23, 1997, http://articles.chicagotribune.com/1997-09-23/features/9709230071_1_music-fans-newsgroup-marillion.

9. 2013CF Crowdfunding Market Outlook Report, www.crowdsourcing.org/editorial/2013cf-crowdfunding-outlook-report/26448 (accessed November 4, 2013).

10. Nathaniel Karp, "Economic Outlook—United States, Second Quarter 2013," BBVA Research, 34.

PART Three

Digital Dynamics in Small Business Funding

CHAPTER 7

Funders and Lenders—
Online Capital Providers

Barely more than a couple generations ago, the idea of getting financing for a small business was confined to a fairly short list of prospective sources. In the years that preceded the concept of junk bonds, equity investors generally tied their money up in a combination of federally insured bank deposits, U.S. government treasury bonds, blue-chip stocks, or AAA-rated corporate bonds.

Likewise for those small businesses who could qualify for debt financing, there were commercial banks so long as the business owner resided in a county that had a bank willing to make business loans. In those days, many states restricted banks to servicing one county, or in some instances required they be confined to operating only in their home states.

By and large, these archaic rules kept banks focused on their home markets—and relatively small. Growth for the bank was a matter of either taking customers from other banks or being fortunate enough to be situated in a high-growth market with a surging population and economy.

Accordingly, small business owners didn't have many options, given that the number, size, and aggressiveness of local banks was closely aligned with the financial vitality of their local economies. Other than banks, financing options were few unless they were connected to individuals with the means who were willing to bankroll the businesses or buy in as partners.

INNOVATIVE FUNDING MARKETPLACE

Today, small business lending seems to be almost chic. It's not, *who's making small business loans?*, but rather, *who isn't making small business loans?*

The perfect storm that combines the rise in technology and data aggregation with a post-crisis, gun-shy banking sector and the slowest recovering job market since post—WWII[1] has benefited small business owners, who suddenly have access to capital from more providers than ever before.

Type the generic search words "small business loan" into the Google search engine and they provide 172 million pages of results. Call it "small business funding" and the number increases to 322 million pages and change it to "small business capital" and the number increases to 577 million. Even the paid ads are robust on all these searches, reflecting the hypercompetition that exists to find qualified business borrowers.

The market is crawling with dozens of funding categories that offer specialized financing products to almost every niche of business imaginable. Companies that used to be considered the pariahs of bank financing—restaurants, retail stores, and web-based enterprises—are star attractions that have legions of funders standing by. While the risk of a market bubble is low, the frenzy for deal flow is already apparent, as witnessed in the constant effort among these funders to be seen in a high volume of search ads, pop-up site ads, and even constant publicity efforts to keep their names in the limelight.

This new marketplace is very different, though, than the general conditions that have accompanied the expansion of business capital over the past 40 years. For one thing, the innovative marketplace is virtual. There are no lunch meetings, office appointments, or checks in the mail.

By design, these funders are accessible through a site visit and maybe an e-mail address. Before an account is set up with them through a password protected loan application, many don't disclose too much information about even who they are or where they're situated.

A second common feature is that there is little customization in what they do—if applicants fit their model, fine. If not, who's next in line? These companies fund a specific set of circumstances in a model that has usually been derived from careful study of millions of blind credit data files, testing different ideas. They've selected lending criteria through carefully evaluated credit parameters intended to lower loan loss risks.

A third common feature is that the pricing is generally multitiered and relatively expensive. A few such funders lead with a pitch extolling the benefits of their low interest loans, while failing to mention that there is an accompanying origination fee, credit default risk fee, and other assorted junk charges that will push the cost charged the best borrowers up to a minimum of the 24 percent APR range.

The sleight-of-hand features used to describe the cost of capital is nothing new in the finance world. And as a rule, no one in this marketplace bends over backward to offer easy comparisons to what an applicant might find in the banking market. There are no references to APR (annual percentage rate), but rather applicants may see funding costs expressed as "cost-on-dollar," which represents the cost of repaying every dollar acquired. So a 1.2x cost-on-dollar would mean that $1.20 was required to repay every $1.00 acquired from this source.

Banks also use loan fees and the 360-day loan calendar to mask their true costs and yields on business loans.

The fourth common feature of these funders is reliance on daily payment transfers from either an automated clearing house (ACH) payment from the borrower's bank account or direct distribution from their merchant account processor. These payments require no human effort to collect other than setting up the account. Check payments have to be delivered, opened, endorsed, deposited, and can bounce. The rapid reeling back of loan funds from the borrower through daily payments serves several purposes. For one thing, the faster repayment of the obligation lowers the risk of getting repaid. Payments are timed to match the revenue stream of the borrower, so payments are pulled out nearly as fast as money is deposited from daily sales.

If the borrowing company's situation began to worsen after funding, it stands to reason that getting the funds back daily chips away at the balance faster and protects the funder from potential losses.

Since the financing cost is largely structured as a fixed sum (remember the reference to multitiered pricing?), faster repayment also increases the yield that will be earned on these financing transactions. The funders that utilize an interest rate as a portion of their funding costs usually set it at a reasonable level in the 10 to 20 percent range. But the remainder of their revenue is locked in fixed fees, regardless of the repayment term.

Therefore, collecting the funds faster significantly improves their financial returns with higher, sometimes astronomical, rate yields.

ONLINE FUNDERS: PURCHASING FUTURE RECEIPTS

Perhaps the most mature of all the innovative funders are merchant cash advance (MCA) companies, an unregulated funding product often mischaracterized as credit card receivable factoring. But unlike traditional factors, these companies buy future credit card revenue streams rather than previous delivered invoices that are expected to be collected.

The idea is not new, dating back to the late 1990s, but digitizing this sector's process has turned a profitable business to an even more profitable one. The original innovation was to tie working capital funding to track day-to-day revenue collections by recapturing as a percentage of future revenues. By diverting funds directly from the merchant processor, MCAs can get control of the cash proceeds faster and avoid the funds going through a bank, where they would be subject to the possibility of getting frozen for competing claims.

While other working capital lenders base their underwriting on the trailing financial performance of the borrowing companies over a two- to three-year period, MCA companies focus on measuring average monthly credit card revenues over a trailing six- to 12-month period. Using that data, they advance funds, usually calculated as a percentage of average monthly credit card cash proceeds.

Virtually all MCA companies are nonbank, nonlenders who choose not to make loans, but rather buy future receivables. In this way, they are completely unregulated as to the maximum credit price ceilings imposed by most states, known as usury laws. Their transaction medium is a "Future Receivables Purchase and Sale Agreement" that positions the transaction as a sale of a specified sum of future credit card proceeds for a discounted sum.

In these agreements, the MCA is referred to as the buyer, and they agree to purchase from the seller (who resembles a borrower) for an amount called the purchase price, payable with a portion of the future credit card proceeds (referred to as the specified percentage), limited to the agreed total that is referred to as the specified amount.

In other words, the MCA provides advance funding to the client for a fixed repayment amount that is repaid with a fixed percentage of the future revenue stream.

There is no mention in these agreements of interest, fees, or other costs. The entire return of the buyer's proceeds plus the premium paid for the advance purchase is all rolled into one number called the specified amount.

All working capital financing is risky business in that funders are providing monies for operations—paying for labor, material, inventory, and so on for the production of a good or service that hopefully will be sold for a future profit. It's tough to provide third party funding for working capital because of the compounded risks. Unlike asset financing, more can go wrong with working capital lending, such as unfinished production or buyers never appearing.

Traditional asset-based lenders (and factors) accounted for these risks by forcing the business to prove it was capable of producing and selling goods with its own capital before advancing working capital. Ideally, in that model the funds were paying for the next round of production rather than the goods that were recently shipped. These funders also could hold a second party accountable for getting repaid—the buyer of the goods. The MCA model does not have these advantages and is a much riskier financial product.

First, they are advancing money in reliance on the expectation of future business revenue generation that resembles past performance levels. If dealing with a seasonal business, these transactions are intended to help carry the business through slack months with the promise that the heavier revenues in months ahead will be sufficient to repay the funding.

Secondly, MCAs are most active in marketing to retail-oriented businesses that rely on a heavy portion of their revenues to be generated through credit card sales. These include merchandise stores, restaurants, convenience stores, hotels, and service businesses. These industry sectors are among the most competitive and suffer relatively high failure rates. MCA clients are already at the end of the money food chain and are not embraced by other financing suppliers beyond their capital asset financing needs.

To address these credit risks, MCAs require daily payments to match the revenue stream of their clients. Since their target customers are open daily for business, revenues are normal on a daily basis. Credit card processors generally remit sales receipts to the merchants two or three days following a client purchase.

MCAs are repaid a percentage of the seller's daily payments, which are remitted directly from the merchant account processor via ACH. Sellers agree to use the merchant card processor determined by the buyer, and to allow that processor to remit the specified percentage of daily revenues to the buyer (MCA) that would otherwise be paid to their own bank accounts. These remittances to the MCA are net of any processing fees, which are exclusively borne by the seller, the funding recipient.

Daily payments also lower the credit risk to the MCA—the sooner the funds are recaptured, the less risk is involved for something to go wrong with the business or their sales volume. Quicker repayment also rewards the MCA with higher financial returns on their capital that can be deployed elsewhere, since their financial reward is fixed.

To compensate for the risk involved with these loans, MCAs charge substantial fees for these advances. Since they are creating unregulated financial transactions, there are no maximum cap or usury rates to worry about. Borrowers are willing to pay the cost for a variety reasons, but one of them is often that they really need the funding and they have no other options.

The transaction cost is the difference between the buy and sell price—MCAs "buy" a future receivable sum ("specified amount") for the purchase price. That cost is not referred to as a fee, interest, or any other word or time restriction that would imply that the funding is related to the time value of money.

Arguably, the absence of the typical pricing markers, such as a defined interest rate or specified fee, which are always required in the regulated financial markets, makes the process less transparent for the funding recipients. Would they accept these funds if they really understood the costs? Certainly many would but it's a good bet that many would not.

TABLE 7.1   Typical Merchant Cash Advance Scenario

Purchase price	= $93,851 (sum that was offered to the business)
Specified sum	= $127,637 (sum that would be recaptured by MCA)
Specified percentage	= 16 percent (portion of proceeds remitted to MCA)

What kind of costs are at stake? In Table 7.1, there actual terms that were taken from a funding proposal to an Atlanta area business in 2013.[2]

On the accompanying Merchant Processing Agreement that was a required part of the transaction, the document information disclosed that the average credit card volume for the business was $100,000 per month, with a high monthly volume in the previous 12 months of $140,000.

While these figures cannot disclose what the actual funding costs will be, since the exact recapture period is determined by future revenues, they can be used to project some possibilities. For starters, with an average volume of $100,000 per month, and 16 percent of that sum remitted to the MCA each month, the contract would be fulfilled in less than one year. But rounding up to the assumption that the company required a full year to generate sufficient revenues to pay it off, the return to the MCA would still be appealing.

The following equation illustrates the calculations on this scenario if a full year were provided to recapture the obligated proceeds.

ROI Calculation for Payment Over One Year

$$\% \text{APR} = \frac{\text{Net Return on MCA's Investment}}{\text{Purchase Price}} = \frac{\$33,786}{\$93,851} = 36\% \text{ APR}$$

Normally, MCAs use the specified percentage to determine the daily payment level from the actual proceeds from credit card revenues handled by the merchant processor for the subject business. Accordingly, using the average volumes, the average payment in this example can be derived as well as the potential repayment terms under these average conditions.

For example, if the monthly credit card volume were $100,000, the average *daily* remittances to the business would total $4,761.91 (based on an average 21 payments per month—merchant processors can only remit ACH payments on the days that the banks are open). Based on the stated percentage, the MCA would be paid 16 percent of that remittance total or $761.90 each day.

Extrapolating that payment amount into the number of payments necessary to recapture a total of $127,637 (the specified amount) comes to 168 payments ($761.90 × 168 ≈ $127,637). But it would probably take an average of at least 240 days to collect that number of payments, accounting for weekends and the ten annual bank holidays.

Based on that calculation, the ROI would be adjusted accounting for the shorter 240-day repayment period, and is illustrated in the next equation.

ROI Calculation for Payment Over 240 Days

$$\text{Adjusted ROI} = \frac{360 \text{ days}}{240 \text{ days}} \times 36\% \text{ APR} = \textbf{54\% APR}$$

What if the business revenue increased significantly? Suppose the average monthly sales increased to their previous high-volume month and provided $140,000 of credit card revenues every month? Using the same calculation method, that would mean the average daily remittances to the business would total about $6,666.66 before the MCA would be paid $1,066.66 every day. At that rate, the $127,637 would be recaptured in about 172 days and the ROI is illustrated in a third equation.

ROI Calculation for Payment Over 172 Days

$$\text{Adjusted ROI} = \frac{360 \text{ days}}{172 \text{ days}} \times 36\% \text{ APR} = \textbf{75\% APR}$$

Most MCAs established the criteria that borrowers must have been in business for a minimum of two years before becoming eligible for funding. However, in the last couple of years competition has heated up to the point that some MCAs will advance funds to companies with as few as two months' receipts. This hypercompetitive ploy is designed to squeeze more funding volume out of the market and hopefully get a customer committed to the funder as early as possible.

But that strategy is even riskier than typical MCA transactions and probably leads most businesses that accept these funds to become addicted early to financing they may never be able to pay off. In actuality, these companies have effectively sold a part of their business for peanuts and will have a tough time breaking the cycle of renewing/extending balances and getting larger advances in perpetuity.

When It Looks Like a Loan, Is It a Loan?

The merchant cash advance business and the future receivables purchase-and-sale agreement are not without controversy. They operate under the legal construct designed intentionally to not be categorized or defined as a lender and are careful to distribute their funds structured as an "advance," not a loan. The language in these agreements attempts to fashion the entire transaction as merely the purchase of a future income stream.

But the problem is that many of these agreements also include dozens of terms that sound exactly like a loan.

Think about an example of selling a car. It's probable that many people have intentionally bought cars for the purpose of earning money with them. But was anyone able to get sale terms that included a provision that the *seller* would personally guarantee that financial return for the buyer? Or offered the buyer additional collateral to assure that financial return? Did any seller provide the buyer with an irrevocable power of attorney to withdraw funds from his or her bank account to assure that the buyer would get his or her prospective financial return?

Beyond page one of the future receivables purchase agreement the language unmistakably starts sounding like loan terms and covenants, although these MCAs go to great lengths to insist that it is not.

The personal guarantee language goes beyond the typical bank loan. In addition to guaranteeing that the MCA will be paid the full entitled sum under the purchase and sale agreement, the signer also guarantees that all information provided to the buyer is true, that the business will not replace the merchant processor that is to be designated by the MCA or add an additional processor, and that the business will not breach several specific covenants.

These covenants include similar terms to what is typically found in a commercial loan transaction, such as the agreement not to change the type of business, not to revoke the MCA's entitlement to the payment stream, not to open new bank accounts or redirect their share of funds where the MCA is not empowered to tap into, to not acquire additional funding from third parties, and to not allow a lien to be placed on the company's receivables. If the transaction were truly a purchase, how are these terms pertinent or acceptable?

More terms that sound like a bank loan:

- **Collateral:** MCA is granted a security interest in all personal property of the subject business including accounts, equipment, inventory, trade name, liquor license, and patents. There's language regarding a power of attorney that provides the right to file and renew a UCC-1 financing statement to perfect their interest.

   Embedded in the paragraphs describing all the rights related to collateral and the MCA's right to perfect their liens with UCC-1 financing statements is the caveat: "Even though the security agreement under this agreement does not create a debt."
- **Inspections:** MCA is granted the authority to inspect and photograph their collateral during normal business hours.
- **Insurance:** MCA requires the seller to maintain insurance "in such amounts and against such risks as are consistent with past practice."

- **Foreclosure:** MCA is empowered to conduct a nonjudicial foreclosure to collect the entitled sums under the agreement in addition to "indemnified amounts" that refer to a litany of costs that potentially could be due if the MCA is sued for the agreement (presumably by the subject business).
- **Confidentiality:** One of the more interesting terms found in the agreement is a confidentiality covenant whereby the seller would agree that the terms and conditions offered by the buyer in the agreement were proprietary and confidential information of the buyer, and accordingly, the seller promises not to disclose them.
- **Representations:** In an effort to legally define and get agreement as to the nature of the agreement between buyer and seller, there is a paragraph specifically setting forth the definition the MCA wants to impart: "Seller is not a debtor of buyer as of the date of this agreement."
- **Power of Attorney:** The agreement term that would make most commercial bankers blanch is where the MCA is granted a power of attorney (POA) to contact any new merchant processor or bank where the subject business has opened a new account.

   The language would authorize the buyer to assert his or her rights with the POA to direct the new proceeds collected by the new processor on behalf of the subject business to be paid to the MCA. Likewise, the language allows the MCA to direct the bank to forward regular payments to the MCA in the amount of the specified percentage.

Judge Disagrees

So, are these MCAs really an alternative funding stream or cleverly structured loans trying to avoid the typical regulation that accompanies business lending?

Apparently at least one judge agreed with the latter description. In June 2011, a California court signed off on a $23.4 million judgment[3] against AdvanceMe, Inc. (AMI), the oldest and largest MCA company. In a class action lawsuit that was filed in California in 2008, the plaintiffs claimed AMI's cash advance program was not actually a series of purchases of future credit card receivables. Instead, they alleged the transactions were just loans with usurious interest rates.

The plaintiffs alleged that several transaction characteristics demonstrated that the AdvanceMe transactions were actually just loans disguised as asset purchases:

- The AMI contracts imposed payment obligations on the business owners that are more typical of loans, instead of covenants that are typical in asset purchase agreements.

- The AMI contracts required personal guarantees from the business owners, which were guarantees of payment obligations more typical of loans, not guarantees of contractual performance.
- Assuming that the AMI transactions are actually loans, they imposed interest rates that violated California's usury laws.

These plaintiffs claimed over $90 million of damages, but ultimately the suit was settled for much less. The MCA also forfeited the right to pursue the plaintiffs for the outstanding sums they borrowed from AMI that had not been collected.

As part of the settlement,[4] AMI also agreed to modify a section of its merchant agreement to read that, "Buyer, Seller and Principals acknowledge and agree that Seller going bankrupt or out of business, in and of itself, does not constitute a breach of the Seller Contractual Covenants" and that AMI would not request payments "from merchants who went out of business in the ordinary course and had not previously breached their merchant agreement."

Enter the Digital Age

For all these differences between how traditional banks operate and how MCAs conduct their affairs, it's important to recognize they are legitimate competitors and according to market estimates are advancing well above $3 billion annually as an industry. They are not going away and have a vested interest in behaving well enough to not draw the attention of regulators.

Some of the top performing companies are achieving impressive results. Consider AdvanceMe, Inc., which is based in Kennesaw, Georgia and was the subject of the 2011 California class action settlement. This company started in 1998 and only took 10 years to have advanced $1 billion. It only took three years for the second billion, two years for the third billion, and in 2013 they aimed for $1 billion in a single year. Compared to the top commercial banks' lending to small business owners, if AMI's numbers were ranked according to FDIC call reports, they would be the 43rd largest small business lender in the nation.

Their growth curve was surely assisted by the financial crisis and the accompanying weakness experienced by the banking sector, but give AMI some credit for boosting their own prospects as well. They approve a very high percentage of the funding applications they receive—reportedly over 70 percent—because they've figured out how to do so profitably.

Having been in the trade longer than the majority of its competitors, AMI has funded about 125,000 different businesses over the years and has never discarded the applications or performance data about them. It is a great example of a company that converted its past experience into valuable data that could be used to predict future performance patterns effectively enough to influence transaction decisions, pricing, and terms. It's *behavioral analytics*.

AMI's proprietary technology platform tracks all of their accounts and can differentiate decisions about the 390 different NAICS codes they lend to based on specific trends and experience they have. So, for example, they recognize that an HVAC contractor has different seasonality than a restaurant, so funding advance decisions can be tailored to those specific characteristics.

Much like a bank grades its credits with various designations, AMI breaks their approved funding accounts down into six risk categories. In this way, the company can budget for the projected performance in each category and designate terms and pricing appropriately. They predict loan losses specific to their risk tiers with impressive accuracy.

While servicing loans, AMI monitors payment levels, constantly comparing them to pre-advance and post-advance averages to recognize business revenue performance. At a certain revenue deterioration benchmark they will make a soft collection call to the business owner, even though payments are continuing as agreed. These calls are to inquire about business conditions and determine whether further action is necessary.

They have figured out how to scale their business to the point that they will make an advance as small as $1,500 or as large as $2 million. Their underwriting target is to project recapturing their funds within 36 months after the advance.

Another key difference between AMI and the commercial banking sector? They currently turn around client requests in an average of 2.6 days—including onsite visits for all transaction requests for over $150,000—but are aiming to lower that average down to one day.

How do small business owners react to the terms and cost offered by AMI? Only they can answer that question, but reportedly about 75 percent of AMI's sellers actually renew their loans (defined as requesting new money in the period from when the original sum is paid down at least 50 percent to six months after payoff).

Do MCA companies take advantage of small businesses with what some observers call "payday type" contracts, terms, and financing costs? Not really. It's fair to say that most small business owners don't really understand why they pay MCAs for the funding they get—at least in more mainstream terms, such as an APR calculation—but it's also realistic to acknowledge that even if they all did, a majority of the companies would take the funding anyway.

Criticizing MCAs over pricing may be a somewhat parochial viewpoint, but consider that most commercial bankers probably are guilty of not charging small companies enough. For many years, small business lending rates have been pegged more to competitive considerations—or, to be blunt—often banks relied on the perceived probability of continued real estate inflation. Most weren't pricing to the credit risk, but rather to what was actually *collateral risk*.

Now that this inflation has passed for some period, many banks can't figure out how to lend money without collateral. These innovative funders have stepped up with financing that is priced according to the risks they are taking. Part of the difference between MCAs and commercial banks is that MCAs overall do a much better job of getting paid on a level that reflects the premium they are entitled to for the risks they accept. It's entirely appropriate and thousands of companies are glad to get it.

That said, the MCA industry also must contend with many rogue lenders among them as well, just as commercial bankers do. Without regulatory oversight, many lenders have entered this business with some practices that border on unscrupulous and give the industry headaches.

Consider a New York State MCA lender whose client document package includes an undated "confession of judgment." Their agreement specifies the terms of the client's default judgment and the rights of the MCA upon filing that document with a court *before the advance is even funded*!

Another issue that challenges the MCA sector is that they are very dependent on third-party originators—loan brokers—for their business pipeline. Remember that perfect storm of the financial crisis that fueled the meteoric rise in MCA? It also left thousands of mortgage brokers unemployed across the country.

Based on the brokers' experience of navigating sketchy *liar loans* through the regulated mortgage industry, making the move to the wild west of merchant cash advance was easy. But it will be a burden on the MCA business, at least those interested in staying unregulated.

One group of 17 MCA lenders formed a trade association—the North American Merchant Advance Association (NAMAA)—to attempt to deal with these problem lenders on several fronts. First, they promised to develop ethical standards and best practices for their industry. Predictably, they also keep an eye on any legislative efforts to restrict their business in the 50 states and Washington.

In addition, they maintain a merchant database and track member activity in an effort to detect potential fraud from merchant companies that might seek funding from more than one MCA.

ONLINE LENDERS: MONEY FROM THE CLOUD

A more recent development in the innovative corridor is the emergence of online business lenders. Unlike the MCAs, these business funders do identify themselves as lenders and register with the various state financial regulators in order to be qualified to engage in commercial lending in most states.

These lenders came into existence through technology, unlike MCAs that started forming more than 15 years ago. Much of the innovation around MCAs was the basic merchant cash advance strategy of matching repayment with daily cash flows, but online lenders bring many more innovations to the practice of business finance.

The online lenders have created many new technical solutions to manage all facets of the business lending, including marketing for clients, gathering applications, making credit decisions, and funding loans. And their key marketing message is that "We're more responsive than a bank and not as expensive as MCAs!"

Online lenders have many similarities to MCAs, though. They are focused on short term (three-month to two-year) working capital loans that are repaid with daily payments (facilitated with ACH transfers withdrawn from the borrower's bank account). Accordingly, online lenders also target retail and service industry sectors that have recurring daily revenues.

And they rely heavily on third-party independent sales originators (ISOs) to generate new loan volume just like MCAs do.

But online lenders are underwriting loans differently than MCAs. To begin with, they seek to recognize all the applicant's income—not just those monies collected through credit card sales—so these lenders require bank account statements to underwrite loans. But that said, they prefer to work with borrowers who do accept credit cards in order to lower the risk of being dependent on cash sales alone. Credit card revenues are stickier—they can be independently verified and are easier to track, unlike cash sales that can be diverted by a business owner before reaching the company's bank account.

They also gather considerable nonfinancial environmental data to contribute to the assessment of credit risk, which provides a more meaningful evaluation that is tailored to each client, rather than a general one-size-fits-all pricing approach of most MCAs.

Online Credit versus Traditional Bank Credit

Online lenders price credit considerably higher than comparable unsecured, short-term working capital loans from commercial banks, but since they are subject to various state usury limitations, their costs are generally cheaper than the average MCA.

Since online lenders also have considerably higher funding costs than commercial banks, it's unlikely that they will ever try to compete with pricing. But, it's also true that commercial banks rarely make unsecured working capital term loans, especially to restaurants, retailers, and service companies. Product rather than pricing will always be an easier way for online lenders to compete head-to-head with banks, when that eventuality arrives.

Most working capital financing provided to small businesses by commercial banks is either in the form of a revolving line of credit (RLOC), generally a secured financing product, or with an unsecured credit card account. The RLOC generally carries plenty of protective loan covenants for the bank and financial statement monitoring obligations. While revolving bank credit lines might be priced better than both credit cards and online lenders, they are also more temperamental.

Constant financial statement monitoring and regular "borrowing base"[5] reports on loan collateral subjects the borrower to living under the threat that funds could be held back or cancelled with little or no notice. And since definitive principal repayment terms are not established, high growth companies frequently need more funding before they can qualify for it and struggle to repay the principal loan balances because their funds are tied up supporting their growth.

The bank's other working capital channel is through bank-issued credit cards that are usually issued on the strength of consumer credit rather than business credit. Like the RLOC, this product is revolving in nature but carries significantly higher interest rates than the RLOC. These accounts do not generally require significant principal repayment schedules and on average fully amortize over 36 years if no future advances are made or additional fees are tacked on.

The long repayment cycle is intended to maximize revenue for the bank. The effect on thousands of small businesses that use credit card advances to finance business growth is that they get in the habit of making minimal payments. Effectively they use this debt as an equity substitute, which would be the financial equivalent of preferred stock with a hefty dividend.

Online lenders generally provide financing with higher costs but also with a defined repayment term that reduces loan principal faster as each payment is made. Overall, for even less astute or disciplined borrowers, these loans can work out to be a lower-cost financing option since the terms are more regimented and not left to the whims of the borrower's self-imposed efforts to get out of debt.

For borrowers who really understand their profit margin and are borrowing funds to take advantage of a business growth opportunity, repaying the loan over a short period actually plays better into their long-term success, regardless of the pricing over a relative short term of 12 to 18 months. Compared to the 36 years it takes to payout a credit card account at the rate it's billed with a minimum payment, the corresponding interest is not really an issue.

Marketing for Clients

Online lenders are technology-driven companies, so it's natural to assume that they would drive their client search and acquisition processes entirely online. Most started with the intention of avoiding the old-fashioned selling techniques employed by everyone else, like loan brokers, print advertising, and cold calling. The problem is that most of their eventual customers either weren't listening or, worse case, didn't agree with that strategy.

With powerful integrated platforms and savvy IT specialists who could grasp and quickly deploy marketing tools that were developing in the same time horizon, online lenders expected a closed loop process that would virtually find, sell, underwrite, fund, and collect loans with virtually minutes of human intervention.

But even with an inherent understanding of data scrapping, microtargeted online ads, and the availability of customer relationship management (CRM), vendors like SalesForce.com, did not make expanding online lending easier. They were either too far ahead of their market or skeptical business owners were hesitant to offer private financial information online to a company they'd never previously heard about.

In any case, early growth was hard to earn and eventually these lenders began to augment SEO strategies, direct mail campaigns, and other virtual marketing in favor of a heavy reliance on ISOs to generate loans. One problem with this strategy was that most of the ISO community had already discovered MCAs, which meant the funding referrals were already spoken for in many cases.

Eventually this galvanized two principal marketing approaches for online lenders using ISOs—either they had to pay more for referrals than MCAs or they had to make their loan terms much more attractive. It was a combination of both approaches that worked best and the ease of use for more technology-savvy brokers that started building loyalty.

While this pivot to more traditional client recruitment has worked out fine—online lending leader OnDeck Capital advertises that they've made more than $700 million in loans since 2007[6]—it has also had negative consequences. One is the cost burden to pay ISOs, which are much more expensive than most digital marketing strategies.

But the other is the human intervention cost—many loan brokers aren't as technically savvy and resist using platform applications. They also don't want their clients to know the lender's identity ahead of loan approval and still submit paper applications. And some loan brokers earn the worst stereotype that many lenders identify with them: dishonest, high pressure, and constantly appealing for exceptions and broader approval guidelines.

Third party origination compensation has ranged from fixed fees by some lenders to "name your price" at others. While the latter is an easy default for those brokers trying to maximize their short-term income, it also meant that their clients were skewed with disproportionately high borrowing costs, as these fees resulted in maximum rates assessed by the lender.

Fixed referral fees place some lenders at a disadvantage and they have to sell the less-sexy benefits of delivering better terms to clients: better customer service to get a decision, more funding, and quick payments to the ISO.

For all the learning curve that online lenders went through to figure out how to sell their funding, they are still growing at a healthy rate, all while in fierce competition with MCAs and with a growing field of online competitors. The OnDeck loan volume may not sound like a threat to commercial lenders, but considering that the average loan size is less than $40,000, it reflects a growing list of adapting clients who have learned they can get capital somewhere other than a bank.

Gathering Application Information

The online application process is very efficient and mostly intended to gather verifiable information to confirm the business and owner's identification, rather than gathering much information with which to underwrite the loan. This point may be the greatest paradigm shift from traditional commercial banking.

Online lenders collect only the exact list of information required to know their client and make their decision, unlike banks that may gather application documentation in a more customary one-size-fits-all, global examination regimen.

For starters, the application form is online. Some lenders use a brief set of screening questions, which helps clarify who they are seeking to lend to and not waste the time spent by applicants needlessly completing the information.

These screening questions delineate the broad qualifications required by the lender. For one example, one lender asks four qualifying questions:

1. Have you been in business for at least two years?
2. Do you accept credit cards for payment of goods or services?
3. Do your clients settle the payments at point of when the goods or services are delivered?
4. Do the average total deposits in your bank account equal a minimum of $10,000/month and your average daily balance a minimum of $3,000?

If borrowers answer no to any question, they are disqualified. It's a very efficient manner of weeding out applications early in the process that are not going to be considered.

Application information is requested to be completed in the lender's website directly by borrowers or their intermediaries. There is no printed edition offered directly by the company, although some ISOs offer a paper application to gather information that they then enter online for their clients.

Paper applications create more work than starting the whole process online with the borrower keying information directly into the platform. (It's a solvable problem—when lenders begin offering ISOs, a white screen application page does not reveal the lender's name or web link information.)

The information itself generally gathers only 40 to 50 bits of data. For example, (1) first name, (2) middle initial, (3) last name, (4) street number, (5) street name, (6) suite or apartment number, (7) city, (8) state, (9) zip code, (10) telephone number, and so on. This information covers about 25 percent of the application!

The application will request a brief explanation of why the money is requested and how the borrower intends to use it. Different uses carry different risks, for example, buying a new piece of equipment indicates growth, while paying back taxes indicates some previous struggles. This data doesn't automatically disqualify anyone (unless they describe an illegal use of the funds) but it does get scored in relation to the other data being collected.

The lender needs only minimal additional information outside the application: a copy of the business tax return (for verification of business ownership), a copy of a photo ID, and a voided check to verify the access to the business checking account. Only one other informational item is needed in addition to this short list.

Online lenders don't gather the usual bank-required personal financial statement, three years' financial statements, and financial projections—all they want is six monthly checking account statements. In developing this business model, the analyzed data bore out the fact that the past six months is more suitable to predict the business performance for shorter-term loans.

One of the frustrations of most loan originators is in unresponsive or often incompetent responses they get from clients and applicants when they need information. If often takes multiple requests to get even incomplete, outdated information. And invariably, when the last bit of information is finally handed over, the applicant wants a response immediately to the loan request!

Online lenders have a different process—they have a fixed list of information that does not change. The technology platform reminds the client constantly of what's needed and how to submit it. If the client lags behind and is not responsive, the application is closed and declined for lack of information. Only motivated borrowers need apply.

Digitally-Assisted Underwriting in the Cloud

Once the client (or his or her intermediary) has input all the required information in the application template and uploaded the requested documents to the online lender, the fun really starts. Recall all the complaints and stories about how long it takes to get a loan decision from a bank? The online lending experience is usually breathtaking in comparison.

First, after all the application information has been acknowledged as received, the final command tap needed to start the application may be a tab called "submit." That command will initiate the automated underwriting process.

The online lending platform will launch a search in the cloud for more information about the applicant, which will provide a significant volume of data to populate their proprietary credit/loan evaluation model and start building a decision score. Some business sectors will have specific and unique information online that is not required or collected about others such as the health department restaurant inspections. Accordingly, the available data is gathered because it's there and can be processed with adjusted scoring in the platform to account for the extra metrics.

No two lenders are alike, but in this marketplace these efforts are being employed with increasing frequency and depth to acquire a broad data set regarding the applicant and/or the business from a number of private sources, social media, and government websites.[7] As more data becomes available, it will be tested against blind credit profiles and if certain parameters reflect indications that they may contribute to identifying risk, they may be added to the model.

In no particular order of importance (since no one knows how various lenders score information), here's a list of some of the kinds of data that's being captured and imputed into the credit decision scoring process of online lenders.

- Private data sources: Many private entities provide data about the market, their clients, or the consumers/businesses that they monitor. While some of these sources are not new to business lenders, the process may be new to some: accessing information through an automated search, a technology platform that's populated with the retrieved data, and a decision process that is initiated instantly. While this technology is currently used by few commercial banks, it will grow in the not-too-distant future and displace plenty of jobs in the transition.

  The established credit information resources are obviously useful to online lenders, who can deploy it to contribute to the profile they're building on the subject loan applicant or even as an instant screening benchmark. But most other sources following are not presently used by traditional business lenders and offer additional metrics that contribute to underwriting credit. Some examples of these private data sources:

- Credit Bureaus: Online lenders check for the borrower's credit score as well; however, most don't use FICO scores. Instead they use the Vantage Score, which provides a different analysis based on a shorter backward-looking horizon of about two years. And, most online lenders are fairly liberal with lower minimum scores, since their studies have concluded that consumer credit scores alone aren't necessarily reliable predictors of future short-term repayment patterns. The major U.S. credit bureaus include Equifax, Experian, and TransUnion.

  These reports are reviewed to understand credit utilization patterns and repayment trends for the most immediate trailing periods, and to reveal signs of lagging cash flow or leverage issues, without punishing client ratings for events that occurred in earlier timeframes.

  In addition, many online lenders employ additional credit bureau tools such as the Bankruptcy Navigator Index (BNI), which can evaluate a series of personal conditions to determine whether there is an elevated risk or probability of a personal bankruptcy or serious liquidity issues in the near term.

- Better Business Bureau: The BBB is a well-known consumer protection agency that manages business complaints on behalf of the buying public. An examination of their files can disclose whether there are outstanding claims against the subject business, a pattern of poor business practices, or a history of unresolved complaints.

- Merchant payment processors: Many payment processors operate to facilitate e-commerce and the data they collect can be very useful to ascertain daily, weekly, monthly, and annual sales volume return rates and other valuable statistics about a business operation.

- eBay.com: Online lenders generally collect the applicant's eBay seller ID number from those that sell goods through this platform. eBay offers plenty of data concerning the client's sales history, revenue volumes, and business practices.

- Amazon.com: Another online merchant aggregator is Amazon.com, which is the checkout counter and marketing platform for thousands of businesses including many that also have real storefronts. A range of data similar to that available through eBay can be obtained from Amazon, although Amazon offers additional services that may produce more analytics.

- Google Maps: By lending to the nation instead of a local market, online lenders are vulnerable to different kinds of risk in assessing an application. One important tool is accessible online, although it has to be reviewed manually. Most online platforms will launch an automatic Google Map search of the subject's business address, with the capacity of the underwriter to zoom in close to a street view. From there they can toggle views up and down the street in an effort to confirm the address and business occupancy, and obtain a sense of the positive (or negative) attributes of the immediate area.

- United Parcel Service (UPS): While not commonly viewed by traditional lenders, shipping patterns, volumes, diversity, and frequency can offer plenty of data to substantiate—or unravel—growth projections and previous performance representations.

- Trade Associations: Some trade associations are learning the power (and profitability) of making membership and industry information data available for other uses outside their organizations. Some associations also collect data about their trade and can provide unique analytics available nowhere else. Membership in a trade organization is not mandatory to be considered for credit anywhere, but it does project a positive management indicator if the applicant is investing in the future of their trade.

- Licensing Boards: Some licensing boards and organizations are opening up to provide confirmation of claimed credentials, which provides online lenders with additional comfort data to validate assumptions that may be inherent with applicants who have a professional designation in their title.

- Social Media Data: When Facebook went public through an IPO on February 1, 2012 for an eye-popping valuation of $38 billion, the most cynical observer must have been forced to admit that there's more to it than entertaining teenagers.

  In fact, there is. Facebook and dozens of other social media sites engage users in what seems to be every way people connect, including blogging (personal publishing), photo exchange, video and music sharing, gaming, business networking, communication forums, social conversations, shopping, information sharing, rating, crowdsourcing, collaboration, and even reputation management.

  Who knew that all the collected data could be harnessed into predictive behavior metrics? Online lenders know and are gathering data from dozens of social media sites to augment their credit approval scoring matrix. Here are a few examples:

  - Yelp.com: Online lending is predominantly focused on retail, restaurants, and other service businesses. Yelp is an online resource that helps consumers find and rate these kinds of businesses. Checking with Yelp can help an online lender grade the connectivity (or disinterest) of consumers to their businesses. This kind of customer satisfaction metric contributes to scoring the business outlook better.

- Angie'sList.com: This site is for service professionals in a broad line of trades—think plumbers, electricians, dentists, and movers, for example—and to be listed the business must be vetted by the company. Subscribers are relying on Angie to recommend only fair, reliable service providers who will perform these services in a competent and reputable manner. Online lenders can tap into these ratings to add more data to their business outlook scoring for businesses in these categories.
- Facebook.com: How does the number of Facebook "Likes" or "Friends" impact a lending decision? It may not judge repayment risks, but it can be a fair assessment of the marketing reach of a business if it is connected to its customers in a positive show of loyalty. Tapping into Facebook by online lenders is more about looking for strengths than weaknesses.
- LinkedIn.com: This business networking site is not just for job seekers but provides web pages for businesses to communicate with a broader network and for individuals to display their professional prowess. Online lenders can tap into this information to determine analytics for the professional and/or client reach of applicants and whether their company is listed. Like other social media platforms, LinkedIn participation or engagement is not needed to qualify, but does potentially add a positive metric as to the marketing efforts and visibility of the applicant.
- Klout.com: This site is a social media scoring service that advises individual users how they rate as an "influencer" across several social media sites such as Facebook, LinkedIn, Twitter, and Google+. Their metrics include the number of connections, the quantity and quality of information offered through social media engagement, and the corresponding responsiveness of their followers and others. Like Facebook, this site is more about looking for strengths than weaknesses.
- Zillow.com: This site is an online real estate database that helps users find, investigate, and value real estate online. While most online lenders are not making real estate-secured loans, the valuation metrics of their business and residential real property is useful information. For the business, this information speaks to the outlook for their business location and whether its value is climbing, which infers that the locale is drawing more neighbors and traffic—or not.

     For residential properties owned by applicant business owners, the valuation information can be measured against personal debt tied to the real estate to establish whether they have personal equity—and therefore a fatter net worth—or whether they are under water on their homes.

There are more social media sites being used and others evaluated for the different information that can be gleaned by both use and interaction with the subject of inquiry. This resource field holds much promise to expand as an important source of financial evaluation metrics.

- Government data resources: Federal, state, and local governments have various resources of information collected that is public and easily accessible. Following are a few examples of the kinds of information online lenders have access to or are currently working to get. Some of it is gathered on demand for a particular transaction while other information has to be downloaded regularly and sorted through a database when needed.
  - Secretary of State: Corporate registration confirmation can be obtained digitally from each state, including details such as when a business was incorporated (years in business), address, and whether the business's annual registration is up to date.
  - Business licenses: Confirmation of whether a business has a current business license can be acquired digitally including details such as business address, category of license, and expiration date.
  - Internal Revenue Service (IRS): Confirmation of tax return transcripts is available from the IRS digitally, although it needs improvement. With an electronic signature from the taxpayer, the IRS will automate the service formerly requiring submission of a form 4506.
  - Local Health Department: For required businesses, such as restaurants, cafés, and caterers, the health department inspection reports provide detailed information about the quality of the business operation and include a public grade that must be displayed to customers. This information and the grade illuminate areas of concern for these businesses that certainly affect the credit risk involved.
  - Census data: Public census data can provide plenty of analytics about geography and the direction particular regions—and ZIP codes—are trending on metrics such as population growth, average household income, per capita income, and aging that can provide an insightful report card on future prospects of the market where the applicant is situated.
  - Immigration and Customs Enforcement (ICE): It's not clear to what extent citizenship or resident alien status can be digitally acquired from ICE at this time to nonemployers. But when available, this data will be useful to affirm the applicant's authorization to be employed in the United States and whether that privilege has an expiration.
  - Labor Department (DOL): Labor statistics and trends data can be digitally obtained to understand the local trends for cost of labor, pool of qualified workers, and outlook for the applicant business.
  - Federal Reserve Bank (FRB): Economic trends and data can be acquired digitally to learn about the local and regional economic

performance of the market where the applicant business is situated, to understand potential economic growth, housing starts, income statistics, and other data trends collected in each region.

- Department of Transportation (DOT): Traffic patterns, projected future routing plans, and volume counts is useful information that can speak to the present potential for an applicant's present location and how it may evolve in the months and years ahead.
- North American Industry Classification System (NAICS): Comparative analytics are available from some sources that track how various industry sectors perform with credit across a variety of financial sectors, based on size, geography, age, and type of financing.

Many traditional business lenders will be skeptical of the approach of gathering so much data in order to compile metrics for a credit decision that they've been making for decades with a much shorter list of information. But they may be wrong. The multiple, seemingly meaningless data points collected through all these cloud resources individually are practically useless. But aggregated into a variety of proprietary patterns, they are proving to provide precedent-setting insight into how businesses are likely to perform given certain characteristics. They offer evidence pointing to the applicants most likely to complete future repayment commitments. And the actual results are being collected over a shorter horizon and deployed immediately into future decision modeling.

The business process of modeling metadata into decision platforms is growing by leaps and bounds, with a staggering amount of data being collected through thousands of sources. The analysis and development of credit modeling around these metrics is really just beginning.

How much data is in play? See for yourself in a graphic representation of various social media sites that are categorized into several distinct media channels at Ethority.com.[8] This visual explanation of the many ways data is being collected is revealing of the future horizon where many decision-making processes are heading—particularly since the end results can be surveyed and tested ahead of any capital being put at risk. One lender in this market claims (off record) that their platform presently accesses more than 2,000 data points during underwriting.

How the data is used and weighted will be unique to each lender. This is pioneer territory, since only time and portfolio performance will determine the real value. But one online lender specifically uses the cloud-sourced data to develop a credit risk score (from 1 to 100) that determines the loan guaranty fee assessed to each borrower. Smaller numbers have higher costs and as the score climbs, the fee comes down.

Old-Fashioned Number Crunching with a Twist

Underwriting these loans for a specific lending decision usually involves loading the deposit account statement data into the lender's platform, and the platform tells the underwriter how the calculations stack up against its proprietary transaction model.

While none of these lending companies discloses how their lending offers are determined, most focus on calculating the average monthly deposit totals of applicant companies and comparing that number to the deposit account's average daily balance over the same period. The loan amount will be determined by the lesser of a percentage of the average monthly deposits or a multiple of average daily balance.

These metrics can be used to calculate a rough sales turnover for the business, its cash cycle trending, and deposit stability. Management and business liquidity assessment is also influenced by the presence and possible frequency of non-sufficient-funds (NSF) charges that may have been assessed against the account by the bank.

These calculations are designed to ensure that the customer can actually pay the loan back. The loan size and repayment period is directly calibrated with the actual cash flow trends—inflows and outflows—that reflect how the business is performing in the immediate trailing period.

Strangely, these metrics have been available to commercial bankers for decades but have not apparently been employed to evaluate either small or short-term lending decision-making heretofore.

Fraud Detection

Operating in cyberspace, these lenders are very aware of the potential for fraud in this business channel since they will not ever meet their clients eye-to-eye. They exercise extraordinary efforts to ensure that they have triple-checked the identities of the parties applying for loans. They also confirm that the subject businesses are in fact viable enterprises for which ownership can be verified. And finally, they must be assured that the checking account is accessible through the authorization of the proper party who owns it.

That checking account will not only be evaluated for determining the loan amount, but it will be "tapped," where a small series of two or three tiny deposits are made and then withdrawn to verify the account existence, and these transactions are confirmed by the authorizing party to verify they have access to the account information online.

This account will be monitored monthly throughout the lending relationship to add ongoing performance metrics in real time, and it is the account to which the loan will be disbursed and from where payments will be collected.

Personal identification confirmation is made by cross referencing information available from the credit bureau reports, which generally contain plenty of information references such as previous residences, employers, and lenders. Small details in the application, such as detailing how long applicants have resided at their addresses, how long they've been in business, and driver's license numbers help the lender use several information verification points at critical stages to validate with whom they are doing business.

Loan Pricing

Online lenders are more expensive than traditional commercial lenders. In that they are either funding loans with private equity, loan sales, or lender finance, their cost of capital is also significantly higher than FDIC-insured deposits, so they have to recapture that in the cost of the capital they distribute.

There are a variety of pricing tools utilized by these lenders as they position and assess costs to their borrowers:

- *Interest rates:* All these lenders charge interest as part of their pricing and it's common in this financing channel to see the interest rate be declared on fairly reasonable terms, from 12 percent to 18 percent. These rates may even be simple interest calculations, meaning some lenders only assess interest on the outstanding obligation while it's actually outstanding rather than assessing a fixed interest fee.
- *Origination fee:* Online lenders break down the financing charges they impose into various fees, and the origination fee is an appealing one. This fee is not paid by the borrower overtly but rather it's *discounted* or withheld from the stated loan sum. In other words, the origination fee would effectively reduce the total amount disbursed from the loan proceeds to the borrower but not reduce the total obligation that the borrower was obligated to repay.

    For example, a five percent origination fee on a $10,000 loan would be calculated to total $500. The borrower would be advanced $9,500 as net loan proceeds after this fee was withheld, but $10,000 would be the sum required to be repaid plus other fees and interest. And interest would be charged on the entire $10,000 loan amount.

    Banks are well acquainted with discounting fees, which serve to not only generate direct non-interest income, but this methodology also fattens loan yields since interest is charged on a sum ($500) that was never advanced by the lender other than moving an entry from the loan account over to their income account.
- *Risk premiums:* Online lenders often assess another fee that overlays the interest cost but is generally not calculated with the other sums that

are assessed interest charges. This fee, which may be called a variety of terms, is essentially added on ostensibly to compensate the lender for the credit risk involved in the transaction, or the premium charged to collect sums to cover the costs of eventually not getting repaid by a certain number of the pool of borrowers.

Different lenders have different ways to derive and calculate this charge, which may range from 2 to 20 percent on top of the discounted fees and interest rate. This sum is generally spread over the repayment period and sometimes segregated outside the regular loan payment, which are the advances subject to interest charges.

Such fees may be determined by the lender based on borrower cash flow tiers, actual credit ratings, proprietary scoring from the environmental assessment, or other calculated repayment exposure faced by the lender.

These various pricing schemes seem to be intended to distort disclosure of what the true financing cost is in toto, since higher pricing chases many borrowers away. It's better to offer a generalization, like "15 percent of total borrowing" to leave the impression with prospective borrowers that the lender is only charging 15 percent interest.

Online lenders mask their lending rates because they can, and in most states they are not subject to any more conforming disclosure that would enlighten their borrowers as to exactly what they are paying. They purposely avoid the commonly referred to APR calculation and instead generalize the approximate cost without tying it to the relative term.

Regardless, these loans are fairly priced in general, based on the higher risk accepted by these lenders, the unsecured nature of the product, and the quick turnaround between application, approval, and funding usually offered to facilitate transactions. Borrowers may find the higher cost less painful than the more difficult and stressful application/approval process required by commercial banks. At least when declined by online business lenders, it's quick and effectively anonymous.

Loan Closing

Maybe the most interesting advancement in how innovative lenders have changed the horizon for business owners is the online closing process. Against the mentality of having to leave their business in prime hours and drive to the bank, shuffle through dozens of pages in detailed documents, and sign their names countless times, online lenders close in real time on the phone.

Closing appointments can be made digitally anytime after loan approval is announced, and since the lender's closing representative is chosen from a pool of staff members, borrowers literally can name their most convenient times.

Both the lender and borrower log into a shared page online in the lender's platform where the loan terms, approval conditions, loan amount, and explanation of fees and interest are discussed. The closing representative will ask two or three questions derived from the borrower's credit bureau file, which was not requested or obtained from his or her loan application, designed to confirm his or her true identity.

The recorded call conforms to a written script that spells out the loan offer provided by the lender, the payment amount, and how it is broken down between principal, interest, and various charges. Lenders request that borrowers verbally acknowledge that their application conditions have not changed and confirm that they can repay the borrowed sums under the stated terms.

If borrowers agree, they sign their names with their computer mouse in a designated area on their computer screen and their loan closing is concluded. The lender then advances the loan proceeds via an ACH transfer to the prescreened bank account, which generally arrives in 24 to 72 hours. Then daily loan payments usually start on the fourth business day after this event once the funds are irreversibly situated in the borrower's account.

Closing and funding loans in this manner is more convenient, less expensive, and probably less prone to errors for all parties concerned.

Loan Servicing

Automated payment gathering via ACH means there's no daily mail to collect, no lockbox, and no sorting, cancelling checks, or making bank deposits every business day. Online lenders just monitor payment performance by figuratively watching debits go out to borrower deposit accounts and credits return into the lender's account.

So long as the daily cash pull established on a given account is cleared with the scheduled payment, online lenders focus more attention on new business development. They do encounter problem accounts, though, and are prepared for a relatively early intervention.

Generally, when a payment skip occurs—that is, when there are insufficient funds in the borrower's account, the online lenders are made aware of the situation with the inclusion of all such accounts on a daily automated report. On the second day, the regularly scheduled payment is debited again, with the hope that normal payments will continue as scheduled.

On a future day in the following week, the missed payment is acquired with a double billing on the account. Of course, the skipped payment carries a penalty that is added to the loan account.

If a second payment skip occurs on a consecutive day, this will generate a telephone call to the owner to determine whether there is an oversight, deposit account problem, or business cash shortage. The representative is empowered to facilitate a number of options, all designed to get the borrower's regular payment stream restored quickly.

A few days of payment holiday or a few weeks of lower payments are but two of the alternatives that can be implemented if the problem is temporary and the borrower just needs some flexibility. Closer monitoring of the situation is much simpler in this world since all borrower information, contact, and decision making is available digitally. Prompted entries of each client contact assures the lender that any future representative will be up to date on the entire history of the account and its problems in very short order.

Even the client's deposit account status and activity can be monitored in real time as the payment issue is discovered and resolved. Financial services company Yodlee.com has the capacity to provide the lender with access to information to monitor the borrower's monthly deposit account activity, including deposits and aggregate withdrawals, to determine the exact condition of the borrower's financial situation.

Coupled with the credit reporting bureau and bank activity reporting services, the lender can also monitor whether the borrower has diverted deposits to a different bank account in an effort to screen payment capacity.

Clients are officially in default when they become three payments behind, which is only three business days in the daily collections business. Write-offs occur if the account gets about 45 payments behind—or about 60 days past due. Online lenders pursue borrowers after charge-off with collection attorneys, depending on the amount involved.

For borrowers stuck in the twentieth century, despite having been funded by a new-age lender, who want to write a check to the online lender to catch up on missed payments or pay ahead, these companies will generally accept these payments—with a $15 service fee added to each payment check received.

Where Do Online Lenders Get Funding?

For anyone in the lending business, it's well known that lending requires plenty of funding. While different kinds of lenders have different funding sources, the lending company itself wants to leverage its own capital to the highest degree possible in order to generate funding to meet the demands of the borrowers they can find.

It's no different for online lenders. They all started out with capital, but instead of using a portion of those funds to build a fancy bank building with teller counters and safe deposit boxes, these online lenders invested in some very sophisticated websites and underlying performance platforms. They spent money on research, programmers, and SEO strategies rather than big desks, lobby furniture, or drive-in windows.

But after that, their funds also went right to work to begin funding the loans they originated and approved. Their cycle is like everyone else's—lend money out, collect payments, and reinvest the proceeds back into more loans.

With any degree of modest success, the funding runs short of the demand for new loans, at which time more funding has to be sourced to cover the lending production. But unlike banks, online lenders can't just offer a special certificate of deposit rate to attract some hot money. Banks are funded by depositors and savers—individuals and companies that need transactional accounts to manage their income and payments along with a safe storage place for saving other funds they don't plan to spend yet.

Online lenders have three primary sources of funding to provide liquidity to help them make new loans:

1. Selling equity: Online lenders can issue more shares to provide blocks of funding cash that will go directly into operating the business plan. Arguably this kind of money is the cheapest and most expensive at the same time. If there are no guaranteed dividends, equity does require any cash flow in the near term.

   In the long term, the more successful the company becomes the more expensive selling additional ownership becomes. But this cost is required because only certain investors willing to accept the high risks of funding an early pre-profit stage enterprise are willing to put capital to work in these companies. Those higher risks require extraordinary returns.

2. Selling loans: After establishing a positive track record of lending out money and getting most of it back, most online lenders have conducted loan sales, meaning that investors buy their loans instead of getting company ownership. These loans are repaid over the same term as the client's loan is repaid at an interest rate that is very appealing to investors.

   These loan sales can be structured in a number of ways, but often are sold at par with the lenders retaining the origination fees and perhaps a servicing fee, and the investor getting to collect the full loan interest and risk premium income. The real expense for online lenders is the absence of these revenues—having to sell off the fattest portion of their income streams is a necessary evil inherent in funding more loans.

3. Lender finance: After establishing a profitable model and proving they can earn respectable profits from these operations, online lenders will be able to tap into bank financing, which should bring their borrowing costs down significantly. Attaining that status will take time, however.

   Most of these lenders face a considerable two- to three-year climb to attain critical mass within reach of profitability. On top of that challenge will be the required absorption of some sizable amortization charges—software is expensed over a much shorter term than property improvements—which pushes profits back in those early years.

Most bank lenders require two full years of profitable operations before offering to support these lenders with credit lines and even once accommodated, these funds are not cheap.

Notes

1. "Great Graphic: U.S. Job Growth Compared to Past Downturns," MarcToMarket .com, www.marctomarket.com/2013/05/great-graphic-us-job-growth-compared .html (accessed November 12, 2013).
2. The referenced transaction terms and calculations present a logical interpretation of the information read from the referenced "purchase" offer from a well-known MCA company. The exact calculations and methodology of determining cost and ROI by the MCAs presumably are proprietary and are generally not disclosed outside those companies. This example was obtained from a business owner who apparently did not receive the offer and was trying to secure better terms at the time this document was provided.
3. Sarah Weston, "A New Chapter Opens for Merchant Cash Advance," Greensheet.com, June 25, 2012, www.greensheet.com/emagazine.php?issue_ number=120602.
4. Ibid.
5. Refers to a daily, weekly, or monthly report designed for borrowing clients to report the details of their current assets to their lenders, usually including accounts receivable and inventory. The details include a complete listing identifying each account by name, the value sum, and aging.
6. "We've Been Helping Small Businesses Grow since 2007," OnDeck.com, https:// www.ondeck.com/our-company/overview (accessed January 21, 2014).
7. Inclusion on this list is not an absolute assertion that all these sites are presently used by the various online lenders. While all are considered pertinent and likely to be employed, online lenders do not publish the actual data they collect to assess client companies and the information they do collect is subject to change from time to time as their assessment of its usefulness is recalibrated against actual portfolio performance.
8. Ethority.com, "Social Media Prism," www.ethority.net/blog/social-media-prism/ (accessed November 25, 2013). (Note: page may require translation to English.)

CHAPTER 8

Crowdfunding with Donors, Innovators, Loaners, and Shareholders

Funding today is as close as the nearest computer keyboard. Whether raising donations, loans, or even equity financing, crowdfunding is now a feasible choice serving for-profit and not-for-profit companies alike. Additionally, it's serving individual artists, social entrepreneurs, and other assorted do-gooders along with consumers wanting to borrow money for convincing reasons, often to refinance themselves out of more expensive debt.

Crowdfunding is proving to be huge. "Registration of Internet domain names containing 'crowdfunding' already has spiked from 900 to 8,800 in 2012," according to the North American Securities Administrators Association, an investor protection group.[1]

According to crowdfunding market analyst Massolutions.com, "Global crowdfunding markets accelerated from an annual growth of 64 percent in 2011 to an 81 percent growth in 2012. We are forecasting $5.1 billion in total global funding volumes in 2013."[2] To put that figure in perspective, 90 percent of U.S. banks have assets less than $1 billion.[3]

In 2012, the Elevation Dock, an aftermarket smartphone cradle for Apple iPhones, became the first individual crowdfunding campaign to reach the $1 million milestone. A few months later, Pebble Technology reached this milestone in only 28 hours, with the eventual campaign totaling over $10 million in total funds raised.

DONORS—FUNDING ARTS, SOLVING PROBLEMS, AND FLOATING LOCAL BUSINESSES WITH NO STRINGS ATTACHED

For any community, aka the "crowd," crowdfunding offers a new phenomenon to immediately convert affinity, fascination, or a temporary (read emotional) reaction to good ideas, projects, solutions, or attractions into cash. Whether an established charitable brand, political campaign, or neighborhood park, the known community is organized with a call to action complete with a well-choreographed pitch describing a pending opportunity to contribute to the greater good.

If successful in communicating their value proposition, establishing a sense of urgency, and offering sufficient, incremental incentives for various participants to pitch in, the campaign will spill over into the attention sphere of other parties who were previously not part of the "community," but find it appealing to add financial support to the idea being financed by the subject crowd.

The Obama presidential campaign broke all barriers in 2008 reaching young and tech-savvy voters in newly emerging social media sites like Facebook, and through e-mail and text messages to appeal for micro-donations. Scoffed at by the McCain campaign for making a pitch for a $3 campaign donation, what they proved was their idea of hooking these smaller donors into making multiple donations.

Any amount of money coming from three million people tends to add up. That's how many donors contributed a total of $600 million through the Obama campaign leading up to his election in 2008. Many made second, third, and even more donations over the course of the campaign.

Donors were offered multiple options to raise their donations and the ease of instant results communicated from their computers or phones linked directly to their bank accounts or credit cards.

The campaign's tactics tracked what specific issues were important to the targeted individual donors and then mailed them regular "cause" messages about that particular issue. Emotive appeals were sent from popular cultural figures who were also identified with various issues.

As explained by Dan Marom,[4] prominent figures in subcultures were used by the Obama Campaign regularly, discussing issues at the forefront of the campaign. However, rather than sending generic e-mails, the campaign solicited help from different figureheads within different subcultures to solicit support and donations. For example:

- Sandra Fluke, a well-known feminist and advocate for gay rights sent e-mails to Obama's e-mail base, discussing contraception, rape, and health choices, issues that are critical for many female voters.
- Kal Penn, an Indian-American actor and cultural figure among younger voters, sent an e-mail to potential donors stating "Friend, (yes, we're friends)," appealing to the younger voting bloc through friendly banter.
- Lena Dunham, a writer, actress, and director, is a prominent figure in the young indie population. Dunham created a video encouraging young people to get out and vote.

And of course, once the election was over, the financial campaign continued.

These tactics have not been lost on the philanthropic world who are training their attention on a new breed of donor who will not be developed with a stamped envelope, glossy brochure, or gala dinner. Crowdfunding has revitalized the arts at a time when public funding programs are steadily dwindling and older traditional patrons are dying off.

Paying for major exhibitions at museums has always been underwritten by foundations, big corporations, and major donors. But the Smithsonian Institution raised more than $130,000 through crowdfunding to pay for a yoga exhibition at the Freer Sackler Galleries.[5] Although two previous campaigns largely failed, the museum pressed on with this third attempt in the face of lower budgets since the Great Recession. Namaste?

An interesting point is that many artists are going directly to the public without wading through traditional grant makers and making their appeals to those who want to support the creation of their art directly, in whatever form. It is widely recognized that this segment represents direct competition to the institutions who are trying to raise money for museums, performance venues, and other cultural enterprises.

Crowdfunding is also growing a market for impact investing in social enterprises that ties entrepreneurship with philanthropy, and is helping to broaden a base of investors to fund companies for both profits and purpose. Exosphere, Inc. launched a crowdfunding campaign on July 4, 2013 to raise money for an open hardware space shuttle with the intention of eventually building and launching a private craft to explore outer space.[6]

And there are more basic charities turning to crowdfunding: medical costs and home down payments. An Orlando, Florida realty company started HomeFunded.com to help raise down payments for clients who have to offer higher prices for homes to compete with hedge funds that have cornered the foreclosure marketplace.[7]

Several crowdfunding sites have opened that facilitate the solicitation and collection of contributions to help sick people defray medical costs, to the tune of $20 million through over 15,000 campaigns.[8] Sites focused on this purpose include GiveForward.com and YouCaring.com.

Crowdfunding site GoFundMe.com suggests a variety of other interesting purposes for which users might launch a campaign: animals & pets, babies, kids & family, celebrations & special events, and weddings & honeymoons. Rival site FundRazr.com has most of these but also suggests contributing to the legal expenses of users.

Maybe the most unsettling sites are DonationTo.com and Graceful Goodbye.com (founded by former Morgan Stanley banker Josh McClung) that solicit contributions for funerals.

So, how does it work? What's the magic formula to attract funding in this online donation marketplace? Well, to begin with, the search for funding is not called a "search" but rather a campaign. That label becomes more apparently appropriate when recognizing the required steps to launch a successful effort to raise money there.

While there are few constraints to launching a campaign, the more successful results come to those who already have some momentum in their venture, organization, or big idea. It's not impossible, but it is rare that anyone decides to launch a new idea started up without any previous work on the ground and raises a ton of money in two weeks. The majority of crowdfunding campaigns flounder, with many sites requiring the goal to be met or zero dollars will be collected from the crowd pledges.

Meaning? The American Cancer Society is more likely to be successful with a targeted crowdfunding campaign as part of a much larger, established fundraising apparatus than another disease-oriented nonprofit effort that is just starting up or has never appealed for contributions.

Here are the common steps to running a crowdfunding campaign, as suggested by a new army of crowdfunding experts and consultants who are available for hire to help guide funding campaigns. These steps are divided into two segments: planning and execution.

Campaign Planning

Like any sales promotion, crowdfunding campaigns require plenty of detailed planning to provide road maps for tactics that will be employed to communicate the message and steer the intended target audience to respond in the desired manner. Typical campaign planning includes the following 10 steps:

1. Establish a prototype of your eventual project and figure out how to launch and accomplish it on a smaller scale before reaching out to the community for funding. Crowdfunding campaigns have proven to be more successful when they're built on top of an existing foundation of an effort already started, and the additional funding can help take that early success even higher, to the next level.

   By opening a more modest project earlier, it demonstrates the faith and commitment in the project by having already invested time and funds into it, which boosts the credibility of the later campaign.
2. Choose the crowdfunding platform judiciously. As the number of crowdfunding platforms increases, the job of choosing the best one gets tougher. Well-known crowdfunding pioneers Kickstarter.com and Indiegogo.com are the largest, but users will compete with many more ideas and campaigns in the hunt for support.

   Plenty of other platforms can offer the same degree of service, but users have to be concerned about who is raising money there, how many categories are available and how many are in the category that best defines your campaign, and how many campaigns actually reach their goal.

3. Create the project page in the platform with flair. Spend plenty of time in several platforms looking at comparable projects that have been successful (or not) and get familiar with the level of detail on their pages and the information included.

   The project page is your mini-website for donors shopping for a place to contribute a portion of their largesse for ideas that they find appealing and have empathy toward. It may be the only opportunity to ever pitch an idea to each individual and convert him or her into a supporter to contribute to the campaign. Make sure the page is well written with a clear objective, is well branded, and offers pictures to tell more of your story.

4. Videos in the crowdfunding arena are an absolute must. Campaigns with short videos (less than 3 minutes) are 50 percent more successful than those without. Plenty of campaigns have garnered remarkable success using videos shot with a digital camera, but if you have a budget that provides access to a more professional-looking production, it should pay dividends. Again, watch videos used by similar campaigns that were successful to see how they approached their pitch message.

5. Choose perks for your donors. Perks may range from worthless tchotchkes to unique and priceless experiences, and are intended to incentivize donors to be generous. Most successful campaigns offer four or five perks at increasingly higher suggested giving levels. It pays to be clever.

   Perks should be related to the cause—for example, a band could offer donors an early release of their new recording, an autographed CD cover, or backstage passes to a future concert. While the cost must remain in check (most consultants say no more than 10 percent of the gift level) some of the best ideas are simply access to whatever donors obviously have a passion for.

   The most common gift levels range from $25 to $50 and across most platforms appear to be definitively tied to the most interesting perks.

6. Be sure to establish a definitive payment system to collect pledged donations. Depending on the platform, there are different methods to collect payment, so organizers must look into what's required by the platform and ensure their banking or other payment arrangements are compatible.

7. Plan a communication strategy that will be launched simultaneously through e-mail to all stakeholders and through social media friends and connections. Include dedicated messaging in the organization's website. Prepare to provide links to the campaign page from all social media platforms.

8. Develop a media target list and publicity materials to support the campaign. Search for media sources that would likely have an interest in the project, including online newspapers, magazines, blogs and even video channels.

   It's unlikely that any attention can be obtained from traditional media, but depending on the organization, if these media outlets already have the subject organization on their radar, include them in all communications. Organize all media information so that it's easy to refer to when needed.

   With any luck, the campaign will be unique enough to garner some attention in the media from outlets that focus on the general target of the campaign. As with all publicity, much or even most of the messaging that's eventually distributed will be ignored because it's not news, not unique, or not as important as a competing story. But send media messages anyway to relentlessly pursue more attention to grow the community.

9. Prepare the existing support community for the campaign with prior notification, explaining the campaign, what will happen, and when it's set to launch. Include the friends and family of the staff and other stakeholders as well.

   This group will be vitally important to the success of the campaign. Their immediate response to the live campaign is imperative to get the attention of other participants in the crowdfunding platform and media that follows the campaign. Most platforms publicize results in real time and rank all the competing campaigns based on pledge results.

   As the core community of supporters begins making pledges, commenting on the campaign's project and messaging through social media to support the campaign, the platform ranking will begin to rise, giving the project valuable exposure to others who may join in with a donation.

10. Recruit any and all known *influencers*, persons with a high profile, gravitas, or who are well known in the industry, state, or national sense, and get their buy-in to participate as a high-profile donor whose donation will be announced strategically to garner more support. You might even consider asking for a matching donation model or challenge.

Campaign Execution

Once thoroughly planned and prepared for, crowdfunding campaigns have to be executed. While many messages, dates, and people can be arranged in a manner similar to a script, the actual execution will actually be more ad hoc. The campaign will have to adjust the script to respond to what actually happens, which will not be known until it does. The following three steps would be a consistent execution of a campaign that had been planned with the strategies just described:

1. Launch the campaign by simultaneously going live on the crowdfunding platform site, announcing the campaign on the organization's social media pages and website, distributing a news release to the entire media list, and sending a personalized e-mail to everyone in the organization's distribution list.

   Make as much noise as possible for everyone that can be reached to hear about the campaign on the same day. The payoff of notifying supporters, friends, and family early will hopefully be a quick response of 20 to 30 percent of the campaign goal to be pledged within the first 1 or 2 days. Only then will strangers take notice and begin getting involved.

2. Start pitching the media regularly with planned "news" as the campaign progresses. Plan for having several unique pitches that describe creative benchmarks of the campaign's success. The goal is to get this information written about to build more awareness beyond the community and raise the profile of the campaign.

   Use positive achievements, like reaching 25, 75, or 125 percent of the goal, for example, to trumpet success in whatever way it can be measured. Announcing the support of the influencers, publicizing good commentary that may have appeared in social media, and other newsworthy tidbits to build excitement for the campaign are desirable.

3. Don't stop. It's important to remain active tracking results, thanking donors, and remaining in touch with all stakeholders, old and new, to provide progress reports, and encourage them to reach out to others for the campaign. Keeping the momentum will ensure that the platform ranking continues to grow and the campaign gets in front of enough new people to be successful.

   Some very organized campaigns send updates hourly, solicit photographs from larger donors for posting with testimonials, and even launch new videos to keep the campaign active. The most active campaigns raise significantly more funding than those that are passive.

Obviously, a crowdfunding campaign requires a lot of effort but if planned and managed well on behalf of good ideas or causes, organizations can do very well raising money in a relatively short period of time.

No two campaigns are alike just like no two crowdfunding platforms are alike. The best known—and most successful—platform is Kickstarter. But they are also very exclusive, in that they must approve or curate the idea before allowing a campaign to be entered on their site.

They publish interesting statistics about the results of their campaigns that can be instructive if thoughtfully analyzed. Their stats are updated in real time daily and can be viewed at www.kickstarter.com/help/stats.

As of this writing in May 2014, Kickstarter[9] had:

- Launched 147,954 campaigns of which 62,219 were successful
- Raised more than $1.12 billion in pledges, of which $965 million was actually collected in successful campaigns and $31 million was currently "live" dollars
- Facilitated contributions from 6,232,807 donors who made 15,349,999 pledges; 1,854,574 donors pledged more than once

Of those 62,219 successful campaigns:

- 6,739 donations were for less than $1,000
- 39,533 were for $1,000 to $9,999
- 8,323 were for $10,000 to $19,999
- 6,405 were for $20,000 to $99,999
- 1,157 were for $100,000 to $999,999
- 62 were for $1 million or more

All these stats are broken down into one of 13 categories, which is instructive of the enthusiasm of some community sectors and the challenges ahead for others.

Obviously, most sites aren't nearly as successful as Kickstarter, but the greater point is that crowdfunding works and represents a profound way to generate donations to support a broad range of good ideas, people, and organization.

Texting/Tweeting for Dollars

Other technologies have developed alternative crowdfunding strategies, but they don't appear to be growing with the same trajectory as website-based platforms. Remember the Haitian earthquake in 2010? With the promotion assistance of the U.S. State Department, the Red Cross launched the first widely publicized text message campaign to raise contributions.[10] That campaign raised $43 million in $10 increments by typing "Haiti" addressed to short code 90999.

Since then, most text-contributing seems to be focused on either direct campaigns using text solicitations to attract donations—meaning the organization must already have the target's mobile number—or at events where people gather and the contributions are frequently impulsive rather than planned. Texting is a convenient payment option that allows people to stay in their seat or at their table rather than having to get up to go present their credit cards. Charges for the donation appear on their telephone bills.

According to mGive.com, they have raised more than $65 million through text solicitations and maintain a database of more than 1 million mobile phone users for various causes.[11] They have conducted over 10,000 campaigns for about 500 nonprofit clients, including the Haitian disaster relief campaign on behalf of the Red Cross.

Service provider MobileCause.com suggests that the average text contribution at an event is much higher than average donations across all text campaigns ($167 versus $107) and that 84 percent of all text pledges received are fulfilled. But when the campaign appeal imposes a $5 or $10 fee to collect text pledges, the rate plummets to 59 percent.[12]

Text donations can take 60 to 90 days to fulfill since the individual donors' telephone carriers must bill them and collect payments before forwarding them to the charitable organization. The process is a little complicated and takes several messages for the first-time contributor to register.

Another medium that held promise was transferring payments via Twitter through an Atlanta-based company called TwitPay.com. Users could register their payment information one time online and then respond to campaigns or send other donations with a tweet. The appeal of the service was that once registered, it only took one message to complete the contribution and in the same tweet appeal to followers to make a contribution as well.

But the tweetdom of Twitter users apparently didn't embrace it and the company shuttered in early 2012.

INNOVATORS—BUY IT, I'LL BUILD IT

There's another new, fascinating business funding model arising through the crowd: "Buy it, I'll build it." Crowdfunding has never been restricted merely to giving donations and many entrepreneurs have created successful campaigns around the notion of "pay me to build it and I'll give you one." The most wildly popular example of this phenomenon so far is the Pebble Watch.

As told by *Entrepreneur* magazine:[13]

> *On April 11, 2012, a young engineer named Eric Migicovsky posted a project request for $100,000 on funding platform Kickstarter. He hoped for development funds from "the crowd" for his Pebble watch prototype, a Bluetooth smartwatch that wirelessly connects with Android and iPhone smartphones to display e-mail, calendar alerts, social media updates and caller ID; play music; run apps like GPS; and, yes, even tells time.*

His project rang the cool vibe for Kickstarter's famously creative geek community. By May 18, Migicovsky had reeled in an astonishing $10.2 million from nearly 70,000 backers—the first $1 million in only 28 hours. Kickstarter's donation model exchanges perks, rewards or products—not company equity—for contributions to fully funded projects.

In this case, depending on the amount they donated, backers will receive one or more Pebble watches before market release, adding up to thousands of presold products. Of course, the Pebble quickly became legend, proving that not only does crowdfunding work, but it can fuel serious money.

Migicovsky had been in development of this project for a few years and had already succeeded in raising about $375,000 at a prestigious incubator. But then the Silicon Valley VCs who'd been tracking his progress walked away, failing to see enough demand for the end product.

Kickstarter was Migicovsky's last resort after he'd already been marketing a working product that generated some buzz. But his struggles after raising $10 million, including manufacturing delays and iOS glitches, offers lessons for anyone who assumes crowdfunding is easy.

"The worst mistake you can make is thinking that it'll be easy," says strategist Jason Best of Crowdfund Capital Advisors. "You have to create a campaign. Anytime you raise money, it's hard, real work and requires a way to be able to engage the customer community."[14]

The big picture to this story is that the digital highway provides a convenient path for entrepreneurs to find a target audience for new goods and services that consumers didn't know they were looking for. Part of why consumers don't know about these products is because some haven't been produced yet.

In this instance, the business bypasses the normal capital market typically needed for funding and the traditional retail sales intermediary needed to market the product, and goes directly to the consumer, who becomes funder and buyer in the same transaction.

Crowdfunding platforms offer the community some validation of the seller and collective confidence from the power of numbers—consumers are more confident if they see that others are jumping in to support such a project. It's assumed by these parties that the platform can be relied on to provide a degree of due diligence on the campaigner.

This sector of crowdfunding will be the place to watch business funding for companies producing innovative consumer products going forward. It's widely known in the venture finance community that many appealing project ideas get passed over for the wrong reasons. It's not because they are bad ideas, produce bad products, or don't have plenty of consumer appeal. But rather, funding doesn't come their way because the venture investors aren't assured of a huge investment return.

LOANERS—BROTHER CAN YOU REFINANCE MY VISA?

In 2005, social enterprise Kiva.com opened a path to provide assistance to low-income entrepreneurs around the globe with a peer-to-peer lending platform, bringing their pitch from prospective micro businesses to the computer screen of empathetic western investors. This same model was later emulated domestically by innovators providing a channel for investors to circumvent banks and finance companies to provide lower-cost consumer financing through peer-to-peer loans.

Peer-to-peer financing has blossomed in the United States and Europe and has generated more than $4 billion in loans to individuals to fund everything from home repairs, automobile purchases, and medical care, and most often to pay off and refinance more ominously priced credit card debt. LendingClub.com, Prosper.com and U.K.'s Zopa.com are the three most dominant companies in this market, each having racked up impressive lending volumes, investor lists, and financial returns.

The concept seems easy: (1) find investors who are seeking better financial returns than offered through bank deposits; (2) offer them 6 to 9 percent returns on their funds; and (3) invest the proceeds in higher yielding consumer loans to consumers who are tired of paying 29.99 percent on their credit cards. In actuality, its much more complicated.

Debt issued by any other entity than a legally exempt chartered bank is a *security*. Therefore, gathering funds from investors to plow into consumer notes is subject to the Securities Act of 1933 and must be registered with the Securities and Exchange Commission, even if the average loan is barely over $10,000. These hurdles have been overcome methodically with technology, but add expense and exposure to the operation.

Lending Club by far is the most successful peer-to-peer lending platform, having issued $3.395 billion[15] in loans since 2006, more than twice the amount disclosed by Prosper.com ($692 million)[16] or Zopa.com (£452 million or $750 million)[17] combined. Given the regulatory hurdles they must maneuver through as a non-bank, issuing securities to represent transactions potentially as small as $1,000, Lending Club is responsible for the dizzying number of loans involved. Yet their model is fairly straightforward for borrowers, given the rules set forth in their term sheet:

- "Members" may complete an online loan application for $1,000 to $35,000 agreeing to a number of terms while the platform agrees only to expose qualified loan applications to its member investors. Members may apply for only one loan at a time, but may have two outstanding loans.

- All member applicants must clear minimum credit criteria prescribed by Web Bank, the functioning lending partner of Lending Club, which includes a minimum FICO score of 660, minimum debt-to-income ratio (DTI), and other undisclosed factors.
- The application completed by members requires income disclosure, which is verified with the member's employer, and a credit report is obtained. Using these data sources along with the application details, the application is graded to a level ranging from "A" to "G," with each grade having five tiers within it, 1 to 5.
- The application also provides that the member agrees to give Lending Club a power of attorney to act on the member's behalf to execute notes for the eventual note agreement and sign an IRS form 4506 needed to obtain a federal income tax return transcript.
- Member applicants agree to pay a nonrefundable origination fee totaling 1.11 percent to 5 percent of the loan amount—to cover the hard costs to Lending Club of processing due diligence and exposing applications to members. This fee is discounted from any loan proceeds to be distributed to the borrower member, but the sum remains part of the principal and accrues interest until the loan is fully amortized.
- Lending Club prices the loan in accordance with the grade and posts it for investor members to review and bid on participation. There is a 14-day limit in which an application can remain posted before final action on the proposal is determined.
- On or before the fourteenth day after the loan proposal is posted for investors to choose whether to purchase a portion of the note, one of the following actions will occur:
  - If the loan is fully committed to by investors it will fund immediately.
  - If 60 percent or more of the requested amount is committed to by investors, it will be funded after the fourteenth day.
  - If less than 60 percent of the requested amount is committed to by investors, the member applicant will be given the choice to accept the lower amount, withdraw the application, or withdraw the application and immediately relist it.
- Lending Club charges its investors a 1 percent servicing fee assessed on each payment received from borrowers.

Lending Club average borrower statistics[18] are stronger than what some may expect, as described in Table 8.1.

The proprietary application grade determines the cost of the loan to the borrower, with loans made to A borrowers charged an average 7.65 percent

TABLE 8.1 Average Borrower at Lending Club (as of November, 2013)

FICO score	703
Debt-to-income	16.2% (excluding mortgage)
Credit history	15 years
Personal income	$71,130
Average loan	$13,490

Source: LendingClub.com.

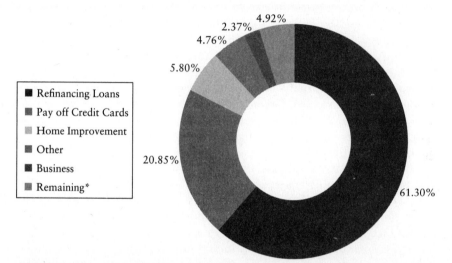

FIGURE 8.1 Reasons Borrowers Seek Peer-to-Peer Loans (as of November, 2013) *Remaining uses include major purchases, car financing, home financing, medical expenses, moving expenses, vacation, learning and training, and green loans. *Source:* LendingClub.com.

APR and G borrowers paying an average 24.44 percent. Likewise, the representative rates projected to be paid to investors[19] are also estimated in a range of 5.11 percent to 9.29 percent for A to C grade borrowers.

Why are borrowers getting peer-to-peer loans? Loan purposes[20] vary, but the overwhelming reason most borrowers (>83 percent) get loans from this source is to pay off and refinance more expensive debt. All these uses are detailed in Figure 8.1.

Technically, all Lending Club loans are directly funded by WebBank. com, a Utah-chartered industrial bank that allows several lending companies to provide private label consumer and lending products available nation-wide. With their bank license easily able to cross any other state line, funding transactions in this way simplifies lender compliance and reduces their cost to do business nationally.

WebBank funds the prequalified loan request underwritten by Lending Club, and after funding it is immediately sold to Lending Club on the same day. At this point, Lending Club only serves clients in 45 states.

Investors buy an interest in Lending Club's "Prime Consumer Notes," which are fixed-income investments that generate a monthly payment stream back to the investor that include principal and interest payments from the borrower. Investors generally choose to spread their risk across hundreds or even thousands of these notes to diversify their holdings. Investors can choose to buy into notes in any of the loan grade categories depending on their appetite for risk and other investment objectives.

Lending Club emphasizes to investors that the investment proceeds are not used directly to actually make loans to borrowers, but rather to invest in what they call "Member Payment Dependent Notes." Each of these notes represents an interest in a portion of the payment stream from a particular loan they've selected, which are forwarded to investors as payments that are collected by Lending Club.

Loans originated in the site are qualified by the underwriting regimen that assures each lender meets an absolute minimum set of credit standards. But then it's necessary that enough investors weigh in to purchase an interest in the related Member Payment Dependent Notes to support that loan in order for it to be funded. Once sufficient investor capital is committed, the actual loan to the borrower is funded by WebBank, which is secured by the proceeds from the particular Member Payment Dependent Notes.

With plenty of qualifications explained, as any investment prospectus should include, Lending Club makes sure investors know that loans may not be repaid at all. But subtle encouragement at diversifying investor portfolios with more loans may be aimed at avoiding losses by simply spreading their money around further.

As noted in a section titled "Benefits of Diversification," two charts[21] reflect that, on average, investors who bought interests in more than 100 notes and did not hold any notes at a level greater than 2.5 percent of the face loan amount had portfolios that performed better than those whose portfolios reflected the opposite.

The site also provides some rough analysis about loan performance as a guideline to temper investor expectations. As illustrated in Figure 8.2, Lending Club demonstrates *loan status migration*[22] over a nine-month horizon based on trailing experience to establish how average loans perform.

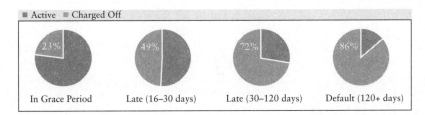

FIGURE 8.2   Loan Migration over Nine Months (as of August, September, and October, 2012)
Source: LendingClub.com.

Their pie charts reflect loan groups that only include loans originated at least three months prior to the sample, and show the percentages of loans that were subsequently charged off after nine months. So, the 23 percent of loans shown to be "in grace period" were charged off within nine months, as were the 72 percent of loans that were late 30 to 120 days.

This information is not thorough but does serve as a benchmark that investors can observe to understand the nature of average risk in these securities.

Historical lending activities are found on the site that reflect how each credit grade performed. Their "Grade Mix Over Time" chart[23] illustrates the volume of loans graded in each of the proprietary grades relative to all lending activities of the company.

Also included in this section of their site is data reflecting the gross loans funded and figures reflecting the sums paid in full versus outstanding in all the credit grades. The outstanding balances are broken down further to current, late, charged-off, or default status. The average interest rates, net annualized return, and an adjusted net annualized return is also provided for each grade category.

The net annualized return is calculated to show the rate of return from collections of loan interest and late fees against the total outstanding sum of unpaid loans. Lending Club nets out charged-off loan principal as well as its 1 percent fee to investors from these sums. Investors can use these results to benchmark their own investing results.

In addition, Lending Club provides an adjusted net annualized return calculation that accounts for future loan loss projections derived from an analysis of the current portion of outstanding loans that are in something other than current status.

Most surprising might be the additional data available to investors (or others) about previous Lending Club activities, less borrower identification information. Views can see the results of all the previous loans made plus loan applications that were declined by Lending Club.

Who invests in Lending Club? Actually, a broad range of investors from banks and credit unions to alternative lenders to smaller investors who buy in to find higher returns. And their investment strategies are just as varied since they have a choice of buying defined risk grades in an amount determined by the investor.

Most regulated lenders restrict loan participation to Lending Club's A and B graded credits only. These loans obviously have lower risks and lower returns, but offer banks the chance to get higher returns than some of their in-house product lines and may target certain market areas to boost their CRA compliance.

Banks and credit unions have the option to white-label Lending Club's platform and connect their own borrowers directly to the decision site. Afterward, the referring bank can decide whether to fund the loan directly.

SHAREHOLDERS—ONLINE MARKET FOR EQUITY

The prospect of raising capital online from the crowd represents some of the most significant changes to American securities law in over 80 years. The JOBS Act allows investors to buy shares in ventures that will be posted in an online brokerage crowdfunding portal. Companies that list on equity crowdfunding platforms will have an opportunity to raise capital funding directly among potential investors whom neither they nor their technological broker may have previously known.

This new capital portal will bring with it new expectations, responsibilities, and obligations to be managed entrepreneurs, regulators, and investors alike.

Under the new law, companies seeking funding from "the crowd" may issue up to $1 million in equity securities in any 12-month period to an unlimited number of investors via one of the crowdfunding platforms approved by the Securities and Exchange Commission (SEC). Initially, only accredited investors[24]—those with an annual income over $200,000 or at least a $1 million net worth—will be eligible to purchase these securities, but the general public will have the same opportunity in 2014 when the SEC implements its new Crowdfund Investing rules.

President Obama signed the Jumpstart Our Business Startups Act or JOBS Act into law on April 5, 2012. This law was constructed from a number of competing bills that would have incrementally changed various security laws to facilitate crowdfunding for equity. But unlike the unregulated donor and innovator crowdfunding activities, the SEC has issued a preliminary 585-page set of rules[25] for crowdfunding for stakeholders, with the delivery date of the final rules uncertain.

What exactly is in the new law? Some of the most important provisions of the JOBS Act include the following terms:

- The act increases the maximum number of shareholders a company may have before crossing the threshold to become a public-reporting company, from 500 shareholders to now 500 "unaccredited" shareholders or 2,000 total shareholders.
- The act provides an additional exemption for certain types of small capital offerings from the SEC registration requirements, subject to conditions. This exemption allows the use of Internet funding portals, which must be registered with the SEC.
- The act provides an aggregate annual investment limit each unaccredited person may make in crowdfunded offerings, tiered by that person's net worth or annual income. These limits are the greater of $2,000 or 5 percent for people earning up to $100,000 annually, or the lesser of $100,000 or 10 percent for people earning $100,000 or more annually.
- The act requires review-level financial statements be provided for investors on offerings between $100,000 and $500,000 and audited financial statements for offerings greater than $500,000 to a maximum of $1,000,000.
- The act relieves emerging growth companies from some disclosure requirements that are typically expected when a company sells shares publicly, for five years after the original registration. The act also waives obligations imposed by onerous Section 404 of the Sarbanes-Oxley Act and related regulations for five years.
- The act lifts a ban on general solicitation and advertising for specific kinds of private placements of securities and loosens rules to permit the various messaging that is contemplated in the crowdfunding sphere.
- The act raises limits for security offerings exempted under Regulation A from $5 million to $50 million, thereby allowing for larger fundraising campaigns under this simplified regulation, and the act raises the number of shareholders permitted to buy shares in a community bank from 500 to 2,000.

After the JOBS Act was signed into law, it took the Securities and Exchange Commission 16 months to publish the rules to which investors and companies would have to conform to in order to legally solicit equity sales via a crowdfunding platform.

While the early crowdfunding market got well-acquainted with donor sites and peer-to-peer lending sites, it will be a new crowd that weighs in to begin crowdfunding with shares. This crowd will be comprised of a completely different kind of participant, one who must navigate through financial statements, due diligences, and the other requisites necessary when their objective is modified to expecting their money to be returned in the future with growth.

An interesting sideshow will surely accompany the evolution of equity crowdfunding as thousands of new investors wade into the financing of less mature and startup businesses, many of whom may have never before invested in a private company. Will they expect faster financial returns than is normal in the startup arena? How patient will they be with future company updates and financial reporting?

Managing investors for these smaller companies is likely to take on a whole new flavor as their investor base expands to include less-experienced investors. Obviously, there are no guaranteed perks such as the t-shirts and digital accolades exchanged with donor crowdfunders.

Introducing new technology to an old-fashioned market doesn't mean there aren't plenty of challenges to slog through to make things work. Raising equity capital from investors is very fairly regulated activity dating back to the 1930s. Opening the cloud as one more exchange for buying and selling equity shares doesn't mean all the old rules have been thrown out.

Having to adhere to the same detailed security rules is coming as a surprise to many excited participants who were initially under the mistaken impression that the web would open up millions of dollars just there for the taking. Instead, they are finding the same rules and most of the same processes are required, with just some digital shortcuts added and former limitations stretched.

Crowdfunding will not exactly be the Wild West. The JOBS Act carries numerous requirements, restrictions, and obligations to provide a legal framework to protect the various participants and create a structured marketplace that will operate tighter than the unsupervised donation crowdfunding sector.

Technology brings much more capacity to facilitate the exchange of capital for shares and for the first time, technology will be employed to confirm that both parties comply with federal law.

To provide transparency to all participants, companies raising capital will be required to provide certain information to the SEC, the platform brokerage through which they're raising funds, and to all potential investors:

- Name, legal status, and address of the business, along with the names of company directors, officers, and key shareholders.
- Company's business plan and a description of business operations.
- Financial information that includes income tax returns, officer-certified financial statements, or audited financial statements if raising $500,000 or more.

■ Description of the purpose and intended use of the new funding, the target offering amount, and the price of the securities being offered.
■ The ownership and capital structure of the business, including the terms of each class of the company's securities and methods of valuation for these securities.
■ Annual reports and financial statements previously issued by the company.

The process is similar to the kinds of information required in the old route to raising capital in that companies seeking money through crowdfunding are required to provide potential investors with sufficient information to make informed decisions. As with the other channels, companies will have significant legal and accounting expenses involved with complying with these requirements on an ongoing basis.

Among the requirements that have not changed:

■ Securities issuers and their officers, directors, or partners can be held liable for any material misstatements or omissions used to promote shares.
■ Security issuers cannot advertise their securities, except to provide a notice that directs potential investors to the crowdfunding platform where their securities are promoted.
■ Security issuers cannot compensate anyone to promote their offerings through communication channels provided by a broker or funding portal.
■ Securities offered through these portals will be restricted and subject to a one-year holding period, except when transferred under certain circumstances.

Another significant point that has not changed, except with rare exception, is the state security laws that add another series of bureaucratic layers onto raising capital for entrepreneurs. Although generally less restrictive than the federal rules, they still must be complied with and generally speaking, have evolved with more similarities than differences. These have long been called blue sky laws in reference to the value of some fraudulent security schemes dating back to around the beginning of the twentieth century.

Small companies have to register their securities in every state from which an investor in their offering resides. So, if 30 investors from six states choose to invest, counting the federal registration, seven different security registrations must be filed to notify regulators of the security sales. These rules are not waived or avoidable under any of the federal safe harbor rules afforded by Regulation D.

Two states, Kansas and Georgia, have been early adapters in passing legislation to accommodate intrastate crowdfunding for equity, before the JOBS Act. In these states, entrepreneurs had the right to raise funds solely within state borders before federal approval and they still have some advantages over multistate fundraising.

In March 2011, the Kansas Securities Commission adopted the Invest Kansas Exemption, which allows companies formed in Kansas to raise up to $1 million from nonaccredited investors, so long as they're state residents. In November of that same year, Georgia adopted similar legislation. While noteworthy, few people took advantage of the new regulations in those two states early on due to the uncertainty about how the market would function and what was expected by issuers.

Reportedly, Kansas is already revising its statute to adopt some features in the Georgia law and there is momentum growing to pass intrastate measures in North Carolina, South Carolina, Wisconsin, and Texas.

What Will the New Market Look Like?

Complying with security regulations is complicated in the stone-age era of legal opinions, written trading orders, and licensing brokers, but the new digital marketplace promises even more turns and twists to navigate. One company set out to create a secure, compliant platform that would facilitate other broker sites—so the shared technology would be less costly for all and not require every participant to build their own site.

CommunityLeader.com started up in 2012 to provide a common platform where other companies can base a crowdfunding portal. Using common technology, tools, and compliance will enable more market participants to mobilize faster, thereby accelerating market growth.

Their platform will provide some of the basic "blocking and tackling" functions for clients that have required development to manage in this electronic frontier. The platform will include functions such as user (investor) identification confirmation, digital signature capacity, and Patriot Act file compliance. In addition, the portal will be able to screen potential investors for their suitability to invest (i.e., sophisticated or accredited investors) and provide escrow solutions to receive and distribute investor funds.

All the client sites within Community Leader (CL) will be *white labeled*, meaning that the public will not know that they are involved. The customized sites produced by CL will be branded only by the clients and will have the features and window dressings they choose.

Another technological feature of CL's product will be to monitor all crowdfunding campaigns for puffering. The term *puffer*[26] originated around auctions, where sellers would be represented by non-buying bidders who purposely called out fake bids in an effort to raise the prices of goods being sold.

In crowdfunding, it's anticipated that some parties could theoretically manipulate their share prices in order to attract more buyers as the share prices rise. Digital detection will be in place to ferret out such efforts. Otherwise the marketplace could be vastly damaged if the promised transparency actually hides manipulated share prices and burns a new league of sucker geeks.

The development of a company like this naturally will raise questions as dozens of companies use their technology to build crowdfunding portals and individually develop followers and clients. How safe is it? Is it really compliant with the new, evolving regulations? And, who owns all that data?

These are not small details and will be sorted out as the first few pioneers go to market, sell shares, and watch the results. Regarding the data, expect both open and closed network approaches, with the client portal deciding whether to protect their client base with their checkbook.

Not Everyone Agrees: The Case against SoMoLend.com

Unfortunately, all states have not been so quick to embrace crowdfunding and if you accept the logic of some insiders at the Crowdfund Intermediary Regulatory Advocates, the crowdfunding industry trade group known better as CIFRA, some states are ready to put up a fight to stop it.

SoMoLend.com, a Cincinnati, Ohio-based online funding platform, was hit with a Notice of Intent to Issue a Cease and Desist Order from the Ohio Commissioner of Securities in June 2013. The company, which connects small business borrowers with corporate, institutional, organization, and individual lenders for debt capital, was cited under accusations for what amounts to charges of securities fraud.

Ohio's Commissioner of Securities, Andrea L. Seidt, contends that SoMoLend Holdings LLC may have committed securities fraud, created and issued fraudulent financial projections, and consistently made false statements about the company's own current and past financial performance.

The only problem was, none of its investors had ever filed a complaint with the Ohio commissioner. The company's president, Candace Klein, was part of the industry leadership that founded CIFRA and initiated meetings with state and federal regulators for years to hammer out reasonable regulations for crowdfunding.

In *Forbes* magazine,[27] DJ Paul, vice chairman of CIFRA, suggests that interested parties take a closer look at the contents of Ohio's notice to SoMoLend[28] and the state's own letter to the Securities and Exchange Commission related to the SEC's[29] regulatory initiatives under Title III of the JOBS Act. "There is a clear correlation and bias against crowdfunding platforms like the one run by Klein," according to Paul.

Title III of the JOBS Act creates a registration exemption under the Securities Act of 1933, for issuers raising less than $1 million through a public offering facilitated by an online funding portal like the one operated by crowdfunding sites.

As for the state's lengthy letter to the SEC, Ohio claimed in January that investors who invest in offerings made pursuant to the new Section 4(a)(6) exemption of the JOBS Act "will lose all or part of their investment."

"Look at the contents of Ohio's letter to the SEC, and then read the state's Notice/Order against SoMoLend," says Paul. "What's clear to me is that Ohio is using Candice (Klein) and SoMoLend to go after an industry and not just SoMoLend.com."[30]

The accusation that the State of Ohio has a bias against crowdfunding seems to be grounded in the state's objections to sections of the JOBS Act, and if true, could have a chilling effect on entrepreneurship in that state. The question to watch is whether overzealous security regulators in other states will push back against the spread of crowdfunding.

Nothing Is Perfect

A significant challenge for crowdfunding will be the essence of one of its very features—raising the cap on the number of shareholders permitted before a company was deemed to be a public-reporting company. The JOBS Act lifts this number from its former 500 shareholders to 500 unaccredited shareholders and 2,000 total shareholders. What's so bad about a higher number, the democratization of the small-cap market?

The issue is that angel investors and venture capitalists may balk at the idea of investing in companies that have hundreds of small, unsophisticated owners amassed from the "crowd round." This should cause some more experienced entrepreneurs to reconsider or avoid crowdfunding their early round, which theoretically should be easier than the normal road show required around dozens of angel pitch meetings.

The consequence of issuing shares to so many parties ahead of the third or fourth round comes down to share dilution versus value. Early investor approval is needed ahead of later financing rounds and the problem would be whether the new share valuation can be reconciled with the number of shares outstanding compared to the return goals established by the later round investors.

Another element of the federal crowdfunding rules may be discouraging to a number of companies anxious to access this capital financing source: tough financial statement requirements. Despite plenty of urging, the SEC refused to modify its demands. IndieGoGo's chief executive, Slava Rubin, called the requirements a "massive deal breaker."[31]

Companies seeking $500,000 that can afford to pay for a CPA review-level financial statement probably can borrow the money at a commercial bank. But even companies that currently can borrow $1 million typically don't pay for audited financial statements and their banks do not require it.

Companies planning to use crowdfunding for equity will undoubtedly be surprised at the annual disclosure rules that are similar to other public companies that raise more money by many multiples. But in an amusing nod to the digital nature of this funding channel, the SEC has permitted some of the disclosures to be made in the form of videos or infographics, so long as they get a full transcript.

The disclosure rules apply as long as the company carries shares that were raised through crowdfunding or goes out of business. The SEC estimates that complying with their rules will cost on average $6,500 for an offering and $4,000 for each annual report.[32] Add to that the intermediary platform commissions and cost of extra financial reporting and it's apparent that few companies will enter this market in the lower funding tiers.

There are plenty of exceptions, but essentially this channel will likely make angel capital investments much more efficient rather than open up new capital to main street businesses. The financial statement and ongoing disclosure rules are intended to ensure that prospective and invested shareholders have access to reliable financial information on companies seeking capital, but is relatively expensive in comparison to the $1 million annual fundraising cap.

But the reality is that companies in a start-up mode typically dedicate every precious dollar to research and development—not costly accounting reports that will only confirm that they've lost money so far. This rule needs to be loosened considerably.

CROWDED ELEVATOR?

As with any new idea, frontier, or market, there are going to be collisions and catastrophes. Remember all those American pioneers who died en route to settle the West? Apollo I? High-frequency trading? All suffered many consequences, some lethal, on the early road to transforming the world from what it was.

One early obstacle to all forms of crowdfunding may be the parties who are left behind by these channels, who will seek to discredit it. Why? At its essence, crowdfunding represents a major power shift. What has been the domain of one party—the local fundraising consultant, a finance company, or local Edward Jones representative—evolves to the benefit of another party.

While crowdfunding is not a zero-sum game, there will be definite losses suffered by many parties, including commercial banks, as their potential market share is anonymously lost to crowdfunding.

Will crowdfunding for financial gifts ever trump philanthropic giving? Absolutely not. According to The Chronicle of Philanthropy,[33] in 2013 U.S. charitable gifts of $1 million or more totaled $9.6 billion. But smaller organizations will probably face the conundrum of having to work one more list of donors, which depending on their resources will either be a blessing or a curse.

As more nonprofit, social entrepreneurs, artists, and others enter the clouds to find the crowds, competition to attract attention will get more challenging. And there's still room for fraud, misrepresentations, and exploitation ahead. But there's no denying that raising funds has permanently been changed for this channel of attracting the benevolence of others.

Peer-to-peer lending will be an interesting place to watch this evolution continue. Even though at least one voice is already predicting a bubble[34] in this market, there are fewer participants and they are moving forward to get into business lending. Who would have believed that we can use our retirement savings to refinance a neighbor's credit card debt or provide their business with working capital?.

This market will continue to grow as more crowdfunding participants find this category because they ultimately want to get their money back, but are wary of equity ownership rather than a promissory note.

As for the crowdfunded equity market, who's going to make this marketplace a full-blown exchange to buy and sell equity interests? The crowdfunding markets are expected to open with smaller, niche-oriented companies that will essentially serve as beta tests for the idea. The functionality of the concept versus the rules imposed to govern it will be tested and most importantly, it remains to be seen whether a sufficient share of investors actually make the market with security purchases.

If there is not a sufficient dollar volume established to attract a stronger, more financially fit set of investment prospects, the market will fade out in the eyes of the larger market.

It will be just as important to watch what happens to all those shares after they enter the market. Will there be a real exchange created where investors can find a place to exit share ownership with willing second-round buyers? Or will they be stuck holding shares that no one wants?

Should there be success in such a rigorous process measured over a period of three to five years, watch for larger investment banks to buy their way into the marketplace.

Notes

1. "How to Prepare a Successful Crowdfunding Pitch," *Entrepreneur*, May 7, 2013, www.entrepreneur.com/article/226576#.
2. "2013CF Crowdfunding Market Outlook Report," www.crowdsourcing.org/editorial/2013cf-crowdfunding-outlook-report/26448 (accessed November 4, 2013).
3. "Community Banking Facts," Independent Community Bankers of America, www.icba.org/files/ICBASites/PDFs/cbfacts.pdf (accessed November 4, 2013).
4. Dan Marom, "A Framework for Political Crowdfunding: Lessons from President Obama," The Crowdfunding Revolution, www.danmarom.com/post/35627344098/a-framework-for-political-crowdfunding-lessons-from (accessed November 4, 2013).
5. Nora Caplan-Bricker, "Crowdfunding Culture: Namaste, and Welcome to the Smithsonian," *NewRepublic.com*, July 4, 2013, www.newrepublic.com/article/113722/crowdfunding-culture-namaste-and-welcome-smithsonian#.
6. "Exosphere Launches Crowdfunding Campaign for Open Hardware Space Shuttle," PR.com, July 7, 2013, www.pr.com/press-release/501598.
7. "Orlando Realtor Launches Down Payment Crowdfunding SiteHomefunded .com," DigitalJournal.com, July 4, 2013, www.digitaljournal.com/pr/1342261.
8. "Crowdfunding for Individual Medical Costs Becoming More Common," NonProfitQuarterly.org, July 1, 2013, www.nonprofitquarterly.org/policysocial-context/22561-crowdfunding-for-individual-medical-costs-becoming-more-common.html.
9. www.kickstarter.com/help/stats (accessed 01/22/14).
10. Amy Gahran, "Donating to Charity by Text Message: Lessons from Haiti," CNN.com, January 14, 2012, www.cnn.com/2012/01/12/tech/mobile/charity-donations-text-messages/.
11. mGive.com, https://mgive.com/resources/faq.aspx (accessed November 18, 2013).
12. MobileCause.com, www.mobilecause.com/mobile-giving-stats/ (accessed November 18, 2013).
13. "How to Prepare A Successful Crowdfunding Pitch," *Entrepreneur*, May 7, 2013, www.entrepreneur.com/article/226576#.
14. Ibid.
15. LendingClub.com, https://www.lendingclub.com/public/about-us.action (accessed January 22, 2014).
16. Prosper.com, www.prosper.com/about/ (accessed January 22, 2014).
17. Zopa.com, www.zopa.com/about-zopa/about-zopa-home (accessed January 22, 2014).
18. LendingClub.com, https://www.lendingclub.com/public/steady-returns.action (accessed November 9, 2013).
19. Ibid.
20. LendingClub.com, https://www.lendingclub.com/info/statistics.action (accessed November 10, 2013).

21. LendingClub.com, https://www.lendingclub.com/info/statistics-performance .action (accessed November 10, 2013).

22. Ibid.

23. LendingClub.com, https://www.lendingclub.com/info/demand-and-credit-profile .action (accessed November 10, 2013).

24. Investopedia.com, www.investopedia.com/terms/a/accreditedinvestor.asp (accessed November 11, 2013).

25. Securities and Exchange Commission, www.sec.gov/rules/proposed/2013/33-9470.pdf (accessed November 18, 2013).

26. Puffer Law and Legal Definition, USLegal.com, http://definitions.uslegal.com/p/ puffer/ (accessed December 22, 2013).

27. Forbes.com,www.forbes.com/sites/mikalbelicove/2013/08/13/ohio-investigating-crowdfunding-platform-somolend/ (accessed November 11, 2013).

28. Ohio Division of Securities, https://www.comapps.ohio.gov/secu/secu_apps/ FinalOrders/Files/2013/13-022%20SoMoLend,%20Candace%20Klein%20 NOH.pdf (accessed November 11, 2013).

29. Securities & Exchange Commission, www.sec.gov/comments/jobs-title-iii/jobs titleiii-199.pdf (accessed November 11, 2013).

30. Forbes.com (accessed November 11, 2013).

31. Robb Mandelbaum, "What the Proposed Crowdfunding Rules Could Cost Businesses," *New York Times*, http://boss.blogs.nytimes.com/2013/11/14/ what-the-proposed-crowdfunding-rules-could-cost-businesses/?_r=0 (accessed November 18, 2013).

32. Ibid.

33. Maria Di Mento, "2013's Biggest Gifts Signal Rebound," Philanthorpy.com, http://philanthropy.com/article/2013-s-Biggest-Gifts-Signal/143743/ (accessed January 2, 2014).

34. Doug Dachille, "How to Rate the Risks of Peer-to-Peer Lending, the Newest Bubble," *PBS NewsHour*, January 1, 2014, www.pbs.org/newshour/business desk/2014/01/how-to-rate-the-risks-of-peer-to-peer-lending-the-newest-bubble .html.

CHAPTER 9

Other Innovative Funding Sources on the Rise

The business finance innovations described in earlier chapters all involved the explicit use of proprietary technology to provide more efficiencies or to scale financing distribution in order to simplify the process of connecting capital to capital users. Actually, innovation does not always require technology, but rather can come in more basic forms, such as strategic ideas and methodologies to navigate capital to the same destination.

And so with financing schemes, a number of good ideas have emerged over the past few years that have offered different, untraditional paths to connect investors and business owners with capital financing. Some of these ideas use plenty of technology to facilitate their ideas, but the distinction here from those other platforms is that the technology is merely the vessel, not the innovation.

At the heart of the companies described in this chapter is this: They have taken an innovative approach to the rules or markets; exploited other weaknesses or vulnerabilities or declined opportunities; taken advantage of tax laws; or deployed technology in a different way. Like the digital innovators, some of the fundamental tenets of the trade have been bent or broken to facilitate these ideas, but none of these particular financing companies innovated strictly with technology so much as they did with finance.

FACTORING IN THE DIGITAL AGE

Factoring is one of the oldest financing vehicles, developed to facilitate international trade in the Mesopotamian culture and was referred to in the Code of Hammurabi. It differs from the two elementary financing vehicles—debt and equity—and provides a means to facilitate the transfer of capital to a business that sells a third party payment obligation to the investor, or *factor*, in exchange for a negotiated discount on the outstanding sum owed. The size of the discount defines the financing cost to the seller, but the combination of the discount and the collection of the debt determine the financial return for the factor.

In a common factoring transaction, a company that is selling goods on open invoices or credit to another company creates a balance sheet entry known as an account receivable (A/R). In the debt market, some lenders will advance loan proceeds against the aggregate total of a company's A/R, which is usually labeled "asset-based lending" (ABL). As such, these lenders generally require all third party customer payments be delivered to an address they control, a "lockbox," so they can account for all the cash receipts of the borrower and ensure that they're repaid first from company cash flow.

The borrowing companies are liable for all debt repayment to the ABL lender even if some of the underlying invoices securing the loan default and do not pay the company.

With factoring, the investor *buys* the A/R. In these transactions, there is a transfer of ownership of the third party customer obligations to pay the company ("seller") to an investor ("buyer"). If the third party defaults on the obligation, the financial loss will be to the buyer, not the originating seller.

In reality, credit cards are a form of factoring, since the card issuer assumes the collection risk of the cardholder, who has agreed to the charges assessed in exchange for goods/services. The card issuer advances cash to the business that accepted the card to settle the debt.

Obviously, the factoring process assumes more risk than ABL lending, since factors depend solely on the debtor to settle their claims in order to be paid, whereas ABL lenders can pursue both the debtor and their borrowing customer. Accordingly, factoring is generally more expensive than ABL lending.

But in the modern era, factoring relationships often looked very similar to ABL lending. Many factors added terms generally reflecting a loan transaction even though at the heart of the deal structure was a legal owner transfer of the underlying obligation. Some of these terms included what might best be described as the terms normally associated with a line of credit.

Like the MCA business, factoring is not a regulated form of financing. In its truest form, it is in fact a transfer of ownership of a debt, which is more discernible than the future cash flow that's transferred in a merchant cash advance transaction. But many factors blur the lines to add lending terms to these relationships in order to lower their investment risk.

For example, some factors require sellers to agree to a two to three year exclusive arrangement to sell all A/Rs to the factor—at least those that would be deemed acceptable by the factor—and agree to a minimum level of annual invoice sales. Should the selling company want to finance operations with another buyer or lender, it would face a penalty payment to be released from the factoring agreement.

Many factors purchase invoices *with recourse*, meaning that if the obligation is not collectible, the business that sold it would have to assume the obligation. Purchasing invoices in this manner should void the transaction being called factoring, since it becomes a loan once the seller/borrower guarantees the invoices it is selling.

Another limitation of factoring, and ABL for that matter, is that both channels have traditionally provided funding to a narrow segment of the small business sector. You can nearly count on two hands the number of industries that can access financing by using their current assets.

Manufacturing and fabrication, printing and publishing, wholesale distribution, trucking, staffing, oil and gas, and limited business services—this short list spells out the limitations of more than half of the factoring companies in the United States. A few factors provide funding for medical receivables or government contract receivables, but factoring has always limited itself with a fairly limited list of eligible client prospects.

A New Twist on an Old Business

When researching its business plan, one innovative company discovered that the aggregate sales volume of all U.S. companies with annual revenues below $25 million selling business-to-business (B2B), totals about $8 trillion per year. And at any given time, the average outstanding A/R amounts to $1.2 trillion. Of that sum, the collective resources of the factoring/ABL financial sector provided funding for only about 5 percent of that sum.

Obviously, the narrow range of business served by the factoring/ABL sector leaves a lot of opportunity up for grabs for other fund providers. A new company, NOWAccount.com (NOW), has taken on the challenge of conquering a large segment of the remaining 95 percent of businesses left untouched by traditional bankers, finance companies, and factors. By using an innovative approach to an old business, they are well positioned to succeed.

NOW operates as a merchant service designed specifically for small businesses selling business-to-business or business-to-government (B2G), instantly buying business invoices, with funds settlement within five days at a flat discount charged for their purchase, similar to a consumer credit card model.

Operating from a web platform, NOW accepts self-enrolling clients with a faster, more efficient due diligence process to get them approved. The company's approval focuses more on future business viability and stability than historical financial records—it needs to determine whether the business will be around to honor potential customer disputes.

Clients choose which of their customer accounts to designate for invoice sales to NOW, which are reviewed by NOW with credit scoring within 48 hours. If approved, clients either sell all that customer's invoices to NOW or none, but retain the choice of which customers to include.

NOW buys invoices on a non-recourse basis, settling the purchase with cash paid via ACH to clients within five days after submission. They hold back a 10 percent reserve, which is payable—less its funding fee—30 days after the original invoice's maturity, meaning if the "net due" date of the invoice is 30 days, the reserve will be refunded after 60 days.

NOW charges a flat fee for the purchased invoices of two and one-half percent for those invoices with net 30 days terms, two and three-quarter percent for invoices with net 60 days terms, and three percent for invoices with net 90 days terms. If the invoices are paid as scheduled, the annualized yield to NOW is approximately 30 percent, 33 percent, or 36 percent respectively. But the customer's cost is roughly the same as it would pay a merchant card processor if the invoice had been charged on a credit card.

And, NOW will buy invoices from international sales, with an additional 1 percent surcharge tacked on to the same pricing grid.

The banking/traditional alternative financing sector provides funding for only about 5 percent of business receivables. At any given time, accounts payable represents a comparably significant percent of the sum of all bank business lending combined. NOW targets the other 95 percent of companies that are selling B2B/B2G. Their operations are performed with more efficient technology and their regulatory burden is very light.

NOW can provide services to start-up companies, since it has no minimum revenue requirements and currently serves companies with revenues of less than $5 million up to over $40 million. These services are without recourse, their pricing is transparent, and there are no junk fees or ISOs to compensate.

eBay for A/R

Online auction service eBay.com was founded in 1995 as a hobby by computer programmer Pierre Omidyar to provide a virtual garage sale for collectible items. By 2006, there was as much sales volume facilitated over this site as was scanned through cash registers at Walmart. Recognize, though, that eBay sells nothing, but merely serves as a market.

They are like an auction house that facilitates a place where buyers and sellers come together to do business, and are paid a fraction of each sale as the price to all parties of doing business there.

The essence of eBay's business model is to allow selling users to offer virtually anything for sale in an auction format, where buyer users have a limited time to enter a competitive bid. The highest bidder within the limited time wins the sale.

What does eBay's model have to do with business finance? Nothing until the founders of The Receivable Exchange (TRE) recognized that an open marketplace for unpaid invoices could improve the flow of capital to thousands of small businesses. Their innovation was to use someone else's innovative technology idea and apply it to a different marketplace.

With investor "buyers" bidding on individual A/R invoices, the idea was that the cost of capital would likely fall for business owners, or at least the pricing would be more appropriately structured for lower to higher risk customers. Likewise, having selling companies offer their A/R to a broader marketplace would create a channel for more investors to participate in a lucrative market with risk spread across many different companies.

And so in 2006, TRE opened a new platform to buy and sell A/R. Factoring was effectively innovated by creating an open marketplace for the exchange of these securities[1] by qualified buyers and sellers. TRE is not the funder on any of the transactions that occur on its platform, but like eBay, created a market where these parties can meet to do business.

TRE's digital trading platform supervises both sellers and buyers to ensure a compliant market, transparent dealings, and a monitored exchange of capital. The company adds sufficient due diligence of sellers to prevent fraud and ensure that participants have legitimate clients and invoices that can be sold for goods or services that have been delivered. Additionally, they regulate who may enter the market as buyers, generally restricted to accredited investors, hedge funds, and banks.

This marketplace has efficiency that can move capital faster, more cheaply, and to a much broader range of industrial sectors than the more restrictive list of sectors financed by factoring or ABL. And another important feature of TRE, their market is void of many customary junk fees and extraordinary costs charged by traditional factors that drive costs through the roof for small businesses.

The old-school factors/ABL lenders advertise funding rates similar to a prime + 2 or 3 percent interest costs but then assess many other fees that reflect their valid hands-on account service costs. In addition, many also charge premiums for dubious conditions or events, best described as fees applied because they can get it in the fine print.

In contrast to the discreet target of 36 to 50 percent (annualized) cost of traditional factoring/ABL, TRE claims to cost participating sellers about 20 percent for the funds generated through sales in their market, a significant savings for small business owners.

WORKING CAPITAL MANAGEMENT
AS A FINANCING STRATEGY

There are also plenty of ways for simpler technology to improve financial management. Considering how accounting software improved information for business management and third party reporting tabulation, it should be no surprise that there are more enhancements ahead.

Over the years, many software providers and web-based technology companies have offered better, more efficient solutions to provide billing, accounts receivable, inventory, and accounts payable management. These efforts improved office efficiencies in tandem to generate and deliver invoices, track inventory, lower shipping errors, and enable companies to manage their payments better.

But one company, Taulia, goes a step further by offering a fully integrated working capital management system that works with both suppliers and their buyers. The company aims to lower the supplier's reliance on expensive working capital financing by automating the billing management system and integrating a transparent schedule of invoice discounting, which they call "dynamic discounting."

Taulia's value proposition is to help smaller supply chain companies manage cash flow better, moderating discount offers and rates according to their real-time cash cycle to maximize the value of their cash float and work their A/R efficiently. The best part, maybe, is that these smaller companies don't have to pay for services—their larger buying companies do.

And their timing is perfect. According to Taulia Vice President Joe Hyland, speaking to *Bloomberg Businessweek*,[2] "Back in the 1970s or 1980s, many of the world's biggest corporations started stretching out payment terms" and earning interest on cash earmarked for suppliers. "Today, those companies are paying suppliers later and later, only now they're earning lousy returns on that money."

Enter Taulia's platform management system, which provides clear communication tracking between these buyers and suppliers, and the purchase discounts offered by suppliers simultaneously can provide buyers a better financial return than the alternative of allowing their cash to sit idle. Faster payment, even discounted, is cheaper than the cost of more expensive financing fees for the supplier.

Consider that proposition from the position of the buyer. If a supplier offered a "2/10, 30 net" discount (2 percent discount for payment rendered in 10 days or net balance due in 30 days), the buyer could shave 2 percent off the material cost for a tangible financial benefit. What kind of benefit? If the full payment was due in 30 days and the buyer paid it 20 days early, that

2 percent discount would effectively earn the buyer a 36 percent annualized return on capital for that advance payment.

Even in the high interest rate environment during the early 1980s, this strategy would have made perfect sense, if it could have effectively been managed. Taulia provides the platform now and to date has signed on more than 100 buying companies and facilitated more than $30 billion in early payments.[3] These larger companies pay an annual fee to use the platform and recruit their suppliers to use it.

And what are the benefits for the suppliers? They are affected just the opposite, with a real 2 percent loss of revenue, which equates to a 36 percent annualized cost of capital. That rate is surely the middle of the cost range they would pay for ABL or factoring. But the difference here is the Taulia platform.

With the working capital management tools, the company automatically tempers the discount offers with real time cash flow needs. The combination of its cash balances, A/R, and A/P calibrates invoice terms. Unlike expensive alternative financing, this management model does not require that every invoice be discounted. And by gradually lowering the discounts, it benefits from the stronger working capital position that requires fewer future discounts.

INVESTING RETIREMENT FUNDS IN SELF, INC.

What a difference a century can make. Think back to 1914, when the average workers were gainfully employed for about as long as they could physically perform the tasks at hand. They retired when forced to by old age or disability and generally only had children and possibly a house as resources with which to enable retirement. Few people had savings or retirement income, but most assumed that they would be cared for by able-bodied children and relatives who generally took care of their own.

In 1935, the Social Security Act began a federally sponsored system of taxing wages to fund retirement benefits that would provide security for aging Americans to avoid poverty when they were beyond their earning years. Workers contributed into a trust fund that would provide a defined benefit intended to support basic subsistence and hopefully augment other retirement resources for retirees.

This program has been expanded and enlarged in several ways since enacted and other anti-poverty measures have been added to provide a basic safety net for U.S. citizens.

Private pension plans were very slow to evolve in the United States. The Presbyterian Church created the Fund for Pious Uses in 1717 that helped its retired ministers. While literature is fairly scarce, after that the American Express Company created the first pension plan in the United States. But it was the Baltimore & Ohio Railroad that in 1884 established the first pension plan by a major employer,[4] after a searing 1877 strike exposed the company's worker abuses, leading to many reforms that spread across most railroads in the years following.

After World War II, an extremely competitive U.S labor market evolved as the nation quickly converted from wartime production to postwar consumption and created jobs for the 12 million returning service veterans. Due to holdover wage controls that had been imposed by the National War Labor Board, employers struggled to find workers as the economy heated up.

The result was that clever employers began offering health care insurance and worker pensions as a means to attract and retain workers during these years, and both lasted for most of the next 60 years. But pensions are expensive and represent an open-ended commitment that many businesses grew to find burdensome.

In the Revenue Act of 1978, the federal government adopted provision 401(k) that provided for tax relief on deferred income. But in 1980, a benefits consultant named Ted Benna[5] realized that such a provision would allow for a simple tax-advantaged retirement savings vehicle and the 401(k) plan was born.

401(k) Accounts

The rest is history—the 401(k) plan became the standard retirement planning strategy for employed savers and a benefit for smaller employers who could not afford full-blown pension plans. Legacy companies started gravitating to end pensions for new employees and instead began contributing to employee 401(k) plans instead.

The difference? Pensions required a defined benefit, meaning retirees were guaranteed a specified financial payout after meeting plan requirements. With 401(k), the investment management and basic savings level were determined by the employees. If they made bad investment choices or did not set sufficient resources aside, they would face the consequences, not the company.

Proceeds gathered through 401(k) plans and individual retirement accounts (IRAs), made popular in the early 1980s, were funneled into a vast range of mostly vanilla mutual funds, depending on the plan administrator. With the plans operated by various investment banks and insurance companies, participants were usually overwhelmed with a great number of investment options intended to meet the employee's risk tolerances.

It's noteworthy to point out that the law did not restrict deferred income to be invested in mutual funds or any other investment, for that matter. Over the years, many creative financial advisers began instructing their clients on how to move retirement savings into a broad range of different assets with the full acknowledgment of the IRS. So, instead of mainstream investments like stocks or bonds, many people began buying real estate (residential and commercial) and other more speculative investments like precious metals and even private company stocks.

Of course, there are rules that prohibit many investments or uses of tax-deferred retirement accounts, chiefly that they not be used to benefit the taxpayer ahead of their ultimate use and subsequent taxation. They must be managed by a third-party administrator or custodian so as to maintain independent supervision of the funds to ensure compliance with IRS regulations.

It was probably only a matter of time before another idea about how to invest retirement funds developed in the late 1990s, using a strategy called Rollover as Business Start-Up (ROBS). It's an interesting acronym that should serve as a warning to individuals considering using it.

As explained by *Forbes*,[6] the way a ROBS program works is as follows: The retirement account owner creates a "C" corporation, which immediately adopts a standard 401(k) plan. The plan allows participating employees to roll their existing 401(k) or IRA account funds into the new plan. The new corporation subsequently issues stock and establishes a qualified profit-sharing plan that allows employees to exchange assets in their 401(k) plan for that corporate stock.

In that way, the account owner has just funded a new business with tax-deferred retirement savings.

Development of this strategy early led many franchise brokers to enlist tax advisers as part of their expansion efforts, particularly when prospective franchise owners were downsized out of work in slow economic cycles. There were controversies swirling around some of these relationships with accusations of inappropriate referral fees exchanged and excessive charges over what a typical tax attorney or CPA might assess.

While there are hundreds of tax advisers who began assisting individuals to structure these arrangements, the two most prominent and nationally recognizable advisers and third-party custodians to facilitate ROBS transactions are BeneTrends and Guidant Financial.

ROBS transactions don't necessarily have to be business start-ups, but can also be a vehicle with which to recapitalize or expand an existing business. They can also be used in conjunction with other third-party financing such as SBA-guaranteed loans, merchant cash advances, or equipment leases.

There are positive and negative aspects to ROBS transactions. They do offer prospective business owners the opportunity to place their retirement savings in a potentially more lucrative investment that can yield much higher returns than might be earned elsewhere. Self-funding business start-ups may utilize them to avoid third-party financing and therefore lower costs and not expose other assets as collateral.

However, using ROBS exposes the individual's retirement savings— sometimes all of it—to a venture at its most vulnerable stage. Reportedly in the franchise sector, a fairly high percentage of start-ups using ROBS ultimately fail, often leading to individual bankruptcy.

Be assured that as with much of federal tax rules, there is much complexity around ROBS, which requires qualified advisers to review the plans for parties contemplating the use of this strategy. In 2009, the IRS conducted a study[7] to determine how this idea was being implemented by various service providers and whether they were acting in compliance with deferred income tax rules.

IRS rules require that the new corporation 401(k) plan be open to all company employees and that they be notified of it. The "C" corporation shares must be professionally valued at the time that they are being sold to the company's 401(k) plan. And the risk of getting it wrong? If the individuals do not correctly set up or administer their ROBS process, they may be subject to taxation on the deferred funds used.

NO STORE, NO HOURS, NO BANK, NO PROBLEM— VIRTUAL LENDERS FOR VIRTUAL MERCHANTS

It used to be that something as ridiculous as the question "Do we finance software?" was met with a blank stare, as the target of the inquiry quickly had to sort out exactly what software is. Those days lasted about a decade ("of course we don't finance software") before evaporating, at least to the point where everyone in the office had a clear definition of all of the components of computing.

But it was not even conceivable back in those days (1980s) that in the future—a mere 10 years later—the Internet would evolve and connect computers all over the world, and among other innovations, facilitate commerce. And going even beyond that bizarre concept, that there would be merchants who would operate exclusively online and generate sufficient business viability and confidence to have their own financial services in the virtual marketplace.

Within 10 years of startup, eBay was to become the platform for about $100 million[8] of merchandise sales each day, an amount equal to the sales volume of the world's leading retailer, Walmart. Over 60 million entrepreneurs set up online stores that bought and sold a limitless list of merchandise around the world, most of which was never seen or possessed by the seller.

In what is probably the most efficient marketplace created to date, eBay provides a medium through which merchants can source goods from an online marketplace of suppliers around the world. Through a vast cottage industry of craftsmen, artists, artisans, growers, and creators, literally millions of items are offered in tiny communities around the global village.

The eBay merchants can sell these goods to their followers or new customers before even committing to buy them from their sources. Essentially, the merchants are brokers for whatever merchandise they sell, connecting manufacturer/seller to the ultimate buyer/user without taking possession of the goods.

The resulting efficiencies in cutting out the step of merchants buying and stocking goods (along with one-half of the shipping cost) mean prices can be more competitive and merchant profits can still be better.

Of course there are many variations of this business. Online merchants often supply resellers who don't order single items but rather a full shipping container of goods. Some online merchants do take possession and add value to the goods, with more attractive packaging or other enhancements. There are many different ways people are performing commerce, but a common challenge did arise as more success was found and opportunities grew in the market realm: Some merchants needed third-party financing to fund expansion.

Are You Kidding Me?

Imagine a client walking into the bank, sitting face to face with a loan officer, and describing her business as follows:

> *My store is in the cloud, I've never met (or seen) my Asian or African suppliers and my customers are spread across all 50 states as well as cities in Europe and Canada. I have no inventory, no accounts receivable and, of course, no building or leased premises. I want to arrange a $10,000 line of credit.*

Laughable? Is that the reaction of most bankers to such a request? Where to start listing all the reasons to decline this request, from the lack of sufficient loan size and lack of collateral assets to the screwy business model (make that lack of understanding). But consider the next couple sentences, which add more information to support the request:

> *My sales last year were $750,000, with a gross profit averaging 60 percent of revenues and a net profit over $200,000. All of my sales are verifiable, since they were collected through either credit cards or PayPal and delivered by UPS.*

While that information will perk up any small business lender, a traditional banker would still find it hard to provide financing to facilitate this business. Who has ever advanced a line of credit to PayPal? How would a banker efficiently monitor sales, evaluate a borrowing base, or even advance funds in a timely manner to fund a 24/7 business?

Meet Kabbage.com, an online lender that started in 2011, designed to meet the credit needs of online merchants 24 hours per day. Applications are online only, credit decisions from $500 to $50,000 are made instantly, and if the merchant has a PayPal account, the funds are transferred immediately.

How can they advance credit without more information and analysis? Who says they don't have plenty of information that's analyzed? Potential clients for Kabbage are exclusively merchants operating online where there is an enviable amount of data. That information is already verified by an independent third party ahead of application and can be quantified and qualified instantly through a digital platform.

To be in that commercial channel, the merchant will likely be connected through one of the principal online marketplaces, such as eBay, Amazon, Yahoo, Etsy, or Shopify. She will probably have payment transfer capacity with both PayPal and another online merchant payment processor, like Authorize.net, Square, or Stripes.com, and of course will be shipping goods with either UPS or FedEx.

There is other data as well, from sources such as government, private companies, and social media sites, that can be aggregated and applied to Kabbage's decisioning model. While the company does not reveal its proprietary formula, one component was revealed in a media interview that offers some insight.

According to *American Banker*, Kabbage uses social media analytics in part to quantify a borrower's propensity to repay. "The underlying logic," says chairman and co-founder Marc Gorlin, "is that a small business actively promoting itself or receiving customer attention through these channels is a better risk candidate than a less socially savvy merchant even with a similar credit score and product line."[9]

Banks depend on business financial statements to assess business operating results, many of which are produced in-house by the business. Kabbage is able to access all these digital records that confirm order volumes (revenues), payments processed (receivables collected less recorded refund volume), and shipping confirmation. Analytics of the full circle of the applicant's operations are tied together to provide validation of customer creditworthiness in real time.

Recognize that this process is done without a loan officer, analyst, underwriter, or credit committee. There are no judgment calls, policy exceptions, "push" deals, or doughnuts at committee meetings. Their innovation is using what's considered mundane data to other funders, aggregated with payment information, to get a more accurate picture of the credit capacity and repayment ability of the applicant faster. They may argue that the resulting conclusions are also more accurate.

Online merchants are free to use the funds for whatever business purpose they see fit, like taking advantage of discounts offered for larger inventory purchases, marketing, hiring more employees, or other business enhancements.

Kabbage presently offers only one repayment term: six months. Their pricing is based on the credit risk they score in their proprietary model that costs borrowers a premium measured as a percentage of the advance, payable with ⅙ of the original advanced sum. For months one and two of the repayment period, the merchant's account is debited ⅙ of the advance plus their price ranging from 2 to 10 percent of the advance sum. Months three through six are charged less, totaling ⅙ of the advance plus 1 percent of the advanced sum. Marc Gorlin, the chairman of Kabbage, said:

> We've learned that if someone has added Facebook or Twitter data to their Kabbage account, they are 20 percent less likely to be delinquent.[10]

Kabbage claims the average cost is about 12 percent, but given that the company is not declaring that figure as an APR, it's not clear how they arrive at it. Needless to say, convenience, niche market, and willingness to fund online merchants places the company in a very competitive position to the companies to whom they are marketing.

And banks shouldn't get too comfortable assuming Kabbage is not a competitor. In early 2013, they started lending to bricks-and-mortar companies.[11] Using financial data exported from Intuit QuickBooks, Kabbage will underwrite loans, instantly analyzing company sales, payroll, and vendor results.

With more than 4 million QuickBooks users, that's a sizable database to begin marketing to before they even close their monthly books. The company's disciples claim that users are better credit risks, given their daily downloading of bank data and use of various financial management modules.

Likewise, Kabbage has also drawn some competition. PayPal, the virtual non-bank deposit holder/payment facilitator, announced in 2013 that it would enter the small business lending arena with a loan product intended to be different than those of the other non-bank business lenders: simple and cheap.[12]

Owned by eBay since 2002, PayPal enters the fray with some distinct advantages over many competitors, particularly Kabbage. First, having more than a decade of managing the deposits and payments for thousands of online businesses, PayPal controls the raw data that other lenders want to understand the cash flow and operating successes of the companies.

Kabbage in particular targets many online companies that are operated on eBay's platform. How competition goes with PayPal will be interesting to watch evolve, but the advantages PayPal has with ties to its parent company are unmistakable.

PayPal's product, dubbed "PayPal Working Capital," was rolled out in September 2013, described as a loan that charges a single, flat fee and nothing else. That is, no interest and no junk charges. Merchants can borrow up to 8 percent of the revenue deposited through PayPal, up to $20,000.

Loans are funded by Salt Lake City-based WebBank, thereby enabling these loans to be funded in all 50 states without PayPal having to become licensed in each of them. After setting the loan fee, PayPal debits borrower accounts for 10 to 30 percent of the merchant's daily receipts until the loan is repaid.

PayPal has not jumped in with both feet, at least not yet. Its original foray targeted only 90,000 merchants, a small fraction of its client base. Still, that's a sizable base of existing clients from which loans can be originated and serviced at a much lower cost than that of any competitor. As e-commerce continues to expand globally, expect that more lenders will enter this lucrative area to facilitate lending and other financial services.

TAKING AS MUCH TIME AS NEEDED TO REPAY

For business owners, which risk is worse: not being able to meet monthly payments due to inadequate revenues or paying a higher rate of interest on obligations? What if a funder were willing to provide the flexibility to the business to take as much time as needed to repay the funding? Really, no rush, take up to five years? Right.

But it's true. Revenue-based financing (RBF) is an old idea that has re-emerged to provide an alternative to bank financing (that generally requires a track record of profits and collateral) and venture capital (that requires critical mass). Long used for speculative venture businesses like filmmaking and oil drilling, RBF is now the model pursued by about a dozen finance companies.

Lighter Capital, an upstart lender founded in 2011, has emerged as the leader of this niche lending vehicle, which requires loan repayment be scheduled as a percentage of top line revenues. Thus, the faster the loan is repaid, the more expensive it will be.

RBF financing is best suited for companies that expect fast growth, have high profit margins (starting at 50 percent and higher), and generally do not have capital tied up in tangible assets that could be used as collateral for cheaper funding. Lighter Capital targets companies in the technology, software, and knowledge-based industries.

Applications for this funding originates online, which serves as a good screening gate to minimize semi-consulting and the expensive use of face time to educate anyone wondering exactly what you do. The company's website offers a very good explanation of what it does, who should apply, what terms are offered, and even the target pricing.

The company's initial request for information begins with a summary of the who, what, and where about the application and an explanation of the purpose of seeking the loan. Management information is requested from relevant LinkedIn profiles along with some cursory financial information about revenues, margins, and profits. Finally, the applicant's web and social media properties are also requested.

Lighter Capital looks carefully at the prospective business growth rate, the existing debt leverage, and the proposed use of funding to drive its credit decision. According to its website, Lighter Capital accepts applications ranging from $50,000 to $500,000, but it's generally limited to 10 to 30 percent of the applicant's annualized runrate. They do not cater to start-up or pre-revenue operations, but will consider companies with as little as $120,000 annual revenues, that have a current runrate pointing toward at least $200,000.

Loans are funding for an expected one to five year repayment period, scheduled with a percentage of revenues between 1 and 10 percent. Their target return for funding is a 25 percent internal rate of return, accounting for the time expected to amortize the financing.

RBF lenders generally do not require collateral, personal guarantees, or any financial covenants that are generally required by bank lenders. Similarly, they relieve borrowers of the management control, equity participation, and exit requirement that would be a part of any potential venture capital funding.

According to *Bloomberg Businessweek*,[13] there are about a dozen lenders that provide revenue-based financing available, which is often used in addition to other financing vehicles.

Notes

1. Debt instruments are legally defined as securities and regulated in the Trust Indenture Act of 1939. Supervised U.S. bank loans are exempted from this regulation.
2. Patrick Clark, "An Alternative to Expensive Alternative Financing," *Bloomberg Businessweek*, May 29, 2013, www.businessweek.com/printer/articles/120286-an-alternative-to-expensive-alternative-financing.
3. Ibid.

4. Elizabeth Fee, *The Baltimore Book* (Temple University Press, 1993), 14.

5. Alyssa Fetini, "A Brief History of the 401(k)," *Time*, October 16, 2008, http://content.time.com/time/magazine/article/0,9171,1851124,00.html.

6. Richard C. Morais, "The IRA Jobs Machine," *Forbes.com*, April 8, 2009, www.forbes.com/2009/04/08/ira-robs-startup-personal-finance-retirement-job-machine.html.

7. Internal Revenue Service, "Employee Plans Compliance Unit (EPCU)—Completed Projects—Project with Summary Reports—Rollovers as Business Start-Ups (ROBS)," www.irs.gov/Retirement-Plans/Employee-Plans-Compliance-Unit%28EPCU%29---Completed-Projects--Project-with-Summary-Report%E2%80%93-Rollovers-as-Business-Start-Ups-%28ROBS%29 (accessed December 15, 2013).

8. Chris Anderson, *The Long Tail: Why the Future of Business Is Selling Less of More* (New York: Hyperion, 2008), 201.

9. Glen Fest, "Kabbage's Fresh Idea for Small Business Finance," *American Banker*, June 1, 2013, www.americanbanker.com/magazine/123_6/kabbage-fresh-idea-for-small-business-finance-1059175-1.html?zkPrintable=true.

10. Ibid.

11. Patrick Clark, "Kabbage Expands Its Cash Advances to Bricks-and-Mortars," *Bloomberg Businessweek*, May 14, 2013, www.businessweek.com/articles/2013-05-14/kabbage-expands-its-cash-advances-to-brick-and-mortars.

12. Patrick Clark, "PayPal Breaks Into Small Business Lending," *Bloomberg Businessweek*, September 24, 2013, www.businessweek.com/printer/articles/154794-paypal-breaks-into-small-business-lending.

13. Verne Kopytoff, "Revenue-Based Financing: The Better You Do, the Quicker You Pay," *Bloomberg Businessweek*, February 5, 2013, www.businessweek.com/printer/articles/95222-revenue-based-financing-the-better-you-do-the-quicker-you-pay.

CHAPTER 10

Capital Guides—Online Resources to Find, Coach, and Assist Borrowers and Lenders

It was inevitable that financial activity would move into the digital sphere, since the Internet offers so many options to scale this business in a variety of ways. Whether or not transactions actually get negotiated online, it makes sense to start matchmaking or processing online. In fact, one of the earliest success stories of financial innovation online was mortgage broker LendingTree.com, which provided users with a portal to obtain a mortgage loan from the convenience of their homes.

Gathering residential mortgage applications and sorting the various offers from competing lenders was a natural place to start brokering online. Why? Because mortgage loans are heavily regulated and standardized. They all have the same application form, disclosure requirements, and a limited range of options. All mortgage lenders ask for almost the exact same information and documentation from applicants in this very homogeneous market.

But business loans are all over the map and funding may be provided by an alternative financing vehicle other than a loan. Business funding applications may require many different sets of information based on the lender's credit culture, transaction size, funding purpose, business location, and so on.

But designing a platform with so many more moving parts required a clear idea of how to monetize whatever would come out on the other side. Given the range of activities performed and the kinds of lending that need connecting, online business loan brokerage is a much more complicated proposition than the earlier mortgage brokerage sites.

And to their credit, there are some very impressive sites available that perform a variety of functions to assist business owners and lenders to source transactions and "meet-up" online with varying degrees of prequalification.

Recognize that these sites serve both borrowers and lenders. For borrowers, it's a place for education, pitch refinement, and a broader search engine for capital. For lenders, it's a screening process to narrow the line to those most qualified by parameters they choose.

These resources are tools at the disposal of all parties to facilitate the connection of investment to user. Business owners have demonstrably shown that they are more open to the idea of connecting in cyberspace. But lenders are coming around—with both deal shopping and internal problem solutions, as is demonstrated by one such online resource.

LOAN BROKERS

The exact origination of loan brokers is a mysterious chicken and egg riddle, but it seems that as long as there has been money lending, there have been independent parties ready to introduce those in need to those with access to resources. And based on the sheer number of these third-party matchmakers across nearly every financing sector, they must be necessary.

What do they do? While there are varying levels of services offered by persons with an enormous range of qualifications (and sometimes an astonishing deficit of qualifications), brokers essentially serve as a conduit to business capital. These parties might be engaged to do anything ranging from serving as a fix-it specialist to being a super sales agent for the business in dire need.

Some business owners need a broker who can organize their application information in a manner that's acceptable for lender consideration. That means the brokers look at everything without bias and try to get the transaction applications completed with all necessary information to ensure they will be reviewed in the best possible light. They are effectively the first sounding board for a deal and work to repair any weaknesses as an advocate for the client.

Sometimes being an advocate means telling owners that they cannot qualify for what they want and advising them about needed improvements to their businesses to qualify later.

But others brokers are simply cheerleaders who throw every scrap of paper they can find at the lender (sans reading them) and then start the hard court press to get the deal heard. They will say anything or do anything to win loan approval.

Obviously there is much ground in between these two extremes and that is where most loan brokers operate. Generally, these people prescribe a set of information that will be needed by the target lender(s), sort through it to ensure everything's in order, and personally present it to the lender. Later the broker arranges a meeting between the parties and works as an aide-de-camp to facilitate progress toward loan approval and closing.

Brokers might be paid by the business owner, or in some lending sectors they are paid by the lender. And it's no secret that many try to be paid by both, which appears to create a conflict of interest to most observers.

Why do these brokers exist? That question can be answered in a number of ways. Some business owners turn to brokers because they have struck out with their own efforts to find capital and in frustration, turn to someone else professing to have all the contacts and know-how. Others engage the intermediary up front because they don't have the time or inclination to negotiate for funding on their own.

It's probably fair to say that finance intimidates many people and they are comfortable gambling on the cost of getting a more experienced person to serve as a short-term representative in their search. And very often this arrangement works out as intended.

It's also fair to say that there are a variety of ways brokers are received by the lending community. Some banks flat out will not consider a transaction walked in by anyone other than the live applicant, while others advertise the referral fees they offer to virtually anyone connecting them to an approval deal.

Is anything wrong with loan brokers? Not really. There are some smart, well-rounded businesspeople that work in this area, the best of whom have a familiarity with a broad range of financing solutions. They advise their clients on the best of these solutions dependent on the short-term/long-term goals of the business. They have strong ethics and assume a fiduciary posture of keeping the client's interest ahead of their own.

And then there are brokers who perform like one-trick ponies. Their clients are steered into financing arrangements and toward lenders that maximize the broker's income, regardless of what's best for the business. They have no loyalty to lenders, either, and have been known to fabricate information in order to get a loan approved. They will move the client to another lender at the drop of a hat for a better fee offer.

Every business has rogue operators who cut across the boundaries in a heated rush to serve their own interest at the expense of all others. They make the rest of the business look bad and damage the reputation of most others who do business responsibly and ethically. So what is one to do?

Part of the solution would be to certify loan brokers, which would provide something attuned to self-policing. With more peer pressure and consumer awareness, the bad apples in this business would have an increasingly difficult time operating on the rough edges.

Link Farms

The pioneers among online loan brokers were simply link farms. These sites were thrown up quickly, some with—and some without—a modest sorting capability for determining the funding purpose of the user and thereby narrowing their search. The user would then be directed to a list of links to lender contacts.

Whether these were effective or not, the business model was for the site operator to be paid a modest fee by the lender for either each party that clicked through to their site or a higher fee if that click resulted in a funded loan. The key for the site operator was finding a domain name that was similar to what the user's search words might be in order to capture plenty of traffic. Think "BusinessLoans.com" or something similar.

For sites without such obvious names, operators had to work with a search engine optimization (SEO) strategy in order to get attention for searches that otherwise would call up only sites with obvious domain names. Although those strategies have largely been rendered useless by Google, there were formerly plenty of ways to game search engines in order to appear higher in user search results.

It was through these kinds of efforts that various sites began adding explanatory content designed to help educate visitors about the nature of funding available. Some sites offer amortization calculators, application tips, and other information to bring value to visitors and impress the search engines.

Value-Added Resources

It was only a matter of time, as website platforms continued to innovate, that more and better online resources would evolve to provide services to help small business owners connect to capital resources. Three distinct leaders have emerged in this space, each with a decidedly different value proposition to bring application sorting, deal channeling, and strategic guidance to small business owners in search of funding.

These features can be invaluable to inexperienced business owners who don't know how to determine who is the most appropriate funding provider for their particular projects. Worse, these business owners often begin these searches not being able to distinguish what kind of lender or lending facility they really need.

Depending on the service provider, these resources can do everything from gathering primary application data that is screened against lender standards to actually coaching business owners through preparation of a business plan and application package. For the average business owner, the very professional service provider can accelerate the capital search for a modest expense.

As a more detailed explanation of what they do, there are three reference titles used to describe and distinguish three ways that innovators are bringing value to business owners. These three distinct approaches are described as Enhanced Self-Direction, Matchmaker, and Application Advisor.

To many users, these three types of companies will each look very similar on the surface with their primary service aiming to connect business owners to funding sources. But it's the added value they deliver and other attributes they offer that distinguish them individually.

Enhanced Self-Direction   Biz2Credit.com is an online broker that provides a superior dashboard to help the user get on the correct path to finding credit. A screen full of icons is used to describe various business loan types, such as start-up loans, franchise loans, business loans for women, and so forth. The fact that many of these clicks are redirected to the same next page is beside the point—this sorting gives the business owners confidence that they are starting at the correct trailhead.

Alternatively, business owners can choose to begin their search on the same page by indicating their industry, which may be chosen from a drop-down list of about a dozen specialty sectors. It's probable that these sectors—like doctors, restaurants, CPAs, and liquor stores, to name a few— are being culled for specific client searches by sponsoring lenders.

Users are then directed to a page that requests four primary application information statistics:

1. Amount of loan request
2. Number of years in business
3. Annual revenues
4. Estimated credit score

With this data, the site sorts lender suggestions according to desirable parameters identified by listed lenders.

The site is noteworthy for plenty of resources for borrower assistance, such as business plan development and a BizAnalyzer. Business plans are offered in three levels, depending on the user's need, ranging from what's needed for a micro loan (price to be requested), to business loans up to $1 million (priced at $1,100), and to loans up to $5 million for business acquisitions (priced at $1,875).

Buying one of these plan packages comes with up to a free month of payroll processing and a free credit report, depending on the plan purchased.

Need to incorporate? One click plus $299 and filing fees can take care of it on the site.

The BizAnalyzer report provides a general opinion about some of the applicant statistics in terms of how most lenders will react, along with a convenient connection to where the business owner can acquire even more detailed (credible?) information for a fee. The report contains direct links to such resources from companies including Equifax, Symantec, Dun & Bradstreet, and The Company Corporation.

The company's business model is apparently to be paid referral fees on all these adjunct services and commission or fees at some level from the 3,500 lenders they claim to be representing and from commissions generated from the referrals to these third-party sales of information.

There are other knowledge resources available on the site as well, such as detailed information about different lending types, a glossary, state business information, and a fairly deep blog library indexed according to a fairly long topic list. Except for the blogs, these resources are rather shallow and will have varying value to users but perhaps do offer sufficient content to point out the direction where user questions need to lead.

Matchmaker   Another online broker, Lendio.com, has a simpler website that is focused squarely on matching the user directly with a choice of lenders, all of whom are interested in the exact type of loan that's been described. In many respects, they are like a business loan version of Lending Tree.

Borrowers are asked to qualify themselves with the same initial application statistics, and as they do the site identifies the count of lenders that may be interested along with a potential range of interest cost. With this information, the site sorts the borrowers' information and directs them to a custom list of lenders who are interested in providing the financing being sought. Contact information is served directly to the user to choose one or more to pursue directly.

This site uses more advanced technology to advance the business owner more accurately to the most likely financing solution available, according to the information disclosed. The stated goal is to deliver at least four loan offers to every business owner. The site's business model is integrated with various ways to be paid, depending on how aggressively the lenders want to search for clients and how they choose to pay.

Some lenders pay up front to be seen prominently by more applicants and recommended more frequently. Some pay higher fees as a percentage on the back end of funded deals. Others pay monthly subscription fees and some pay a little of all three, depending on the kinds of transactions that may be sorted to them.

There are no fees charged to the business owners. This site has plenty of resources behind it as well, including more detailed descriptions of the various loan products and significant financing information about some states. But the main focus is a quicker path to getting business owner's profile in the platform and compared to their lender database for purposes of matchmaking.

Application Advisor Finally, the third major online broker offers a different approach. Boefly.com, the company in this category, which was founded by former small business lenders, provides a unique platform designed to draw in more participants around the same goal, connecting business owners with capital. Perhaps their advantage is having started from a position of deeper understanding of the small business loan market than their competitors.

This company offers business owners free access to post application information that is screened and will be matched to its network of lenders, like the other broker sites. But what's different is a more robust platform of services to advise these users about the fundability of their proposals, and three options to enhance their applications with online and live tools.

The "basic" option ($249) offers access to an online application template that assembles the self-loaded information into a readable format that can be transferred digitally to appropriate lenders. An enhanced "'premium" version ($699) comes with live telephone support and a one-on-one assessment of the application with advice offered on how to increase the odds of getting funding.

Finally, most impressive is the "full service" ($1,499), where the company's team will produce an application package, complete with financial analysis and business plan, on behalf of the borrower for a fixed fee good for one year. This plan also promises more prominent contact with matched lenders.

Not only does this company offer a place for business owners to search for financing, it facilitates other brokers to access the site as a portal to find lenders from its stated 3,600 lender network. These brokers have access to the online tools to prepare borrower packages and a variety of other backroom technology to support their business.

Broker services are offered on a monthly subscription basis with a small charge added for each deal posted. Brokers get in line with borrowers to find lender matches when they use the gold service level ($99/month + $25/deal). When they use the platinum service option ($149/month + $10/deal), they get live support from Boefly's staff to provide feedback on deals and telephone support to interface with lenders concerning deal status.

Lenders also get access to the marketplace Boefly facilitates by being listed with a monthly subscription. There is a free lender option that plugs lenders into the platform with a profile of borrower preferences, but they are limited to three deal referrals each month. The premium lender option ($99/month) offers lenders a profile page on the site with 48-hour advance access to deals before free option lenders and the ability to refer borrowers to other lenders.

Finally, the elite lender option ($250/month) offers the features of the other two plans, plus these lenders can access Boefly's market for loan sales, as either a buyer or seller.

And perhaps these latter features for the elite lenders are where the real insight of company founders can be best demonstrated. Boefly extends its marketplace even further by providing a platform for investors interested in buying loans. Investors can subscribe for $250/month and get access to all the lenders in Boefly's network.

Readers with experience in the government-guaranteed lender sector will be familiar with a robust market for loan sales that exists for the portion of loans guaranteed by the U.S. Small Business Administration (SBA) and U.S. Department of Agriculture (USDA) loan programs. There are plenty of other loans and portfolios sold, but the Boefly platform offers a new option—arranging loan sales directly between buyer and seller without facilitation by a securities broker.

OTHER ONLINE RESOURCES

Before there were online loan brokers there was FTrans.com, a bank service provider that was attempting to reintroduce asset-based lending into community banks. With the backing of an experienced financial services software guru and a major regional bank, they built a digital backroom lending management platform that would help smaller banks overcome the expertise/expense barriers to providing working capital financing to smaller companies.

There was a secondary benefit in that banks making small lines of credit secured with only a blanket lien on unmonitored A/R or inventory could begin keeping a better eye on those assets so as to provide better risk management. By connecting the service platform to company accounting software, lenders could keep closer tabs on what was happening at the borrower's operation in real time.

Maybe it was the Great Recession or maybe a lack of vision, but bankers did not flock to this product, which from all indications provides a cost-effective alternative to the grinding labor needed to monitor borrowing bases and business accounts. The services are still offered and are used by 80 banks around the United States. As community banks continue to search for competitive advantages for survival, this platform may be a more promising alternative in the years ahead.

In the meantime, FTrans is expanding its business to provide direct financing to borrowers, who are often referred to them by community banks.

■ ■ ■

Like pondering who answered all the world's questions before Google, where were all these credit applications going before there were online loan brokers? One of these sites claims to receive about $500 million of business loan applications monthly, while another claims to have matched borrowers to more than $1 billion in financing. Both are very impressive figures for a business that hasn't existed for more than five years.

One of these sites claims that 85 percent of all application profiles get matched to at least one lending source, while 60 to 70 percent are approved for financing. That figure would seem to be very successful based on the approval rates of most lenders.

But for all these sites, the same issue provides challenges: customer acquisition. Remember, they are competing to find the very same clients that the lenders they are representing are searching for directly. And the search criteria with which lenders represent as their standards to sort client applications—such as number of years in business, minimum loan size, and FICO scores—can change at any time, altering results overnight.

It's even possible to ponder that the lenders can hold these sites to different and higher standards than they might accept directly, so as to pass the costs back to the clients for payments required on transactions acquired through online loan brokers.

CHAPTER 11

What Innovation Means for Bank Lending

For readers making it this far without calling a headhunter, be rewarded with confidence that the banking business is going to be just fine. Even small business lenders and community banks will weather these changes and likely emerge with some interesting competitive advantages as the small business financing marketplace continues to evolve.

There are major changes still ahead and competition will likely be even more fierce for business, but those bankers/lenders willing to embrace change and leverage their franchise value will do well. Embracing change, though, may mean adapting to change more often than leading it. Much innovation in lending and other banking operations will be derived from non-bank companies' decidedly lower levels of regulation. The author of an April 2013 article, "The Future of Banking—and Why it Won't Be Determined by Banks," said the following:

> The day-to-day of banking is changing worldwide, and banks are not the ones driving the innovation. For instance, by some measures, Starbucks is among the 200 largest banks by deposits in the US, having $3 billion on their in-store card in 2012. Both Google and Amazon are also talking about providing finance to users of their marketplaces. At the other end of the economic spectrum, 31 per cent of Kenyan GDP now flows through M-Pesa, which is so simple it can be operated on a very modest Nokia phone and has no physical bank branch presence.[1]

Many questions remain regarding how far U.S. bank consolidation will go during the next few years, whether or when economic growth will accelerate to previous expectations, and the role of globalization and innovation ahead in changing the banking industry.

COMPETITION ERODES BANKS' SHARE OF SMALL BUSINESS LOANS (AGAIN)

The pie is shrinking for commercial banks that have been losing market share of small business loans for most of the past 40 years. It probably began when they chose to begin shedding many business lines in favor of more lucrative lending and to address the problem of scaling some business lines in the face of institutional growth.

Deregulation opened the door to many new competitors in the 1980s and 1990s who continued to peel away more product volume. Later, profitable securitization made it much more attractive for many banks to originate, bundle, and sell loans than be stuck dealing with a portfolio of Mom and Pop shops.

And now innovation has continued or perhaps hastened the next generation of market share erosion for the banking sector. Innovation is a broad word that encompasses many paths to the same destination:

- New ways to use old systems, like credit card processors redirecting merchant proceeds to bypass banks, which produced merchant cash advance companies providing funding to merchants based on the expectation of future revenues.
- Technology platforms that offer new ways for lenders to find borrowers, borrowers to apply for credit, and lenders to make credit decisions, as well as fund loans without meeting the borrower.
- Revisions of old ideas of how to transfer capital from communities to fund businesses in the form of gifts, buy-it-I'll build-it innovators, peer-to-peer loans, and equity sales.
- Connecting investors directly to third-party receivables that can be purchased from small businesses at a discount.
- Buying third party receivables without recourse for a fixed fee using a merchant processing model.
- Connecting businesses and suppliers through technology to manage working capital with more strategic use of invoice discounting.
- Exploiting tax laws to produce a self-funding option for businesses with their own retirement savings to support their enterprises.
- Capital funding for companies that only exist in the cyberspace of other technologies.
- Funding that schedules repayment as a percentage of future revenues with an open-ended repayment term.

There are surely more innovations to come in the months and years ahead.

When does the erosion end? Will banks as small business lenders become just a fond memory of the baby boomer-era entrepreneurs like passbook savings accounts and safe deposit boxes? Hardly.

If accurate or even conservative, the estimated $100 billion that this emerging sector has peeled away in small business financing is still a small fraction of the bank business lending marketplace. And much of that would have never been provided by bank lenders anyway. Banks are firmly limited in capacity to finance small businesses for a fundamental reason—cost of capital.

FDIC-insured deposits provide the banking sector with access to a mammoth percentage of the nation's money supply. The innovative funders will spend the next five to seven years sorting out market leaders and profitability just to get access to that same funding indirectly from the banks as borrowers. Lender finance will be sorely needed to replace the more expensive equity funding and loan sales that make profitability so elusive in this channel today.

In fact, the innovative lenders will probably grow the banking sector's penetration into small business lending, albeit indirectly, through growth in lender financing and the direct investment by many banks into the leading innovative funders and lenders. These funds will not appear in the bank's quarterly call report as small business loans.

Many of the nation's largest banks are already there. Sources contributing background information for this book identified Bank of America, BB&T, Fifth Third Bank, JPMorgan Chase, RBC Citizens Bank, Wells Fargo, and U.S. Bank as among the largest banks funding innovative capital providers. Whether by lender finance, securitized loan purchases, or equity capital, some major funding is already fueling the growth of the innovative channel.

How much? One MCA funder described selling portions of just one $300 million lender finance facility in $10 to $50 million shares. That speaks volumes about product interest, loan quality, and the diversity of banks queuing up for this market.

Aside from larger banks, which will benefit from this emerging innovative sector, the funding erosion does represent a challenge for smaller community banks. While a majority of these loans funded by innovative lenders are generally untouchable loans for most banks, there are plenty of exceptions. Those exceptions are expensive, lost opportunities that community banks sorely need to provide earning assets and fee income.

And given how much closer these bankers are to their clients, how much more quickly they can respond to opportunities, and how most business owners still seem to launch their funding searches with their own local banks, maybe it's time community bankers started paying closer attention to this innovative sector.

WHAT BANKS CAN FUND (BUT WON'T) VERSUS WHAT BANKS CANNOT FUND (BUT WILL)

Small businesses are very popular among policy makers. No one seems able to name a Dunkin Donuts owner or dry cleaner operator who's been a guest in the Lincoln bedroom in the White House, but most presidential candidates go out of their way to extol the importance of entrepreneurship and small business ownership. After election, though, all that adulation fades quickly.

Perhaps it's the same with banks. While small business loans are specifically highlighted in the quarterly call report and most banks jockey for relationships with small business owners, lending to them is a love/hate relationship. It's sort of like bank branches—one year you can't get enough of them and the next year you want to dump as many as you can.

Part of the schism around small business lending market share involves banks choosing to avoid making loans in this sector while aggressively marketing for the transaction accounts, money management business, and other financial services. Such decisions around lending are usually grounded in strategic, economic, or risk-management reasoning that makes perfect sense.

For very large banks, small business loans are inefficient to originate and manage. Being structured differently than small community banks, larger banking companies seem awkward in the kinds of business development efforts it takes to meet business owners. Chairing the United Way campaign and having the most television ads are no match for smaller, more nimble competitors who attend local real estate board meetings, drop in on business openings, and foster relationships with referral sources that last for years.

Past origination, larger banks probably find it more challenging to underwrite loans, since their organization and its incumbent credit authority are more centralized. Delegating loan authority down far enough to be effectively competitive is hard for loans that might average only $600,000. Hence, it's easier to not make loans in that territory and use those resources in middle market lending, CRE, and other business lines.

By choosing to avoid small business loans, though, these lenders also take a pass on a good, lucrative market that often fronts a rich banking relationship with many needs. Deposits and other services follow the loans. Not doing what everyone expects that they naturally would do—that is, to hold a commanding lead in small business banking—is the irony that puzzles many prospective customers and policy makers.

The answer is simple—small business loans funded by live bank officers sitting in a bank branch are very expensive to scale and generally fall outside the largest banks' credit culture.

But conversely, witness that many of these same megabanks are deeply vested in business that's almost universally frowned upon. Debates have raged around the country over the past 10 years over the emergence of payday lending. This business involves a non-bank funding company that advances funds—usually measured in hundreds—to consumers against a future paycheck.

The advances are designed to be outstanding for days, and the fees assessed are fixed sums, just like the models described for merchant cash advance companies. Predictably, given the short duration of the advances, these fees cost the consumers 100 percent to 1,000 percent-plus if measured as an APR.

This funding is not regulated because they're not loans, and predictably, several state legislatures have entered the fray to either ban this activity or embrace it. Consumer advocates rail about the exorbitant costs and resulting credit addiction, while these companies are making substantial profits. While there are large, franchised payday lending companies, there are also thousands of locally owned funders, totaling more than 22,000 offices nationally.

According to a leading advocate against this business, the Center for Responsible Lending,[2] the statistics around it are ugly:

- The typical two-week payday loan has an annual interest rate ranging from 391 to 521 percent.
- Churning existing borrowers' loans every two weeks accounts for three-fourths of all payday loan volume.
- Repeated payday loans result in $3.5 billion in fees each year.
- Loans to non-repeat borrowers account for just 2 percent of the payday loan volume.
- The average payday borrower has nine transactions per year.
- Ninety percent of the payday lending business is generated by borrowers with five or more loans per year, and over 60 percent of business is generated by borrowers with 12 or more loans per year.

Who funds a large percentage of this sector? Commercial banks. Just like the MCA sector, banks are funding large chunks of loan pools, credit lines, and securitized loans for these funders who draw the ire of many policy makers and consumer protection advocates.

And similarly, merchant cash advance, title advance, pawnshops, private auto lenders, and hard money lenders also represent other indirect ways in which very expensive funding gets distributed from banks that wouldn't dare make the loans directly.

Why don't banks fund these kinds of loans directly? Because banks are regulated and the charges for payday and MCA funding is nearly always in the usurious range. Banks also would still face the scale problem they have with more desirable small business loans, which means it's cheaper to let another company do the heavy lifting of sorting through all the deal prospects to find what's acceptable.

Finally, banks are sensitive to the reputation risks that would accompany having their branches filled with low-income consumers and high-risk business owners willing to pay a king's ransom for credit.

They fund these loans indirectly, even though they would absolutely refuse to fund them directly to the recipient. Indirect lending allows these banks to avoid the cost (expense and reputation) of originating these kinds of loans while earning higher interest rates through lender finance lines of credit—all with another financially capable guarantor ensuring portfolio performance.

THE BEST DEFENSE IS STILL A GOOD OFFENSE

Consider the $100 billion of capital distributed by the innovative funding sector as a wake-up call. By producing a plethora of new ideas, technologies, and channels to get funding into the hands of small business owners long shut out of anything much more than credit cards, this expansion is much more than a simple democratization of money. It's economic stimulus, where the banking industry has been sidestepped by private investors—some of whom invest millions and many others chipping in $25, $50, or $100.

But recognize that while few banks have noticed, much less felt, the effects of that redirected funding, to date this sector has only been picking the low-hanging fruit. Much more volume will be mined by relieving small companies directly of the onerous burdens of carrying aging, unpaid invoices to the doorstep of the local bank for businesses they don't expect to lose.

If innovative lenders can profitably fund loans averaging in the mid-$30k range to more than 300 NAICS classifications, with loan losses/charge-offs in line with those of regulated commercial banks, it's obviously easier for them to scale up to loans valued by bankers than for bankers to reach down for smaller deals. And if one of these innovative lenders gets a bank charter or merges with a small business lending company (SBLC) licensed by the SBA, this is in the government guaranteed lending market, where it poses a much greater threat to community banks.

Instead of ignoring the innovative sector, banks—particularly smaller banks—should look at online loan sites as a marketplace to buy performing assets. Not unlike other securities, these purchases would offer short-term earnings with better yields than can be earned with the average net income margin (NIM) produced by most bank lending.

Think of the possibilities. No need to pay for a round of golf or extra processing staff, and someone else pays for the credit report.

Sure, the bank would have to do some due diligence on the lender. It would have to develop credit guidelines, lending authorities, documentation protocols, and oversight, all of which most surviving banks are pretty adept at already managing. There's also the question about how this would fit into their CRA mandates, but certainly targeting specific ZIP codes would provide automated analytics to monitor the results.

Think about how such a proposition to buy loans from the innovative lending/funding marketplace might work:

- Bank credit management decides what the bank's ideal portfolio should look like in terms of credit risk, loan size, industry penetration/concentration, geographic location, and exposure.
- The bank vets the most appealing participants in the innovative space with direct management interviews and documentation review. Assurances will be needed for information security, underwriting standards, portfolio performance, pricing, fraud detection, and platform access. Independent sources would need to be researched to understand reputational risks, legal issues, or other barriers.
- An internal policy has to be formulated describing exact risk limitations and a desirable range of loans including client profiles, industry, location, loan size, pricing, and a credit rating system.
- Approval authority and decision procedures have to be worked out to authorize the appropriate person to make decisions in real time. Exposure limits on a daily, weekly, and monthly basis would need to be settled. Documentation and recording processes have to be determined so there is sufficient accounting for all purchases/advances.
- Instead of making a lunch appointment, authorized lenders review loan pools, individual transactions, or even small company invoices to buy in real time. The bank can open or close the spigot at a moment's notice, meaning that its balance sheet management gets easier with a readily available supply of loans they can ramp up or down in short order.

The upside of this strategy is fairly attractive, with lower costs, faster product development, and better funding returns. The bank could test it ad nauseam, but it is valuable to get accurate historical data from the originator that will spell out plenty of analytics. And depending on the size of the bank, it's likely that many of these kinds of loan purchases—all smaller loans—would not even show up on a regulator's radar.

Some bankers may scoff at the notion of relying on a different underwriting schematic, investing in higher priced debt, and documenting the application records in a digital folder rather than an upright filing cabinet. And there are those muttering about their unwillingness to consider a business loan without understanding the company's business plan.

Business plans? Please, let's end this charade now: A majority of bankers rarely read business plans. Yes, it's a checklist item and the executive summary almost always gets a quick read. But the truth is that most business owners don't write very well and most bankers never reach the midpoint of a well-constructed business plan anyway.

BANKS STILL HAVE THE MOST CUSTOMERS AND CHEAPEST BUCKS IN TOWN

Innovative lenders/funders, for all intents and purposes, are unregulated banks. That fact has some upsides and downsides. No, they don't have as many regulators or regulations; yes, by operating in the cloud their costs are significantly lower; and yes, their technology pivots from a 200-year-old legacy of paperwork they don't have to touch or file.

But innovative lenders/funders are vulnerable to the two most valuable assets that the commercial banking sector holds firmly: cheap funding and legions of indoctrinated, trained customers. While the latter will continue to evaporate, the former is unlikely to change in our lifetime.

While much of the world is rapidly going digital on laptops, tablets, and mobile devices, many people over 30 years old—those who are beginning to aggregate assets and start businesses—still do not associate those connections with business lending. Recall the Pepperdine Survey, which illustrated that more than two-thirds of business owners headed to banks first to get credit even though a majority expected that it would be difficult to be approved.

Time and more technology adaptation will change that paradigm, but for now, many more people line up in banks for credit than are cruising websites. Most business lenders have experienced more than a few meetings with business owners who had no idea of where to turn for capital other than to a bank, despite that they may be entirely unfundable there and would have to be rerouted to another source.

Entrepreneurs as a group are generally more concerned about doing the business they are in. An overwhelming majority will get fewer than five loans in the life of their business, so they don't develop much expertise navigating through the process. But what they do understand is that the search for capital begins in a bank.

Even if a majority of the business borrowing public lines up at their computers for credit, there is still the issue of funding. Non-bank lenders/

funders alike will need to acquire funding to meet the demand they create, and without depositors, will have to either sell shares, sell loans, or get bank credit. Clearly the latter option is the most economical, although they'll pay a premium.

Josh Koplewicz, founder of Thayer Street Partners, said:

> *There's been an explosion of new companies using the internet to originate loans. The barriers to entry are low. There are people setting up shop with a couple hundred thousand dollars. But aside from a few big names like Lending Club, it may be difficult to create enterprise value without some edge in access to borrowers.*[3]

And even at this date, profits have been elusive for most of the innovative companies for that very reason—their expensive funding costs or the sacrifices made to revenues by necessary loan sales. Without a solid profit level, they will find it difficult to transition into the lender finance department at a bank, meaning they will be forking over a disproportionate share of income to buy funding. It will be a difficult conundrum to beat: no profits due to high funding costs, no cheaper bank funding due to no profits.

Another interesting problem emerging in the sector is that despite the seemingly boundless funding capacity of these innovative funding companies, all of them seem to be scrambling for customers. Sourcing loans is already a problem for many of them for a variety of reasons, including the general lack of confidence in most business owners about expanding at this time.

New lenders are still coming online each month, meaning that the pie gets a little smaller as more participants vie for a share of the market that does not seem to be growing as fast. Even LendingClub.com has more investors seeking borrowers than they are able to match.

Few business owners get the benefit of a bidding war now, but what new market entrants use cost as their selling point? There are already a few attempting to carve out pricing as their competitive advantage.

If the banking industry compared those conditions to the fact that, according to the Pepperdine Survey, banks are turning away as much as 73 percent of their loan applicants, there's an obvious solution. It's easy to connect the dots to where these banks could refer some of those declined applications—to an innovative lender/funder—and turn them into earning assets instead of nasty statistics.

Even better, since most innovative lenders/funders use checking account data to form loan decisions, remember who's holding all that data. (Hint—that would be the banking industry.) It would be very simple for a bank to digitally measure the business checking account activity of their client base by NAICS code and auction the resulting business leads to innovative lenders/funders.

WHAT'S NEXT? CHARACTER REDUX, RISE OF ALTERNATIVE PAYMENTS, AND?

Has anyone noticed the subtle shift in websites over the past 10 years? Circa 2006, conventional wisdom was that sites have an appealing homepage to which all traffic should be directed. Information there was to be restricted to "above the fold," so to speak, which meant users would not have to scroll down to find any content. The homepage would include plenty of neatly arranged buttons and links to sort and direct visitors to access to other information they wanted to see.

By 2009, this arrangement was passé, particularly with those sites with dozens or hundreds of pages, whose homepages looked like a foreign language newspaper. The new movement was send visitors directly to the intended page of their interest, allowing them to skip the homepage and its laborious extra clicks. Former secondary pages all became as fancy as the homepage, with users able to navigate deeper, faster.

With the advent of tablets, websites are changing again to a rolling homepage that scrolls downward, seemingly for miles, and all the other site features can be navigated to other site pages from two or three different link tabs found at the top, bottom, and along the main content. Scrolling is finally cool because that's how tablet users view sites and, of course, tablets will be replacing laptops any day.

With a career in banking, where not much of anything really changes often, it's fascinating to see changes in technology that are happening in real time and learning about more big ideas under construction. Where will it end? Who says it will end? Here are a couple ideas and trends to keep an eye on that will continue to weigh in on the business lending marketplace ahead.

Measuring Character

Lenders have struggled for years to find an accurate measurement for a prospective borrower's character, one of the hallowed five Cs of credit. Measuring a person's prior credit history through a credit report or FICO scores was an adequate, if imperfect, measurement to screen out some applicants, but fell short of truly reflecting the profile of a person's moral compass. Character is a tall test that speaks to someone's intentions to repay a debt and will to hang tough when adversity tests that intention.

The best FICO can really do is to definitively say that the subject person hasn't displayed poor character yet. There have been more than a few perfect credit scores that turned out to describe people with lousy character when the going got tough.

The days of relying on such simple measurements are winding down rapidly as several information service companies are developing behavioral analytics, to provide more detailed predictive profiles for individuals that will offer an accurate assessment of a person's character according to customized traits.

How will this work? From the information that's already being collected in multiple places where we shop, ship, chat, write, correspond, read, browse, donate, support, and even where we're governed. ProPublica provides a glimpse of the kind of data and sources that are already being collected in a 2013 article titled "Everything We Know About What Data Brokers Know About You."[4]

It's been estimated that more than 1,600 different data bits can be collected on individuals, including basic identification, physical traits, personal interest, job history, romantic interests, hobbies, and whether they're left or right handed. Obviously, bankers will steer clear of any assessment that uses sensitive data points that one might construe as discriminatory, but other data that has never been quantified can make a meaningful contribution to their analysis.

When will these models be available? One has already launched from the Entrepreneurial Finance Lab, which is the outgrowth of a Harvard doctoral project.[5] The enterprise started using a psychometric test to predict future behavior that has been deployed in 16 countries where there are no credit bureaus. To date, over 70,000 small businesses have taken the test in an effort to qualify for credit.

The article details how this model asks questions that don't necessarily have a right answer; using an algorithm, it aims to predict whether an individual is likely to default based on how the answers relate to one another.

For example, to assess their sense of personal control over outcomes—which tends to correlate with loan repayment—respondents might be asked to rate how much they agree or disagree with the statement: "I believe in the power of fate."

Another question on risk tolerance might ask them to choose between opposing responses with equal social desirability, such as: "I plan for every eventuality," "I'm in between," or "Planning takes the fun out of life."

There are some unexpected findings: Optimism and self-confidence are good signs among seasoned entrepreneurs, but high levels in younger business owners do not bode well, statistically.

And the math and reasoning questions meant to measure fluid intelligence can also assess integrity—of the loan officer. Too many correct answers can reveal that an applicant was coached.[6]

Expect these kinds of platforms to slowly creep into banks through familiar names including Experian, Equifax, and TransUnion. While they are already providing some credit scoring models that analyze credit reports and some limited environmental data, wait for this information to be much more revealing about who to lend to and who to avoid.

Cash Substitutes

Payments and money transfers have historically been of little interest to business lenders, who are glad to leave that to the other side of the house. But the growing number of disruptive technologies facilitating the movement and storage of capital may impact lenders in the next few years.

Lenders will need to be able to understand and find confidence in multiple new ways that business owners generate payments and store their cash. Balance sheets will begin listing new accounts and even currencies that will rarely intersect with checking accounts and other places bankers could readily confirm.

For example, consider two rapidly growing options for people to store value and transfer payments:

- PayPal: This alternative money service is well known and an early disruptive technology to facilitate the movement of payments among Internet-based retailers and their customers. Without the benefit of federal deposit insurance, PayPal has millions of customers storing billions of dollars there. And now, instant access to those funds is beginning to appear with retail merchants like Uber, the personal transportation service, and Home Depot, which includes PayPal as a point-of-sale payment option.
- Bitcoin: Perhaps the oddest innovation that's arisen in years, Bitcoin is a new digital currency created by an anonymous programmer (or group of programmers) known as Satoshi Nakamoto. In a story that sounds like it must have been from a B movie, Bitcoins are "mined" from a network that releases a block of Bitcoins every 10 minutes until the finite supply of 21 million is exhausted.

    How do they derive value? Who issues, regulates, or controls Bitcoins? Actually, part of their purpose and appeal for many investors is that this currency is used entirely outside of any government. Bitcoins are transferred digitally with a trailing authentication code. The value is theoretically derived in a pure marketplace through the exchange among investors, outside of anyone's monetary policy or manipulation.

What's the Next Big Idea?

For any readers who have been in the trenches for more than the past 20 years, these many different innovations are truly transformational. And if business lending experiences continued technological innovation like most other sectors have, the pace of change will only increase in the years ahead.

Clearly the shadow banking system, which is an unregulated counterpart to the regulated banking sector, is alive and growing. Access to capital is getting easier, faster, and more narrowly focused on smaller niches of the broad small business market. These changes are channeling new sources of funding to business owners who will enjoy a growing smorgasbord of capital sources.

But along with that greater access comes more accurate assessment models that might welcome—or dismiss—funding applications in record time. Risk-based pricing for capital, delivered by investors rather than banks, will likely mean borrowers will be paying much more for capital, at least until there is broader competition in the market.

So what will be the next big idea? eBay for CRE lending? Pre-approved, self-generated SBA guarantees? Google sending you a loan check based on assessing your bill pay and e-mail? We can only speculate. But what is certain is that advancements are being made daily that will rapidly change the nature of small business funding, with implications for both borrowers and funders in the years ahead.

Notes

1. Anil Stoker, "The Future of Banking—and Why it Won't Be Determined by Banks," SmallBusiness.co.UK, www.smallbusiness.co.uk/financing-a-business/business-banking/2347068/the-future-of-banking-and-why-it-wonand39t-be-determined-by-banks.thtml (accessed January 2, 2014).
2. "Fast Facts—Payday Lending," ResponsibleLending.org, www.responsiblelending.org/payday-lending/tools-resources/fast-facts.html (accessed January 6, 2014).
3. Randal Smith, "Not Banks, but Still Lending Money and Drawing Investors," DealB%k, August 7, 2013, http://dealbook.nytimes.com/2013/08/07/not-banks-but-still-lending-and-drawing-investors/.
4. Lois Beckett, "Everything We Know About What Data Brokers Know About You," *ProPublica*, September 13, 2013, https://www.propublica.org/article/everything-we-know-about-what-data-brokers-know-about-you.
5. Sarah Wheaton, "Credit Score, by Multiple Choice," *New York Times*, December 30, 2103, www.nytimes.com/2013/12/31/business/credit-scores-from-a-test-not-a-history.html?_r=0.
6. Ibid.

About the Companion Website

To support the book and offer additional resources and value, an online database of innovative lenders and service providers is available at www .wiley.com/go/bankersguide (password: green14).

Sources are identified by major categories, such as business lenders, crowdfunding, peer-to-peer lenders, merchant cash advance companies, and so on, consistent with the book contents. The listing provides contact information and a brief description of the services provided.

This database has been compiled from industry sources and news accounts of companies and individuals that are available to provide a variety of funding and other financial services.

Download the listing in .xlsx or .pdf format, and be sure to check back for updates.

Index